THE TRANSITION FROM FEUDALISM TO CAPITALISM

Paul Sweezy
Maurice Dobb
Kohachiro Takahashi
Rodney Hilton
Christopher Hill
Georges Lefebvre
Giuliano Procacci
Eric Hobsbawm
John Merrington

THE TRANSITION FROM FEUDALISM TO CAPITALISM

Rodney Hilton

The Transition from Feudalism to Capitalism
Rodney Hilton

First Published in India 2006
Reprinted 2009
Reprinted 2015
Reprinted 2018
Reprinted 2021
Reprinted 2022

ISBN 978-93-5002-334-1

Published in agreement with Verso (The Imprint of New Left Books), London for publication and sale only in South Asia

Published by
AAKAR BOOKS
28 E Pocket IV, Mayur Vihar Phase I
Delhi 110 091, India
aakarbooks@gmail.com
www.aakarbooks.com

Printed at
Sapra Brothers, Noida

Contents

Bibliographical Note

The essays in this volume were first published in these journals: Paul Sweezy, 'A Critique', and Maurice Dobb, 'A Reply', in *Science and Society*, Spring, 1950; Kohachiro Takahashi, 'A Contribution to the Discussion', in *Science and Society*, Fall, 1952; Maurice Dobb, 'A Further Comment', and Paul Sweezy, 'A Rejoinder', in *Science and Society*, Spring, 1953; Rodney Hilton, 'A Comment', and Christopher Hill, 'A Comment', in *Science and Society*, Fall, 1953; Georges Lefebvre, 'Some Observations', in *La Pensée*, February, 1956; Giuliano Procacci, 'A Survey of the Debate', in *Società*, XI, 1955; Rodney Hilton, 'Capitalism – What's in a Name?', in *Past and Present*, February, 1952; Eric Hobsbawm, 'From Feudalism to Capitalism', in *Marxism Today*, August, 1962; Maurice Dobb, 'From Feudalism to Capitalism', in *Marxism Today*, September, 1962; John Merrington, 'Town and Country in the Transition to Capitalism', in *New Left Review*, No. 93, September–October, 1975.

Biographical Note

Paul Sweezy is Editor of *Monthly Review*; Maurice Dobb is a Fellow of Trinity College, University of Cambridge; Kohachiro Takahashi is Professor of History, University of Tokyo; Rodney Hilton is Professor of History, University of Birmingham; Christopher Hill is Master of Balliol College and Professor of History, University of Oxford; Georges Lefebvre was Professor of History at the University of Paris; Giuliano Procacci is Professor of History, University of Florence; Eric Hobsbawm is Professor of History at Birkbeck College, University of London; John Merrington is Lecturer in History, Middlesex Polytechnic.

Introduction

Rodney Hilton

Maurice Dobb's *Studies in the Development of Capitalism* was published in 1946. Karl Polanyi, who reviewed it very critically in the *Journal of Economic History*, in 1948, nevertheless described it in the following terms: 'a scholarly and original volume on the decline of feudalism, on mercantilism, the industrial revolution and the nineteenth century, the period between the two wars, in effect the whole history of western capitalism short of the Marshall Plan.' Polanyi thought that Dobb had retained from Marx what was bad (the labout theory of value) whilst discarding what he, Polanyi, thought was Marx's 'fundamental insight into the historically limited nature of market organisation.' Unfortunately, Polanyi's review was not long enough to develop this interesting criticism, but it indicated, on the reviewer's part, a serious attitude to the problems of a Marxist analysis of feudalism as a mode of production (which Marx himself had not systematically undertaken) and of the transition from feudalism to capitalism (about which Marx necessarily said more, though not enough).

R. H. Tawney's long review article of the book in the *Economic History Review*, in 1950, showed little interest in the theoretical problems of a Marxist approach. However, it was appropriate that a lengthy, appreciative, yet critical, review should be written by the one British historian of high calibre who had not only made the whole period of the 'transition' a lifetime's study based on original research, but had actually acknowledged the reality of capitalism as a distinct economic and social order – this at a time when economists, historians and politicians were trying to pretend that it had never existed. Many of Tawney's criticisms are of great practical interest to the historian of the 16th and 17th centuries and have to be taken seriously. However, although Tawney said in the review that 'the combination of history with theory is one of the merits of the book' he did not raise any of the general theoretical problems which Polanyi hinted at, and which have also exercised Marxist students of Dobb's work. All the same, Tawney, and presumably the editor of the *Economic History Review*, thought, with Polanyi, that a scholarly and original volume on a subject of such importance justified a sympathetic, even if sometimes severe, consideration.

Unfortunately this interest was not shared by the editors of some other historical journals nearer to the centre of what one might call the British 'historical establishment' than the *Economic History Review* was then. There was no review in the *English Historical Review*, supposed shrine of high scholarship, nor in *History*, through whose pages the message of that high scholarship is conveyed to history schoolteachers and others outside the circle of professional researchers. Nor were there reviews in the principal journals of economic theory, such as the *Economic Journal* and *Economica*.

The reasons for the general neglect of Dobb's book are fairly obvious. British academic historians do not like Marxism. In any case, the decade after the end of the war was hardly propitious for the unprejudiced discussion of a Marxist interpretation of capitalism. This is not the whole story, of course, which has to have added to it the suspicion, not only of theory and abstract concepts, but even of generalising interpretations which may have relatively little theory about them, such as the Whig interpretation of history. What is preferred in the British academic tradition, at any rate since the end of the 19th century, is exact and detailed scholarship directed towards the amassing of verifiable data. The training of the historian does not lie in the discussion of hypotheses by which significant historical developments can be explained, still less in the attempt to penetrate to the essence or 'prime mover' of socio-political formations. It is in, supposedly, removing all elements of subjectivity from the study of a sequence of events over the short term, or in identifying the constitutive elements in the major (usually the ruling) institution of society. This is done by recourse wherever possible to supposedly 'objective' administrative record sources, and by critical assessment of chronicles, narratives or letters, which are deemed liable to the risk of human bias.[1]

This type of historical scholarship is not, of course, exclusively

[1] Interesting assessments of the nature of modern historical writing are to be found in *Ideology in the Social Sciences*, ed. Robin Blackburn, London, 1972. They are 'History: the poverty of empiricism' by Gareth Stedman Jones and 'Karl Marx's contribution to historiography' by E. J. Hobsbawm. Jones somewhat over-estimates the revolutionary character of the *Annales* school, which, however innovative, is by no means Marxist.

British, but European. It was well exemplified by the French historical school of the pre-Bloch, pre-*Annales* period. Its achievements have been considerable and should in no way be underestimated, particularly in the field of medieval research which particularly interests us here. For, as readers of the debate will appreciate, it was not Dobb's treatment of the later history of capitalism which aroused the interest of the participants, but what he had to say about those forces which destroyed feudalism. For the most part the problems of the transition are tackled from the medieval, rather than from the modern end. Indeed it was largely on the basis of the work of the deservedly famous non-Marxist historian, Henri Pirenne, that Paul Sweezy launched his critique of Dobb. Pirenne's work is not, of course, to be classed with the narrower type of academic scholarship to which reference has been made, although he was as capable as anybody of a meticulous and critical treatment of source material. He was also, however, capable of wide-ranging generalisation and it was no doubt the problem-orientated character of his research which inclined Marxists to treat him very seriously. Giuliano Procacci, in his assessment of the initial debate, rightly drew attention to the formidable backing of non-Marxist scholarship which Sweezy was deploying against Dobb when he cited Pirenne. Perhaps Procacci rather overestimated the big guns of Sweezy's side. After all, whom does Sweezy quote apart from Pirenne? And as we now know well, Pirenne's interpretation of medieval European economic history has been severely criticised by many, other than Marxist, historians. His interpretation of the decline of the Mediterranean trade and of the de-urbanisation of Western Europe, has suffered some hard knocks. His view that it was the revival of long-distance trade which re-vivified the European economy in the 11th century, is not generally accepted; nor is his opinion concerning the social origins of the urban merchants of the period of revival.[2]

Nevertheless, Procacci's general point was entirely justified. The British Marxists may have had good ideas, but they needed to back up these ideas with research which would match that of the established schools of non-Marxist historiography which they were, in effect, challenging.

Dobb's book, as he himself admits, and as his reviewers have reiterated, was the work of a Marxist economist who had made himself

[2] See the collection of essays edited by A. F. Havighurst, *The Pirenne Thesis*, Boston, 1958, and A. B. Hibbert, 'The Origins of the Medieval Town Patriciate', *Past and Present*, No. 3.

familiar with the then existing range of secondary works. His opponent in this controversy, Paul Sweezy, was in a similar situation – that is, of a Marxist analyst of contemporary capitalism who ventured into the field of medieval economic history on the basis of secondary work by non-Marxist historians. The same is true, though to a lesser degree, of the most formidable of the subsequent participants in the debate, for although Takahashi is an original worker in the field of Japanese feudalism and the problems of the transition to capitalism in the 19th century, his perceptions of the same problems in the history of the classic area of the formation of capitalism, Western Europe, are again based on secondary works. The most recent of the longer contributions to the debate, that of John Merrington, is again not concerned with the research problems of the historian of the feudal economy. Thus, with the exception of Hill and Hilton, whose contributions to the original debate were relatively slight, the argument has been conducted by Marxists who have put their fingers on certain fundamental problems with regard to the feudal and capitalist modes of production but who, for lack of support from Marxist specialists (at any rate in the 1950s, when the debates began) were necessarily obliged to do much of their own spadework among non-Marxist secondary authorities.

Now it is evidently essential for anyone who takes the general concept of 'mode of production' seriously to establish the components of different modes. The practising historian, whose aims may not be the same as those of the sociologist or philosopher,[3] cannot rest at this point. There is a law of motion of feudal (as of other) societies, as well as a particular set of structural relationships in them. To define and elaborate the law of motion and the particular shifts which eventually generate the conditions for the transition from feudalism to capitalism requires an effort of research and not only of logic. It means the critique and the utilisation of the achievements of bourgeois scholarship. It also means the application of critical method to contemporary sources. Such a critical method must be Marxist, based on an understanding of the concept of the mode of production. It must also take into account the critical methods developed by historians since at the latest the 17th century.

Marxist historians have significantly altered our understanding of the bourgeois revolution and of the development of capitalist society from the 17th century onwards. One need only mention the original

[3] As L. Althusser seems to admit, *Reading Capital*, London, 1970, p. 14.

researches of such leading English Marxist historians as Christopher Hill, Eric Hobsbawm and Edward Thompson, not to speak of Albert Soboul in France, Giuliano Procacci in Italy and many others in the capitalist countries. B. F. Porchnev, A. D. Liublinskaya and J. V. Polisensky, well known in this country, are again only a few of the historians working on similar fields in the socialist countries. Marxist work on feudal society and on the medieval preconditions for the development of capitalism has been much more restricted, at any rate in the West, though E. A. Thompson's writings on early Germanic society deserve to be singled out. Otherwise the main focus of Marxist medieval research has been confined to the field of agrarian history. There are various reasons which could be suggested for this limited development. The young Marxist is likely to have a political commitment to socialist or communist politics, and therefore to be attracted to the study of the capitalist mode of production in all its political, social and cultural manifestations. This study, moreover, not only has the appeal of the direct influence of Marx's and Engels' own theory and practice, but the aid of a considerable company of Marxist practitioners who are engaged in constant theoretical and practical discussion of the problems of the Marxist historian of capitalist society, and the transition from capitalism to socialism. The study of feudal society has few such advantages for most younger historians, who are therefore somewhat isolated, practically and theoretically. The republication of this transition debate will, it is hoped, help to encourage further consideration of the theoretical issues and further research on the unsolved problems posed in the earlier contributions and in this introduction.

* * *

It is now more than twenty years since the original debate in the pages of *Science and Society*. A considerable amount of research has been done by Marxist and non-Marxist historians which is relevant to the main topics which were discussed. It is not proposed in this introduction to produce a laborious historiographical memorandum of this research, but rather, as far as the author is capable, to re-examine some of the problems at issue in the original debate in the light of subsequent work – and subsequent thinking. These problems include: the definition of serfdom; the origin of towns; the role of handicrafts; merchants and the money economy; the unfettering of simple commodity production; the alternative paths for the emergence of capitalist production; the concept of the 'prime mover'.

Serfdom

The term 'serfdom' in Marxist discussion is often unnecessarily ambiguous, an ambiguity which seems to be derived from non-Marxist historical research. Surely Takahashi is right to insist that serfdom is the existence-form of labour in the feudal mode of production. Its essence was the transference to the use of the lord of the labour of the peasant family which was surplus to that needed for the family's subsistence and economic reproduction. The surplus labour could be used directly on the lord's demesne (home farm of the manor), or its product could be transferred in the form of a rent in kind or in money, from the family holding.

Given the effective possession of the subsistence-producing holding by the peasant family, the transfer of the surplus must be forced, since the peasant, as contrasted with the wage labourer, does not need to alienate his labour power in order to live. Having accepted this broad definition of serfdom as the enforced transfer, either of surplus labour or of the product of surplus labour, many different juridical and institutional forms of serfdom can exist which in many – perhaps most – cases are not necessarily considered to be 'servile' in the eyes of the law. This has given rise to much confusion among historians. For example, Marc Bloch examined the enfranchisement charters of villages in ecclesiastical estates in the north of France and observed that the peasants who received those charters, constituting the majority of the inhabitants of the villages, were thereby freed from a range of obligations, such as *formariage* and *mainmorte*, which were generally regarded as servile. The families which were designated as servile in those same villages in the estate descriptions of the 9th century were much fewer in number than those who had to be emancipated in the 13th. Bloch, therefore, concluded that there had been a process of enserfment between the 9th and the 13th centuries. However, the Belgian historian, L. Verriest, showed that the proportion of families specifically designated as 'serfs' (*servi*) had not changed in the intervening period. The majority of the peasants enfranchised in the 13th century were juridically free *vileins* who had been subjected to obligations which were analogous to those of the 'true' serfs. As we shall see, although formally Verriest was right, it was Bloch whose interpretation was nearer to the truth.[4]

During the early period of European serfdom, there was, during the

[4] M. Bloch, *French Rural History*, London, 1966 and 'Liberté et Servitude Personelles au Moyen-Age' in *Mélanges Historiques*, I, Paris, 1963; L. Verriest, *Institutions Médiévales*, Mons, 1946.

period in which the feudal landowning aristocracy was emerging in its classical form, a great variety of forms of peasant subordination resulting from different developments of the period. These included the establishment of demesne slaves on landed holdings, with or without manumission of servile obligations; the subordination of free peasants to powerful or threatening neighbours; the submission of free men to the protection of a saint (i.e. to a monastic landowning community supposedly devoted to the worship of the saint), and so on. The nomenclature of the subordinated peasants varied from place to place according to the nature of the subordination, or even, as R. Boutruche suggested, according to the fantasy of the lords' clerical administrators. As Boutruche goes on to say, this led some historians into similar fantasies of erudition so that the characteristics of the peasantry as a social class were altogether forgotten.[5]

There was a real change in the nature of European, particularly Western European serfdom, between the 9th and 13th centuries. I propose to discuss this briefly because it illustrates an important element of confusion in some of the discussion about the character of the feudal mode of production.* This confusion concerns the role of labour rent in the social relations of the period. Labour rent has often been regarded as the characteristic form of servile subordination of peasant to lord. Consequently, most of the English Marxists in the transition discussions have – even when acknowledging that labour rent is not the only form of feudal rent – regarded the commutation of labour services into money in England in the 14th century as being of special significance in the transition. This was, on their part, the consequence of a certain insularity of historical training, for the survival in 14th-century England of large estates characterised by big demesnes using labour services from peasants on dependent tenures was exceptional, as Dobb had mentioned. But the general history of European feudalism shows quite clearly that labour rent was not an essential element in the feudal relations of production, although the coercive character of these relations perhaps appears most clearly in the organisation of forced labour on the demesne.

We first become aware of the demesne-based form of estate organisation in the estate descriptions (mostly ecclesiastical but also royal) of the 9th century. It may well be that the accident of documentary

[5] R. Boutruche, *Seigneurie et Féodalite*, I, Paris, 1959, pp. 128–9.

* For the problem of the definition of feudalism. See my note, p 30.

survival focuses our attention on Northern France and the Rhine valley, as well as on this particular period. The form of organisation was certainly older than the 9th century, though whether there was direct continuity from the late Roman Empire is still disputed. It was also widespread, being found in Central Italy as well as in England by the end of the 10th century, if not earlier. All the estate descriptions emphasise the importance of labour obligations from the holdings of both free and servile peasant holdings, so that although there were rents both in kind and in money, labour rent was apparently predominant. It is probable that at this period this was just as inefficient a form of the use of surplus labour as it was in Eastern Europe in the early modern period.[5a] At any rate it seems clear that the system was beginning to disintegrate at about the time when the descriptions were being drawn up.

Various features of the European economy and society in the 10th and 11th centuries made it necessary to change this mode of appropriation of surplus labour. The capitularies and ordinances of the Frankish and Ottonian monarchies suggest that there was considerable peasant resistance to labour services as well as to legal enserfment. Although the severity of the Scandinavian and Magyar invasions must not be overestimated, they necessarily weakened the ramshackle structure of the Carolingian imperial hegemony. State power was not so much fragmented (or parcellised) as confined within practical limits, given the slow communications and effective radius of the exercise of military force. It is probably that there was a considerable increase in population, with a consequent subdivision of peasant holdings. The population increase may also have encouraged an increase in the number of families of the feudal warrior class which were enfeoffed on holdings. Although one must not exaggerate, it seems likely, too, that technical improvements increased agricultural yields.

There was, during this period, a noticeable change in the character of the feudal ruling class. Jurisdictional power, that is the right to try the subject population and to derive profit from the exactions implicit in jurisdiction, was devolved downwards not only to the counts, but to castellans (lords of districts controlled from a castle) and even to simple lords of one or two villages. The big estates, especially the monastic, preserved to a certain extent their outward structure, but the demesnes

[5a] W. Kula's *Théorie Économique du Système Féodal*, Paris–The Hague, 1970, analyses the serf run estates of early modern Poland and contains many useful hints for students of similar estates in medieval western Europe.

tended to be broken up and taken over by estate officials or sub-let to peasant tenants. Within their judicial immunities, jurisdictional power was decentralised in the same way as it was in the counties. Labour services tended to disappear as the main form of feudal rent. Indeed, by the 12th century, peasant surplus was transferred to the landed aristocracy less in the form of a rent calculated on the size of the peasant holding, whether in labour, kind or money, than in seigneurial taxation (tallage) and in the profits of jurisdiction. These profits included not only court fines but the profit from various monopolies, such as the right to force the inhabitants, free or serf, of the area of jurisdiction, whether tenants or not, to grind corn at the lord's mill, bake in his oven or press grapes in his wine-press. In addition some extra labour services were demanded, but as from subjects rather than from tenants, being mainly for road and castle building, perhaps even to mow what remained of the demesne meadows or to cultivate the demesne vineyard. The sum total of these new aspects of feudal rent, it has been calculated, considerably exceeded the previous landlord income which had been based on the yield from the demesnes and the rents from the holdings. Yet, as the burdens increased, the term 'serf' was disappearing so that few peasants so called were left by the middle of the 12th century.[6]

It was from these new forms of seigneurial exaction that the leading strata of many European peasant communities obtained some form of enfranchisement in the 12th and 13th centuries, usually at a heavy price in cash. Nor is this the end of the history of the complex evolution of feudal rent. However, I do not propose to pursue the subject further, for the purpose of this discussion of the change in the character of feudal rent between the 9th and 13th centuries has simply been to emphasise how varied were the forms in which the surplus was pumped out of the basic producers, and also how closely connected with these forms was the institutional superstructure.

The Origin of Towns[7]

Of further importance in the history of feudal rent in this earlier period is the probable connection which it had with the growth of towns, small market towns as well as the bigger urban centres; for the urban revival of the 11th and 12th centuries coincided with the development

[6] The ideas in the preceding paragraphs are based on a number of monographs, but some of the evidence will be found in the work of R. Boutruche (n. 5) and in G. Duby's *Rural Economy and Country Life in the Medieval West*, London, 1962.

[7] See H. van Werweke' article 'The Rise of the Towns', with bibliography in *Cambridge Economic History of Europe*, III, Cambridge, 1963. The author is a follower of H. Pirenne.

of the new forms of serfdom. The enlargement of the surplus transferred from peasant production, more in the form of jurisdictional and monopoly profits than in the form of rent from landed holdings, meant that lords' incomes were in fact realised more and more in cash. The division of labour between town and country, the development of towns not simply as markets where rural produce was sold so as to raise cash for the satisfaction of lords' exactions, but as centres of craft production, can no doubt be *explained* in general terms, as the response to the more efficient concentration of surplus in the hands of a more differentiated (and from the point of view of its cultural demands more sophisticated) aristocracy. The processes themselves must be *described* in more complex fashion. Some small towns undoubtedly were founded through seigneurial initiative simply to provide convenient market centres which could also yield profits from market tolls and stall rents. In other places, the nuclei around which developed urban crafts, and markets for local produce as well as for the luxury commodities of long distance trade, were pre-existing settlements of churchmen (cathedrals, collegiate churches, monasteries) or groups of warriors in the retinue of some great feudatory, such as a duke or a count. The necessary precondition in all cases was the increasing size and disposability of seigneurial incomes. At the same time it is likely that the increased population which provided the artisans, petty traders and providers of services in these new (or revived) towns was itself generated by the break up of the old domanial system. For certain aspects of that break up provided the conditions for population growth, namely the fragmentation of peasant holdings; possibly greater scope for the operation of partible inheritance; and increased productivity of peasant agriculture resulting from the concentration of technical resources on the holding instead of their diversion to the demesne.

Max Weber[8] laid great stress on the political autonomy achieved by the urban communities of Western feudalism as compared with the cities of Asia. Non-Marxist historians (especially in France) described the same phenomenon when they referred to communes as 'collective lordships', inserted like other vassals in the feudal hierarchy.[9] Undoubtedly the independent urban commune has been an important component of the special features of European, as distinct from other feudalisms. It would, however, be as wrong to attribute to communal independence the development either of merchant capital, or of urban-

[8] *The City*, London, 1958.

[9] See C. Petit-Dutaillis, *Les Communes Françaises*, Paris, 1947, Bk. I, iii.

based craft industry, as it would be to lay stress on the fragmentation of sovereignty (itself a concept of non-Marxist historiography). There was a very considerable range of urban autonomy from feudal control, and the towns which enjoyed the greatest political independence were not necessarily the most developed economically or socially; Paris, the biggest town in medieval Europe, being a case in point. Nor was the political autonomy of an independent commune the necessary condition for that type of urban or craft monopoly to which Marx referred, when he said that the towns exploited the countryside economically where the countryside (i.e. the feudal ruling class) exploited the towns politically.

Many an English borough had its gild merchant in full control of the terms of trade on the market without, at the same time, enjoying the higher ranges of urban privilege. The problems of the divisions of labour between town and country are many, and however much we may learn from the labours of the best non-Marxist specialists in urban constitutional history, it would be unfortunate if it were thought that the problems of the urban element in feudal society were to be solved in these terms.

What is needed is detailed work on the degree of occupational specialisation in towns of various sizes, various functions and at various stages of development. To give some examples, the presence of the feudal aristocracy in the Italian towns is a historical commonplace, while it is often asserted that the North European feudatories lived rather in the country; but these generalisations need testing, especially in England, where every sizable town had its ecclesiastical and feudal or royal-official enclaves. The agriculturally occupied element in urban populations is often referred to, but seldom measured and analysed. Lists of organised crafts within the urban jurisdiction are often available but the total numbers of separate occupations, mainly unorganised, have not been systematically compared from town to town, so as to estimate the whys and hows of functional separation from the agricultural hinterland. Nor is the contrast between the gild dominated urban industry and the free industry of the countryside, the supposed theatre of development of capitalist Way I, as straightfoward as it seems. Were the East Anglian industrial villages of the late 14th century town or country? Were not medieval Manchester and medieval Birmingham, often thought to typify the progress of rural industrialisation, referred to at the time as boroughs or *villae mercatoriae*?[10]

[10] In other words, the dividing line between town and country is not necessarily the same as that between the regulated and unregulated urban areas.

Handicrafts

These questions are not posed in order to suggest that the contributors to our symposium are wrong in saying that the social differentiation developing within agricultural and industrial petty commodity production is the foundation for the subsequent development of capitalism. There is, however, a serious lacuna in our knowledge. English Marxists (and non-Marxists), fortunate in the documentary riches at their disposal, have investigated with some success the history of the later medieval peasantry. This contrasts sharply with our ignorance of the artisans of town and country, whether organised in gilds (the best known) or not. This ignorance, as so often, is not altogether the consequence of a shortage of evidence; it also results from an absence of theoretical analysis of the nature of this type of labour and its situation within the relations of production of feudal society, which are predominantly the relations between 'servile' peasants and ruling landowners.[11]

There was, of course, a primitive division of labour in prehistoric (in effect pre-class) society, whereby some members of the community specialised in weaving, iron work, making pottery and other necessary artefacts. This is well attested by the archaeological record, but the archaeological record is not able to reveal how these workers acquired their subsistence. Was there an exchange of manufactured goods and foodstuffs in the form of use values within the community, or did the artisans also work as agriculturalists, providing substantially, if not entirely, for their own subsistence? There seem to have been survivals in feudal class society of both these situations. On the one hand we find specialist artisans within the households or the demesne economies of lay and ecclesiastical magnates. On the other hand we find village craftsmen, especially smiths, who have landed holdings but whose surplus labour is appropriated as a rent in horseshoes, repair to plough shares, and so on.

Neither of these types of craft work implies simple commodity production, but when the craftsmen of large households of monasteries or feudal potentates began to produce not only for their lord, but for others who clustered around those centres of power, and for peasants

[11] It is significant that George Unwin's works, especially *Industrial Organisation in the 16th and 17th centuries*, London, 1908, still provide us with one of the best theoretically oriented analyses in English of craft production. It will be remembered that Dobb relies heavily on Unwin in the *Studies*... But see also the work of the Polish historian, B. Geremek, *Le Salariat dans l'Artisanat Parisien aux XIII–XVe Siècles*, Paris–The Hague, 1968.

bringing in their produce for sale as well as in the form of rent in kind, then we have the beginning of urban-based simple commodity production. Traces of feudal household provisioning by these urban artisans remain for a surprisingly long time; in Paris for instance where, in the 13th century, the king nominated feudal lords as official masters of the leading crafts, or in the much smaller cathedral town of Metz, where the bishop, who was also lord of the town, did much the same.

These were institutional relics throwing some light on previous relationships. But long before the 13th century, industrial craftsmen had become separated both from their rural and feudal-household contexts and appeared as apparently autonomous industrial households within urban communities, producing for sale to anybody who had money. But what was the nature of these households? How are we to categorise the labour which produced shoes, knives, plough-parts, carts, cloth and other commodities (as we are entitled to designate these artefacts)? In view of the labour embodied in the craftsmen's product, in view of the fact that there was evidently a considerable exchange of values between peasants and artisans, the craftsman's income cannot simply be regarded as part of the redistributed surplus from the peasant economy, mediated through the demands of the feudal aristocracy, as was the case with the profit on alienation which constituted merchant capital.

It is true that as monopolistic gilds developed, the exchange between peasant and artisan became unequal, but the relation between peasant and artisan was not exploitative in essence. In fact in the small market towns,[12] whose aggregate population probably constituted the greater part of the total urban population of Europe, the feudal exploitation of the artisan was parallel to the exploitation of the peasant, for the lords of those towns also skimmed off the product of the surplus labour of the artisans through house and stall rents, mill and oven monopolies, tolls and taxes. This exploitation was direct in the case of the unenfranchised towns, and was not entirely absent in the independent boroughs and communes which often had to pay a cash commutation for rents and tolls, as well as paying a high rate of taxation, whose weight fell more heavily on the artisans than on the ruling mercantile élites.

These tentative suggestions about the categorisation of artisan labour within the feudal mode of production assume artisan households which are internally undifferentiated, as well as minimum differentiation between producing units. By the time we have adequate records, this

[12] *English Medieval Boroughs: a Handlist*, by M. W. Beresford and H. P. R. Finberg, Newton Abbot, 1973, gives a good idea of the large number of these smaller centres.

state of affairs is mainly found in small market towns of about 500 inhabitants, whose functional separation from the countryside was complete (in the sense that agriculturalists were an insignificant or non-existent element in the population). In the bigger centres we can no longer assume the equality of labour within the household, nor equality between artisan households. As the market for the artisans' commodities extended, we not only have the familiar process, well described in Dobb's *Studies*, by which the merchant interposes himself between the craftsman and the buyer. Inside the workshop the apprentice ceases to be simply a trainee (often the son of the master craftsman) and becomes an exploited labourer in receipt of his subsistence only. In addition, journeymen are hired – not in great numbers, for the scale of production does not permit this – and represent another subordinated element within the workshop. To begin with, however, the journeyman was not simply a wage labourer, a direct source of surplus-value for the employer. In the 13th-century Flemish textile towns there was still confusion concerning the payment made to the textile craftsman by the merchant putter-out. It was not quite a wage, and yet it was not simply a payment for a job done by an independent craftsman. Whatever it was, it is of interest for our present purposes that a municipal rate was fixed by the piece of cloth, so much to the master, so much to the journeyman – a smaller quantity for the latter of course, but a smaller difference than one would expect.[13] The same arrangement is found as late as the 15th century in some English towns. In other words, although the process of differentiation was beginning within the workshop, master and journeyman were still the common objects of exploitation by merchant capital.

Merchant Capital

By contrast with the producer of manufactured goods, the medieval merchant capitalist has been the subject of many studies, based on the survival of a considerable amount of documentary evidence. Some of the most spectacular fortunes were accumulated by the merchants of the Italian towns, who illustrate in their activities the normally unspecialised character of the European merchant class as a whole – whether in Northern or in Mediterranean Europe, whether operating modestly in the regional markets or on a large scale in the international luxury trade. The Italian merchants, of whom the Florentines and the

[13] G. Espinas, *La Draperie dans la Flandre Française au Moyen-Age*, Paris, 1923, pp. 617–49; Little Red Book of Bristol, II, ed. F. B. Bickley, Bristol and London, 1900, pp. 58–61.

Venetians were the most successful, had as the basis of their profits the trade in high priced commodities, such as spices, jewellery or silk textiles, from the Far and Middle East, high quality woollen textiles from Flanders and Central Italy, gold from West Africa. They also dealt in money, as bankers to the Papacy and other rulers (mainly war finance). Some of them, like the great merchants of the Flemish towns, organised the provision of the raw materials for the manufacture of cloth as well as the sale of the finished product, without in any way altering the character of the productive process. Other products entered international trade, such as wine from the Île de France, from Gascony, Burgundy and the Rhineland; grain, timber and fur from the Baltic; salt from the Bay of Bourgneuf; alum from the Black Sea; woad from southern France, fish from Iceland, iron and steel from Sweden, not to speak of the standard commodities of regional trade, such as cereals or medium-priced textiles. The technical sophistication of the trading methods, the ability to concentrate funds to finance (at usurious rates of interest) governments and landed aristocrats who were always short of easily realisable assets, the cultural patronage of these medieval merchant capitalists, has brought forth a chorus of admiration from their historians.[14] None, however, has been able to alter the estimate which Marx made of their historical role, that their capital remained always within the sphere of circulation, was never applied either to agricultural or industrial production in any innovative fashion. The so-called commercial revolution in no way altered the feudal mode of production.[15]

One might well ask, therefore, what reality can be attributed to the suggestion that 'the money economy' acted as a solvent of feudal relations. We have seen that feudal rent could be paid as well in money as in labour or kind, without affecting the relationship between lord and tenant. It has been suggested that other relationships, such as those between kings and barons, or between barons and their vassals, which had once been based on personal and especially military service, became transformed as a result of the replacement of the personal by the cash

[14] Much detail and full bibliographies in volumes I and III of the Cambridge Economic History of Europe, 1952 and 1953. The title of a recent text-book by an expert on the subject, Robert S. Lopez, is significant – *The Commercial Revolution of the Middle Ages 950–1350*, Englewood, 1971. There are up-to-date bibliographies in N. J. G. Pounds, *An Economic History of Medieval Europe*, London, 1974, one of the better text-books to have been published recently.

[15] It seems to me that Marx modified his views about the role of merchant capital in the middle ages between writing the *Grundrisse* and the chapters in Vol. III of *Capital*, in the sense of believing less in the positive role of merchant capital at the later date. See K. Marx, *Grundrisse*, London, 1973, pp. 504–8.

nexus. Examples of this include the granting of fiefs consisting of money incomes charged on state revenues instead of revenue-yielding landed property; the payment of cash scutage instead of military service in the royal host; the giving of loyalty by retainer to lord in exchange for a cash annuity; the mobilisation of all military service on the basis of the payment of wages. Unfortunately for the advocates of the money-as-solvent theory, cash scutage is found as early as the beginning of the 12th century, and money fiefs not much later. Divided loyalties, treachery and self-seeking were just as prevalent when the feudal contract was based on the landed fief in the 11th and 12th centuries as in the days of so-called 'bastard feudalism', when it was based on money payments. Nor did big cash incomes transform the behaviour of the feudal ruling class, as any student of the English aristocracy between the 13th and 15th centuries can testify. If anything, it was the declining cash incomes of the feudal aristocracy which was the first symptom of the end of the feudal mode of production; for these incomes to the end represented peasant surplus, coercively extracted, and their diminution was the monetary sign of the failing grip of aristocratic domination of the old type.

The solvent qualities of money, as Marx has emphasised, only came into operation once the historic processes of the dissolution of the feudal modes of production were well under way. In the *Grundrisse* Marx pinpoints as the essential aspect of this dissolution the separation of the labourer from the objective conditions of his existence – land, craftsman's property, even (suggested Marx) subsistence as a lord's retainer.[16] In England, as in other areas of Western Europe, the failing grip of aristocratic domination was indeed a significant feature of the preliminary processes of dissolution to which Dobb and Takahashi, in the course of the Transition debate, have drawn particular attention. This was something which, before Marx, the pioneer English economic historian, James Thorold Rogers, had already documented.[17] Subsequent research has shown that the appearance for a short time of what seemed to Marx to be a predominance of free peasant property was the

[16] It must be emphasised that, contrary to the suggestions of some critics, Marx presented by no means a simple picture of the actual historical process by which peasants in England lost their landed property and communal rights. See *Capital*, I, Bk. VIII, 30; *Grundrisse*, p. 511.

[17] See chapters VIII and IX of his *Six Centuries of Work and Wages*, based on the material already published in his *History of Agriculture and Prices*, Oxford, 1866. Marx used this work in writing *Capital* and thought reasonably well of him, even though he was a liberal economist.

direct outcome of the class struggle between landowner and peasant. Marx was thinking particularly of developments in England, where the evidence is good. The disturbed situation in the middle of the 14th century, with the population collapse resulting from the bubonic plague and governmental financial shortage resulting from the Anglo-French wars, could very well have led to the strengthening of serfdom. The shortage of labour so strengthened the economic position of tenants and labourers vis a vis landowners and employers that one way in which the ruling class could have reacted would have been the tightening up of controls on the movement of unfree persons, increase in rents and jurisdictional fines, and a freeze on wages. For about two decades after 1350 this policy was tried, but with complete lack of success. The peasants already had considerable experience in resisting seigneurial encroachments. Village communities, though internally divided between rich and poor peasants, were very tough bodies to deal with, as many a local rebellion had demonstrated. Although major risings, such as the French Jacquerie of 1359 and the English revolt of 1381 were defeated, local resistance could not be overcome. The English situation is very instructive. Villein (or servile) land tenure, without changing its essential juridical character, was attenuated into copyhold. In the atmosphere of peasant self-assertiveness, copyhold became hardly distinguishable from free tenure, to such an extent that members of the landowning gentry were prepared to take portions of copyhold land to round off their estates.

Rents were sufficiently low and the ability of both landowners and the state to control the free movement of peasants and labourers so minimal in practice that, at the end of the 14th century, and for the greater part of the 15th century, the feudal restrictions on simple commodity production virtually disappeared.[18] One must not expect to find, during this period, any dramatic developments in the direction of capitalist production. The yeoman farmer employing wage labour certainly prospered; there was a free movement of craft production from the older gild-dominated towns to the village and the less restricted smaller towns, but no drastic social differentiation in the sense of a mass of wage labourers selling their labour power to agricultural and industrial employers. This was to be a long drawn out process, by no means completed even in the 17th century. The point is, however, that during the course of the relatively unfettered commodity production in the

[18] My *English Peasantry in the Later Middle Ages*, Oxford, 1975, is an attempt to discuss this phase of relatively unfettered simple commodity production.

15th century, the necessary pre-conditions were created for later capitalist development.

Feudal relations of production were by no means abolished during this period; the essential characteristics of a feudal ruling class and a feudal state (in the Marxist sense of the word) remained. The enormous incomes of the great aristocrats, such as the Dukes of Lancaster and York (founders of short-lived royal dynasties), the Earls of Warwick or Salisbury, were still largely based on rent, though they increasingly pillaged the resources of the monarchy in their efforts to keep effective patronage over their retainers and political supporters. The machinery of state, even after its re-shaping in the early 16th century, was essentially that of the medieval *regnum*. Moneyed wealth, which was not based on the possession of landed property, came from trade which was in the hands of monopoly companies of merchants like the Merchant Adventurers and the Merchants of the Staple. It did not come from industrial production, although the principal export from England was finished and unfinished cloth – the profit went to the sellers rather than to the producers. In other words, however important were the changes which gave free rein to the agricultural and industrial commodity producers, there was no transformation of the basic relationships constituting the feudal mode of production.

The Prime Mover

The contributors to the original debate, with the exception of Paul Sweezy (and whatever their own reservations about Maurice Dobb's formulations) all rejected the argument that the feudal mode of production was static and self-perpetuating, did not generate the preconditions for its own transformation and therefore needed an outside force to upset its equilibrium. Sweezy, following Pirenne, had found this outside force in the merchant capital accumulated in the Middle-Eastern–Mediterranean trading area, which was, as it were, injected into the stable feudal system through the agency of a set of traders of unknown social origin. Since feudalism was, according to Sweezy, a mode in which all production was for use, not for exchange, the future progress of feudal Western Europe, after the 11th century was due to factors external to it. Sweezy did not explain what was the nature of the social formation which generated this mass of merchant capital or indeed why it should be regarded as a separate social system from that of non-Mediterranean Europe. In response to criticism, however, Sweezy quite rightly asked what was the prime mover within the feudal mode which gave it an internal dynamic both for development and dissolution.

In my own short comment towards the end of the debate I suggested that the necessary if fluctuating pressure by the ruling class for the transfer to itself of peasant surplus labour or surplus product was the root cause of the technical progress and improved feudal organisation which made for the enlargement of the disposable surplus. This was the basis for the growth of simple commodity production, seigneurial incomes in cash, international luxury trade and urbanisation. This side of the story has been developed with great brilliance by Georges Duby in his recent book on the early development of the medieval economy. As I have explained elsewhere, I believe that his explanation is one-sided.[19] He stresses the pressure of the lord on the peasant. He does not pay the same attention to the efforts of the peasants to retain for themselves as much of the surplus to subsistence as was possible given the socio-political balance of forces. But this peasant resistance was of crucial importance in the development of the rural communes, the extension of free tenure and status, the freeing of peasant and artisan economies for the development of commodity production and eventually the emergence of the capitalist entrepreneur.

As has already been mentioned, the history of the English agrarian economy in the 14th and 15th centuries illustrates very well the consequences of successful peasant resistance to the lords' pressure for the transfer of surplus. In fact, this must be regarded as a critical turning point in the history of the 'prime mover'. The long period of the successful and multiform exploitation of peasant labour ended, at any rate in most Western European countries, between the middle and the end of the 14th century. Only with the successful re-imposition of forms of legally enforceable serfdom could the landowners have continued their previous success. In the West this was politically and socially impossible. In Eastern Europe the story was different. In the West more and more of the disposable surplus was retained within the peasant economy. When the harsh yoke of landlordism was next felt by the rural population, it was something quite different in essence, if not always in form – the beginning of the emergence and long and uneven development of a new triad, landowner–capitalist farmer–farm labourer.

Meanwhile, since the original debate, other non-Marxist historians have made their own proposals about a prime mover in feudal society.

19 G. Duby, *The Early Growth of the European Economy: Warriors and Peasants*, London, 1974. My review of the French edition was published in *New Left Review*, No. 83, January–February 1974.

The most persuasive of these are variants on demographic interpretations of medieval development. One of these, which might better be called an 'ecological' theory of history, has been cogently argued by M. M. Postan in various works.[20] It also emphasises the agrarian, peasant base of the economy. However, it concentrates rather on the relationship of the cultivator to the environment, to the earth as his natural workshop as Marx would have put it, than on the relations between the cultivator and the exploiting landowner. Hence, the important events were the pressure of an increasing peasant population on scarce resources, the consequent fragmentation of holdings, exhaustion of the soil and impoverishment of smallholders. Nevertheless this expanding agrarian economy, before it choked itself, was dynamic and market oriented, a dynamism to be seen especially in certain sections of the upper strata of society, such as the supposedly capitalistically inclined owners of manorial demesnes and the enterprising and innovating merchant capitalists of the great cities. When the equilibrium broke, however, at the turn of the 13th century and especially after the population collapse of the mid-14th century, the pressure on scarce landed resources relaxed and the peasant economy became more prosperous. But it also became more self-sufficient, less market-oriented. Regional and international trade contracted, so that until the last quarter of the 15th century when population once again began to rise, the late medieval economy was stagnant.

There is another type of 'prime mover' interpretation, less wide-ranging than that briefly described above. This focusses on the internal composition of peasant families in their communities. Historians of this school examine family constitution, inheritance customs, problems of the absorption or rejection of younger sons and daughters by family and village communities and the associated question of non-agricultural by-occupations in the countryside. These topics are of great importance and must certainly enter into any serious research by Marxists into the detailed functioning of the feudal mode of production. This is all the more important in that this field of study can be made to bear conclusions of a very dubious character. Some of its devotees present the medieval family and community as though they were isolated and self-regulating social groups abstracted from the wider world, and in particular unaffected by the expoitative pressures of landowners, the church and the state. In so far as this outside world has to be acknowledged, the

[20] Summed up in *The Medieval Economy and Society*, London, 1972.

emphasis is on harmony rather than pressure. This leads to an interpretation of feudal society as part of a continuum of pre-industrial 'traditional' societies, whose main characteristic is stability, not to say stagnation. Medieval clerical estate theory, with its emphasis on the unchanging and organic relationship of the social orders, each fulfilling its proper function (ruling, fighting, praying, buying and selling, working) under God, is rehabilitated as the rational explanation of this type of social order. At the village level, the difference between rich and poor families is explained in terms of the ruling functions of the rich and the service functions of the poor. It is even suggested that this distinction is genetically determined.[21]

Some of the irrational excrescences of non-Marxist historical research into demographic aspects of the medieval economy should not lead to the rejection of the positive contributions made by certain historians of this school. Although kinship relations were not as important in feudal as in primitive societies, they still played a vital role in the distribution of resources at all social levels. This must be acknowledged while at the same time the primacy of the exploitative relationship between lord and peasant in the feudal mode of production must be reasserted. The same applies to the inter-relationship of peasant populations and landed resources, the positive contribution of the Postan school to our understanding of the late medieval economy. Marxist scholarship cannot operate as a hermetically sealed system. Not only must it absorb the positive contributions of non-Marxist scholarship but it can and should show that Marx's concept of the mode of production gives us the best tool for the analysis of the dynamic, not only of capitalism, but of feudalism.

[21] Current work produced by the school of Father J. A. Raftis of the Pontifical Institute of medieval studies exemplifies this approach. See for example E. B. Dewindt, *Land and People in Holywell-cum-Needingworth*, Toronto, 1972 and J. A. Raftis, *Warboys*, Toronto, 1975.

A Note on Feudalism

It is to be hoped that the contributions in this volume to the debate on the transition from feudalism to capitalism will be of interest to others than *cognoscenti* of Marxism. Generally speaking, the terminology of Marxism is well enough known. But it may still be worth while at this point to dwell on the word 'feudalism' which, by now, has rather divergent meanings, as between Marxist and some non-Marxist historians.

Marx, when writing about 'feudalism', was using the term in a way which would have been, to some degree, familiar to his contemporaries, that is to describe a whole social order whose principal feature was the domination of the rest of society, mainly peasants, by a military, landowning aristocracy. Marx, of course, analysed that domination in a way which was peculiar to him, basing his analysis on the specific form in which the labour of the direct producer, once that producer's subsistence necessities had been fulfilled, became the income of the ruling class. By analogy with his full analysis of the capitalist mode of production, which was Marx's principal objective, we refer to the feudal mode of production as composed of the forces of production (the material basis of the productive process) and the relations of production (the relations between the main classes). The essence of the feudal mode of production in the Marxist sense is the exploitative relationship between landowners and subordinated peasants, in which the surplus beyond subsistence of the latter, whether in direct labour or in rent in kind or in money, is transferred under coercive sanction to the former. This relationship is termed 'serfdom', a term which, as has been seen, causes some difficulties.

As we have mentioned, Marx's contemporaries, while not necessarily agreeing with his analysis of the essence of feudalism, would have known what he was talking about. Since his day, non-Marxist historians have refined the meaning of the term, so that it is no longer the description of a whole social order but of certain specific relationships within the medieval ruling class. These relationships, briefly, were those of the free vassals with their overlords, and were based on the tenure of landed holdings (fiefs or in Latin *feoda*). Fiefs were held by vassals in return for military service in the lord's host; attendance at the lord's court of jurisdiction; aid and counsel to the lord. When taken in this refined sense, feudalism has little to do with the relationships between lords and peasants (who probably constituted at least 90% of the population in the early middle ages) and, strictly speaking, lasted for only about a couple of centuries. This very narrow interpretation of the word has been abandoned by many non-Marxist historians, following Marc Bloch, but is still very influential, especially in English academic circles. Its exponents claim that their interpretation has a rigour which is absent from broader interpretations, but one could well argue that rigour may be wasted when devoted to categories of analysis of limited significance.

The Debate on the Transition

A Critique

Paul Sweezy

We live in the period of transition from capitalism to socialism; and this fact lends particular interest to studies of earlier transitions from one social system to another. This is one reason, among many others, why Maurice Dobb's *Studies in the Development of Capitalism*[1] is such a timely and important book. Something like a third of the whole volume is devoted to the decline of feudalism and the rise of capitalism. In this article I shall confine my attention exclusively to this aspect of Dobb's work.

Dobb's Definition of Feudalism

Dobb defines feudalism as being 'virtually idential with what we usually mean by serfdom: an obligation laid on the producer by force and independently of his own volition to fulfil certain economic demands of an overlord, whether these demands take the form of services to be performed or of dues to be paid in money or in kind' (p. 35). In keeping with this definition, Dobb uses the two terms, 'feudalism' and 'serfdom', as practically interchangeable throughout the book.

It seems to me that this definition is defective in not identifying a *system* of production. *Some* serfdom can exist in systems which are clearly not feudal; and even as the dominant relation of production, serfdom has at different times and in different regions been associated with different forms of economic organisation. Thus Engels, in one of his last letter to Marx, wrote that 'it is certain that serfdom and bondage are not a peculiarly (*spezifisch*) medieval-feudal form, we find them everywhere or nearly everywhere where conquerors have the land cultivated for them by the old inhabitants.'[2] It follows, I think, that the concept of feudalism, as Dobb defines it, is too general to be immediately applicable to the study of a particular region during a particular period. Or to

[1] London, 1946. Reprinted 1963 and 1972.

[2] Marx-Engels, *Selected Correspondence*, p. 411 f.

put it otherwise, what Dobb is really defining is not *one* social system but a family of social systems, all of which are based on serfdom. In studying specific historical problems, it is important to know not only that we are dealing with feudalism but also which member of the family is involved.

Dobb's primary interest, of course, lies in western European feudalism, since it was in this region that capitalism was born and grew to maturity. Hence it seems to me he ought to indicate very clearly what he regards as the main features of western European feudalism and to follow this with a theoretical analysis of the laws and tendencies of a system with these principal features. I shall try to show later that his failure to follow this course leads him to a number of doubtful generalisations. Moreover, I think the same reason accounts for Dobb's frequent practice of invoking factual support from a wide variety of regions and periods for arguments which are applied to western Europe and can really only be tested in terms of western European experience.

This is not to say, of course, that Dobb is not thoroughly familiar with western European feudalism. At one point (p. 36 f.) he gives a concise outline of its most important characteristics: (1) 'a low level of technique, in which the instruments of production are simple and generally inexpensive, and the act of production is largely individual in character; the division of labour . . . being at a very primitive level of development'; (2) 'production for the immediate need of the household or village-community and not for a wider market'; (3) 'demesne-farming: farming of the lord's estate, often on a considerable scale, by compulsory labour-services'; (4) 'political decentralisation'; (5) 'conditional holding of land by lords on some kind of service-tenure'; (6) 'possession by a lord of judicial or quasi-judicial functions in relation to the dependent population.' Dobb refers to a system having these characteristics as the 'classic' form of feudalism, but it would be less likely to mislead if it were called the western European form. The fact that 'the feudal mode of production was not confined to this classic form' is apparently Dobb's reason for not analysing its structure and tendencies more closely. In my judgment, however, such an analysis is essential if we are to avoid confusion in our attempts to discover the causes of the downfall of feudalism in western Europe.

The Theory of Western European Feudalism

Drawing on Dobb's description, we can define western European feudalism as an economic system in which serfdom is the predominant relation of production, and in which production is organised in and around the manorial estate of the lord. It is important to notice that this definition does not imply 'natural economy' or the absence of money transactions or money calculation. What it does imply is that markets are for the most part local and that long-distance trade, while not necessarily absent, plays no determining role in the purposes or methods of production. The crucial feature of feudalism in this sense is that it is a system of *production for use*. The needs of the community are known and production is planned and organised with a view to satisfying these needs. This has extremely important consequences. As Marx stated in *Capital*, 'it is clear . . . that in any given economic formation of society, where not the exchange value but the use value of the product predominates, surplus labour will be limited by a given set of wants which may be greater or less, and that *here no boundless thirst for surplus labour arises from the nature of production itself*.'[3] There is, in other words, none of the pressure which exists under capitalism for continual improvements in methods of production. Techniques and forms of organisation settle down in established grooves. Where this is the case, as historical materialism teaches, there is a very strong tendency for the whole life of society to be oriented toward custom and tradition.

We must not conclude, however, that such a system is necessarily stable or static. One element of instability is the competition among the lords for land and vassals which together form the foundation of power and prestige. This competition is the analogue of competition for profits under capitalism, but its effects are quite different. It generates a more or less continuous state of warfare; but the resultant insecurity of life and possession, far from revolutionising methods of production as capitalist competition does, merely accentuates the mutual dependence of lord and vassal and thus reinforces the basic structure of feudal relations. Feudal warfare upsets, impoverishes, and exhausts society, but it has no tendency to transform it.

A second element of instability is to be found in the growth of population. The structure of the manor is such as to set limits to the number of producers it can employ and the number of consumers it can support, while the inherent conservatism of the system inhibits overall expansion. This does not mean, of course, that no growth is possible, only that it tends to lag behind population increase. Younger sons of serfs are pushed out of the regular framework of feudal society and go to make

[3] *Capital*, I, p. 260. Italics added. (All references to *Capital* are to the Kerr edition).

up the kind of vagrant population – living on alms or brigandage and supplying the raw material for mercenary armies – which was so characteristic of the Middle Ages. Such a surplus population, however, while contributing to instability and insecurity, exercises no creative or revolutionising influence on feudal society.[4]

We may conclude, then, that western European feudalism, in spite of chronic instability and insecurity, was a system with a very strong bias in favour of maintaining given methods and relations of production. I think we are justified in saying of it what Marx said of India before the period of British rule: 'All the civil wars, invasions, revolutions, conquests, famines . . . did not go deeper than its surface.'[5]

I believe that if Dobb had taken full account of this inherently conservative and change-resisting character of western European feudalism, he would have been obliged to alter the theory which he puts forward to account for its disintegration and decline in the later Middle Ages.

Dobb's Theory of the Decline of Feudalism

Dobb summarises the commonly accepted explanation of the decline of feudalism as follows:

'We are often presented with the picture of a more or less stable economy that was disintegrated by the impact of commerce acting as an external force and developing outside the system that it finally overwhelms. We are given an interpretation of the transition from the old order to the new that finds the dominant causal sequences within the sphere of exchange between manorial economy and the outside world. 'Natural economy' and 'exchange economy' are two economic orders that cannot mix, and the presence of the latter, we are told, is sufficient to cause the former to go into dissolution (p. 38).'

Dobb does not deny the 'outstanding importance' of this process: 'That it was connected with the changes that were so marked at the end of the Middle Ages is evident enough' (p. 38). But he finds this explanation inadequate because it does not probe deeply enough into the effect of trade on feudalism. If we examine the problem more closely, he

[4] It might be thought that the vigorous colonisation and reclamation movement of the twelfth and thirteenth centuries disproves this argument. I think, however, that this is not the case. The colonisation movement seems to have been a reflex of the growth of trade and commodity production, not a manifestation of the internal expansive power of feudal society. See Henri Pirenne, *Economic and Social History of Medieval Europe*, New York, 1937, ch. 3, sec. ii.

[5] Emile Burns, ed., *A Handbook of Marxism*, London, 1935, p. 182.

argues, we shall find that 'there seems, in fact, to be as much evidence that the growth of money economy *per se* led to an intensification of serfdom as there is evidence that it was the cause of the feudal decline' (p. 40). In support of this contention, he cites a considerable body of historical data, the 'outstanding case' being 'the recrudescence of Feudalism in Eastern Europe at the end of the fifteenth century – that "second serfdom" of which Friedrich Engels wrote: a revival of the old system which was associated with the growth of production for the market' (p. 39). On the basis of such data, Dobb reasons that if the only factor at work in western Europe had been the rise of trade, the result might as well have been an intensification as a disintegration of feudalism. And from this it follows that there must have been other factors at work to bring about the actually observed result.

What were these factors? Dobb believes that they can be found inside the feudal economy itself. He concedes that 'the evidence is neither very plentiful nor conclusive', but he feels that 'such evidence as we possess strongly indicates that it was the inefficiency of Feudalism as a system of production, coupled with the growing needs of the ruling class for revenue, that was primarily responsible for its decline; since this need for additional revenue promoted an increase in the pressure on the producer to a point where this pressure became literally unendurable' (p. 42). The consequence of this growing pressure was that 'in the end it led to an exhaustion, or actual disappearance, of the labour-force by which the system was nourished' (p. 43).

In other words, according to Dobb's theory, the essential cause of the breakdown of feudalism was over-exploitation of the labour force: serfs deserted the lords' estates *en masse*, and those who remained were too few and too overworked to enable the system to maintain itself on the old basis. It was these developments, rather than the rise of trade, which forced the feudal ruling class to adopt those expedients – commutation of labour services, leasing demesne lands to tenant farmers, etc. – which finally led to the transformation of productive relations in the countryside.

A Critique of Dobb's Theory

In order to make his theory stand up, Dobb must show that the feudal ruling class's growing need for revenue and the flight of serfs from the land can both be explained in terms of forces operating inside the feudal system. Let us see how he attempts to do this.

First with regard to the lords' need for revenue. Here Dobb cites a number of factors which he regards as inherent in the feudal system. Serfs were held in contempt and were looked upon primarily as a source of income (p. 43 f.). The size of the parasitic class tended to expand as a result of natural growth of noble families, sub-infeudation, and the multiplication of retainers – all of whom 'had to be supported from the surplus labour of the serf population'. War and brigandage 'swelled the expenses of feudal households' and 'spread waste and devastation over the land'. Finally, 'as the age of chivalry advanced, the extravagances of noble households advanced also, with their lavish feasts and costly displays, vying in emulation in their cult of *magnificentia*' (p. 45).

Two of these factors – disregard for the interests of the serfs, and war and brigandage – existed throughout the whole period, and if they became more intense with the passage of time, this requires to be explained: it cannot simply be taken for granted as a natural feature of feudalism. Dobb makes no attempt to explain such a trend, however; and even the special drain which he attributes to the crusades during the decisive period of feudal development is of doubtful significance. After all, the crusaders fought in the East, and they naturally lived for the most part off the land; the crusades were to a certain extent looting expeditions which brought material rewards to their sponsors and participants; and they were in large part substitutes for, rather than additions to, the 'normal' feudal warfare of the time. On the whole, it seems to me that these two factors provide little support for Dobb's theory.

It is somewhat different, however, with the other two factors, namely, the growth in the size of the parasitic class and the growing extravagance of noble households. Here we have *prima facie* evidence of a need for increased revenue. But whether we also have the necessary support for Dobb's theory is more doubtful. The growth in the size of the parasitic class was matched by a growth of the serf population. Moreover, throughout the Middle Ages there was plenty of cultivable land to be brought into use. Hence, despite its extremely conservative nature, the feudal system did expand, slowly but steadily. When we take account of the fact that warfare took its main toll from the upper orders (since they alone were permitted to bear arms), we may well doubt whether there was a significant *relative* growth in the size of the parasitic class. In the absence of any clear, factual evidence one way or the other, we would certainly not be justified in attributing decisive weight to this factor.

On the other hand there is no reason to doubt the reality of the growing extravagance of the feudal ruling class: here the evidence is plentiful and it all points in the same direction. But was this growing extravagance a trend which can be explained by the nature of the feudal system, or does it reflect something that was happening outside the feudal system? It seems to me that on general grounds we should expect the latter to be the case. Even under such a dynamic system as capitalism, spontaneous changes in consumers' tastes are of negligible importance,[6] and we should expect this to be true *a fortiori* in a tradition-bound society like feudalism. Moreover, once we look outside the feudal system we find ample reason for the growing extravagance of the feudal ruling class: the rapid expansion of trade from the eleventh century onward brought an ever-increasing quantity and variety of goods within its reach. Dobb recognises the existence of this relation between trade and the needs of the feudal ruling class, but it seems to me that he passes over it altogether too lightly. If he had given it the weight it deserves, he could hardly have maintained that the growing extravagance of the ruling class was due to causes internal to the feudal system.

Let us now turn to the problem of the flight of the serfs from the land. There is little doubt that this was an important cause of the crisis of the feudal economy that characterised the 14th century. Dobb assumes that it was due to the oppression of the lords (which in turn had its origin in their growing need for revenue) and can thus be explained as a process internal to the feudal system. But has he made out a convincing case for this assumption?[7]

I think not. The serfs could not simply desert the manors, no matter how exacting their masters might become, unless they had somewhere to go. It is true, as I have argued above, that feudal society tends to generate a surplus of vagrant population; but this vagrant population, constituting the dregs of society, is made up of those for whom there is no room on the manors, and it is hardly realistic to suppose that any considerable number of serfs would deliberately abandon their holdings to descend to the bottom of the social ladder.

This whole problem, however, takes on an entirely new aspect – to

[6] Thus, for example, Schumpeter feels justified in assuming that under capitalism 'consumers' initiative in changing their tastes . . . is negligible and that all change in consumers' tastes is incident to, and brought about by, producers' action,' *Business Cycles*, (New York, 1939), I, p. 73. Needless to say, this assumption is in full accord with the Marxian theory of the primacy of production over consumption.

[7] It should be stressed that it *is* an assumption, not an established fact. Rodney Hilton, a student of medieval economic history to whom Dobb acknowledges indebtedness in the Preface, states in a review that 'there is not anything like adequate statistical proof that an appreciable number of peasants left their holdings for the reason stated [i.e., intolerable conditions of oppression],' *Modern Quarterly*, II, Summer, 1947, p. 268.

which Dobb pays surprisingly little attention – when we recall that the flight of the serfs took place simultaneously with the growth of the towns, especially in the 12th and 13th centuries. There is no doubt that the rapidly developing towns – offering, as they did, liberty employment, and improved social status – acted as a powerful magnet to the oppressed rural population. And the burghers themselves, in need of additional labour power and of more soldiers to enhance their military strength, made every effort to facilitate the escape of the serfs from the jurisdiction of their masters. 'There is frequently', Marx commented in a letter to Engels, 'something quite pathetic about the way the burghers in the twelfth century invite the peasants to escape to the cities'.[8] Against this background, the movement away from the land, which would otherwise be incomprehensible, is seen to be the natural consequence of the rise of the towns. No doubt the oppression of which Dobb writes was an important factor in predisposing the serfs to flight, but acting by itself it could hardly have produced an emigration of large proportions.[9]

Dobb's theory of the internal causation of the breakdown of feudalism could still be rescued if it could be shown that the rise of the towns was a process internal to the feudal system. But as I read Dobb, he would not maintain this. He takes an eclectic position on the question of the *origin* of the medieval towns but recognises that their *growth* was generally in proportion to their importance as trading centres. Since trade can in no sense be regarded as a form of feudal economy, it follows that Dobb could hardly argue that the rise of urban life was a consequence of internal feudal causes.

To sum up this critique of Dobb's theory of the decline of feudalism: having neglected to analyse the laws and tendencies of western European feudalism, he mistakes for immanent trends certain historical developments which in fact can only be explained as arising from causes external to the system.

[8] *Selected Correspondence*, p. 74.

[9] As I shall argue below, it was the relative absence of urban life in eastern Europe which left the peasantry there at the mercy of the lords and brought about the recrudescence of serfdom in that region in the fifteenth century. Dobb, it will be recalled, cited this 'second serfdom' in eastern Europe against the view that trade necessarily tends to bring about the disintegration of feudal economy. We can now see that the problem is in reality much more complex. Near the centres of trade, the effect on feudal economy is strongly disintegrating; further away the effect tends to be just the opposite. This is an important question to which we shall return later.

More on the Theory of the Decline of Feudalism

While I find Dobb's theory of the decline of feudalism unsatisfactory on several counts, I think he has nevertheless made an important contribution to the solution of the problem. Most of his specific criticisms of traditional theories are well taken; and it seems clear that no theory which fails to take into account the factors which Dobb stresses – especially the growing extravagance of the ruling class and the flight of the serfs from the land – can be regarded as correct. Hence the following notes and suggestions owe much to Dobb even where they depart from his views.

It seems to me that Dobb has not succeeded in shaking that part of the commonly accepted theory which holds that the root cause of the decline of feudalism was the growth of trade. But he has shown that the impact of trade on the feudal system is more complicated than has usually been thought: the idea that trade equals 'money economy' and that money economy is a natural dissolvent of feudal relations is much too simple. Let us attempt to explore the relation of trade to the feudal economy more closely.[10]

It seems to me that the important conflict in this connection is not between 'money economy' and 'natural economy' but between production for the market and production for use. We ought to try to uncover the process by which trade engendered a *system* of production for the market, and then to trace the impact of this system on the pre-existent feudal system of production for use.

Any but the most primitive economy requires a certain amount of trade. Thus the local village markets and the itinerant peddlers of the European Dark Ages were props rather than threats to the feudal order: they supplied essential needs without bulking large enough to affect the structure of economic relations. When trade first began to expand in the tenth century (or perhaps even before), it was in the sphere of long-distance, as distinguished from purely local, exchange of relatively expensive goods which could stand the very high transport

[10] It should be noted that the problem of the growth of trade in the Middle Ages is in principle separate from the problem of the decline of feudalism. Granted the fact that trade increased, *whatever the reason may have been*, feudalism was bound to be influenced in certain ways. There is no space here for a discussion of the reasons for the growth of trade; I will only say that I find Pirenne's theory – which stresses the re-opening of Mediterranean shipping to and from the western ports in the eleventh century, and the development by the Scandinavians of commercial routes from the North Sea and the Baltic via Russia to the Black Sea from the tenth century – to be quite convincing. But clearly one does not have to accept Pirenne's theory in order to agree that the growth of trade was the decisive factor in bringing about the decline of western European feudalism.

costs of the time. As long as this expansion of trade remained within the forms of what may be called the peddling system, its effects necessarily remained slight. But when it outgrew the peddling stage and began to result in the establishment of localised trading and transshipment centres, a qualitatively new factor was introduced. For these centres, though based on long-distance exchange, inevitably became generators of commodity production in their own right. They had to be provisioned from the surrounding countryside; and their handicrafts, embodying a higher form of specialisation and division of labour than anything known to the manorial economy, not only supplied the town population itself with needed products but also provided commodities which the rural population could purchase with the proceeds of sales in the town market. As this process unfolded, the transactions of the long-distance traders, which formed the seed from which the trading centres grew, lost their unique importance and probably in the majority of cases came to occupy a secondary place in the town economies.

We see thus how long-distance trade could be a creative force, bringing into existence a *system* of production for exchange alongside the old feudal system of production for use.[11] Once juxtaposed, these two systems naturally began to act upon each other. Let us examine some of the currents of influence running from the exchange economy to the use economy.

In the first place, and perhaps most importantly, the inefficiency of the manorial organisation of production – which probably no one recognised or at least paid any attention to, as long as it had no rival – was now clearly revealed by contrast with a more rational system of specialisation and division of labour. Manufactured goods could be bought more cheaply than they could be made, and this pressure to buy generated a pressure to sell. Taken together, these pressures operated powerfully to bring the feudal estates within the orbit of the exchange economy. 'Of what use now', Pirenne asks, 'were the domestic workshops which on each important manor used to maintain a few score serfs to manufacture textiles or farming tools, not half as well as they were now made by the artisans of the neighbouring town? They were allowed to disappear almost everywhere in the course of the twelfth century'.[12]

[11] In this connection, it is important to recognise that the contrast between the two forms of economy is by no means identical with the contrast between town and country. Rural as well as urban production for the market is included in exchange economy. Hence the relative importance of the two forms of economy can never be measured by a simple index like the proportion of urban to rural population.

[12] Pirenne, *op. cit.*, p. 82.

Second, the very existence of exchange value as a massive economic fact tends to transform the attitude of producers. It now becomes possible to seek riches, not in the absurd form of a heap of perishable goods but in the very convenient and mobile form of money or claims to money. The possession of wealth soon becomes an end in itself in an exchange economy, and this psychological transformation affects not only those who are immediately involved but also (though doubtless to a lesser degree) those who come into contact with the exchange economy. Hence not only merchants and traders but also members of the old feudal society acquire what we should call today a businesslike attitude toward economic affairs. Since businessmen *always* have a need for more revenue, we have here a part of the explanation of the ruling class's growing need for revenue, on which, as we have seen, Dobb places so much emphasis in accounting for the decline of feudalism.

Third, and also important in the same connection, is the development of the tastes of the feudal ruling class. As Pirenne describes the process,

> 'in every direction where commerce spread, it created the desire for the new articles of consumption, which it brought with it. As always happens, the aristocracy wished to surround themselves with the luxury, or at least the comfort befitting their social rank. We see at once, for instance, by comparing the life of a knight in the eleventh century with that of one in the twelfth, how the expenses necessitated by food, dress, household furniture and, above all, arms, rose between these two periods.'[13]

Here we have what is probably the key to the feudal ruling class's need for increased revenue in the later Middle Ages.

Finally, the rise of the towns, which were the centres and breeders of exchange economy, opened up to the servile population of the countryside the prospect of a freer and better life. This was undoubtedly the main cause of that flight from the land which Dobb rightly considers to have been one of the decisive factors in the decline of feudalism.

No doubt the rise of exchange economy had other effects on the old order, but I think that the four which have been mentioned were sufficiently pervasive and powerful to ensure the breaking up of the pre-existing *system* of production. The superior efficiency of more highly specialised production, the greater gains to be made by pro-

[13] *Ibid.*, p. 81.

ducing for the market rather than for immediate use, the greater attractiveness of town life to the worker: these factors made it only a matter of time before the new system, once strong enough to stand on its own feet, would win out.

But the triumph of exchange economy does not necessarily imply the end of either serfdom or demesne-farming. Exchange economy is compatible with slavery, serfdom, independent self-employed labour, or wage-labour. History is rich in examples of production for the market by all these kinds of labour. Dobb is therefore unquestionably right in rejecting the theory that the rise of trade automatically brings with it the liquidation of serfdom; and if serfdom is identified with feudalism, this is of course true *ex definitione*, of feudalism too. The fact that the advance of exchange economy actually went hand in hand with the decline of serfdom is something which has to be explained; it cannot simply be taken for granted.

In analysing this problem we can, I think, safely pass over the uneven character of the decline of serfdom in western Europe. Dobb points out that for a time in some regions of western Europe the progress of trade was accompanied by an intensification rather than a relaxation of the bonds of serfdom. This is no doubt true and important, and he succeeds in clearing up a number of apparent paradoxes. But these temporary and partial reversals of trend should not be allowed to obscure the overall picture which is one of the steady replacement of demesne-farming using serf labour by tenant farming using either independent peasant labour or (to a much smaller extent) hired labour. The real problem is to account for this underlying trend.

It seems to me that of the complex of causes at work, two stand out as decisively important. In the first place, the rise of the towns, which was fairly general throughout western Europe, did a great deal more than merely offer a haven of refuge to those serfs who fled the manors; it also altered the position of those who remained behind. Probably only a relatively small proportion of the total number of serfs actually packed up and moved to the towns, but enough did to make the pressure of the higher standards enjoyed in the towns effectively felt in the countryside. Just as wages must rise in a low-wage area when workers have the possibility of moving to a high-wage area, so concessions had to be made to serfs when they had the possibility of moving to the towns. Such concessions were necessarily in the direction of more freedom and the transformation of feudal dues into money rents.

In the second place, while the manor could be, and in many cases was, turned to production for the market, it was fundamentally inefficient and unsuited to that putpose. Techniques were primitive and division of labour undeveloped. From an administrative point of view, the manor was unwieldy: in particular there was no clear-cut separation of production from consumption, so that the costing of products was almost impossible. Moreover, everything on the manor was regulated by custom and tradition. This applied not only to the methods of cultivation but also to the quantity of work performed and its division between necessary and surplus labour: the serf had duties, but he also had rights. This whole mass of customary rules and regulations constituted so many obstacles to the rational exploitation of human and material resources for pecuniary gain.[14] Sooner or later, new types of productive relations and new forms of organisation had to be found to meet the requirements of a changed economic order.

Is this reasoning refuted by the 'second serfdom' of the sixteenth century and after in eastern Europe, on which Dobb places so much stress? How did it happen that in this case the growth of opportunities to trade led to a dramatic and enduring intensification of the bonds of serfdom?

The answer to these questions will be found, I think, in the geography of the second serfdom, in the fact that the phenomenon becomes increasingly marked and severe as we move eastward away from the centre of the new exchange economy.[15] At the centre, where town life is most highly developed, the agricultural labourer has an alternative to remaining on the soil; and this gives him, as it were, a strong bargaining

[14] Dobb often seems to overlook this aspect of feudalism and to assume that only the villein stood to gain from the abolition of serfdom. He tends to forget that 'the enfranchisement of the peasants was in reality the enfranchisement of the landowner, who, having henceforth to deal with free men who were not attached to his land, could dispose of the latter by means of simple revocable contracts, whose brief duration enabled him to modify them in accordance with the increasing rent of the land,' Pirenne, *A History of Europe from the Invasions to the XVI Century* (New York, 1939), p. 533.

[15] Pirenne gives the following graphic description: 'To the west of the Elbe the change had no particular consequences beyond a recrudescence of corvées, prestations, and arbitrary measures of every kind. But beyond the river, in Brandenburg, Prussia, Silesia, Austria, Bohemia, and Hungary, the most merciless advantage was taken of it. The descendants of the free colonists of the thirteenth century were systematically deprived of their land and reduced to the position of personal serfs (*Leibeigene*). The wholesale exploitation of estates absorbed their holdings and reduced them to a servile condition which so closely approximated to that of slavery that it was permissible to sell the person of the serf independently of the soil. From the middle of the sixteenth century the whole of the region to the east of the Elbe and the Sudeten Mountains became covered with *Rittergüter* exploited by *Junkers*, who may be compared, as regards the degree of humanity displayed in their treatment of their white slaves, with the planters of the West Indies,' *ibid.*, p. 534.

position. When the ruling class turns to production for the market with a view to pecuniary gain, it finds it necessary to resort to new, more flexible, and relatively progressive forms of exploitation. On the periphery of the exchange economy, on the other hand, the relative position of the landlord and the agricultural labourer is very different. The worker cannot run away because he has no place to go: for all practical purposes he is at the mercy of the lord, who, moreover, has never been subjected to the civilising proximity of urban life. When the expansion of trade instills a lust for gain into a ruling class in this position, the result is not the development of new forms of exploitation but the intensification of old forms. Marx, in the following passage (even though he was not specifically concerned with the second serfdom in eastern Europe), went to the root of the matter:

> 'As soon as people, whose production still moves within the lower forms of slave-labour, corvée labour, etc., are drawn into the whirlpool of an international market dominated by the capitalistic mode of production, the sale of their products for export becoming their principal interests, the civilised horrors of overwork are grafted on the barbaric horrors of slavery, serfdom, etc.'[16]

Dobb's theory holds that the decline of western European feudalism was due to the overexploitation by the ruling class of society's labour power. If the reasoning of this section is correct, it seems to me that it would be more accurate to say that the decline of weste. n European feudalism was due to the inability of the ruling class to maintain control over, and hence to overexploit, society's labour power.

What Came After Feudalism in Western Europe?

According to Dobb's chronology – which would probably not be seriously disputed by anyone – western European feudalism entered a period of acute crisis in the fourteenth century and thereafter disintegrated, more or less rapidly in different regions. On the other hand, we cannot speak of the beginning of the capitalist period until the second half of the sixteenth century at the earliest. This raises the following question: 'how are we to speak of the economic system in the intervening period between then [i.e. the disintegration of feudalism] and the later sixteenth century: a period which, according to our dating, seems to have been neither feudal nor yet capitalist so far as its

[16] *Capital*, I, p. 260.

mode of production was concerned?' (p. 19). This is an important question, and we should be grateful to Dobb for raising it in this clear-cut form.

Dobb's answer to his own question is hesitant and indecisive (p. 19–21). True, the feudal mode of production 'had reached an advanced stage of disintegration'; 'a merchant bourgeoisie had grown to wealth and influence'; 'in the urban handicrafts and in the rise of well-to-do and middling-well-to-do freehold farmers one sees a mode of production which had won its independence from Feudalism'; 'the majority of small tenants . . . paid a money rent'; and 'the estates were for the most part farmed by hired labour'. But Dobb qualifies almost every one of these statements and sums up by saying that 'social relations in the countryside between producers and their lords and masters retained much of their medieval character, and much of the integument at least of the feudal order remained'. In other words, Dobb's answer, I take it, is that the period was feudal after all.

This answer, however, is not very satisfactory. If the period is to be regarded as feudal, even from the point of view of Dobb's comprehensive definition, then at the very least it ought to have been characterised by the continued predominance of serfdom in that countryside. And yet there is good authority for the view that this was precisely the period during which serfdom declined to relatively small proportions all over western Europe.

'In England [Marx wrote] serfdom had practically disappeared in the last part of the fourteenth century. The immense majority of the population consisted then, and to a still larger extent in the fifteenth century, of free peasant proprietors, whatever the feudal title under which their right of property was hidden.'[17]

It seems that Marx had reservations about how widespread this development was on the continent, but before the end of his life he must have given them up. At the end of 1882, three months before Marx's death, Engels wrote a paper dealing with the *Mark*, the old German land system. He sent the manuscript to Marx, commenting that 'the point about the almost total disappearance (*Zurücktreten*) of serfdom – legally or actually – in the 13th and 14th centuries is the most important to me, because formerly you expressed a divergent opinion on this'.[18]

[17] *Ibid.*, I, p. 788.
[18] *Selected Correspondence*, p. 408.

Two days later Marx wrote back: 'Returning the manuscript: *very good.*'[19] And to this Engels replied: 'I am glad that on the history of serfdom we "proceed in agreement", as they say in business'.[20]

These passages show that it was the considered judgment of Marx and Engels that by the 15th century the substance had largely gone out of feudal forms and that serfdom had ceased to be the dominant relation of production throughout western Europe. There is nothing in the evidence cited by Dobb to convince me that we would be justified in reversing this judgment.

Dobb might answer that he does not disagree, that he concedes the substantial disappearance of serfdom, and that his characterisation of this period as essentially feudal is based on the fact that the peasant was still restricted in his movements and in many ways dependent upon the landlord. What he says (pp. 65–66) could, I think, be construed in this sense; and Christopher Hill, who is in a good position to know Dobb's meaning, lends support to this interpretation. According to Hill:

'Mr. Dobb's definition of feudalism enables him to make clear what rural England in the fifteenth and sixteenth centuries was like. He rejects the view which identifies feudalism with labour services and attributes fundamental significance to the abolition of serfdom in England. Mr. Dobb shows that peasants paying a money rent (the overwhelming majority of the sixteenth-century English countryside) may be dependent in numerous other ways on the landlord under whom they live . . . Capitalist relations in agriculture were spreading in sixteenth-century England, but over most of the country the dominant relation of exploitation was still feudal . . . The important thing is not the *legal form* of the relationship between lord and peasant, but the economic content of this relationship.[21]'

It seems to me that to stretch the concept of feudalism in this way is to deprive it of the quality of definiteness which is essential to scientific usefulness. If the fact that tenants are exploited by, and 'in numerous ways' dependent on, landlords is the hallmark of feudalism, we should have to conclude, for example, that certain regions of the United States are today feudal. Such a description may be justified for journalistic

[19] *Briefwechsel*, Marx-Engels-Lenin Institute ed., IV, p. 694. This letter is not included in the *Selected Correspondence*.

[20] *Selected Correspondence*, p. 411.

[21] *The Modern Quarterly*, II (Summer, 1947), p. 269.

purposes; but if we were to go on from there and conclude that the economic system under which these regions of the United States live today is in fundamental respects identical with the economic system of the European Middle Ages, we should be well on the way to serious confusion. I think the same applies, though obviously in less extreme degree, if we assume a fundamental identity between the economic system of England in the sixteenth century and the economic system of England in the thirteenth century. And yet to call them both by the same name, or even to refrain from giving them different names, is inevitably to invite such as assumption.

How, then, shall we characterise the period between the end of feudalism and the beginning of capitalism? I think Dobb is on the right track when he says that the 'two hundred-odd years which separated Edward III from Elizabeth were certainly transitional in character' and that it is 'true, and of outstanding importance for any proper understanding of this transition, that the disintegration of the feudal mode of production had already reached an advanced stage *before* the capitalist mode of production developed, and that this disintegration did not proceed in any close association with the growth of the new mode of production within the womb of the old' (p. 20). This seems to me to be entirely correct, and I believe that if Dobb had followed it up he would have arrived at a satisfactory solution of the problem.

We usually think of a transition from one social system to another as a process in which the two systems directly confront each other and fight it out for supremacy. Such a process, of course, does not exclude the possibility of transitional forms; but these transitional forms are thought of as mixtures of elements from the two systems which are vying for mastery. It is obvious, for example, that the transition from capitalism to socialism is proceeding along some such lines as these; and this fact no doubt makes it all the easier for us to assume that earlier transitions must have been similar.

So far as the transition from feudalism to capitalism is concerned, however, this is a serious error. As the foregoing statement by Dobb emphasises, feudalism in western Europe was already moribund, if not actually dead, before capitalism was born. It follows that the intervening period was not a simple mixture of feudalism and capitalism: the predominant elements were *neither* feudal *nor* capitalist.

This is not the place for a detailed discussion of terminology. I shall simply call the system which prevailed in western Europe during the 15th and 16th centuries 'pre-capitalist commodity production' to indicate that it was the growth of commodity production which first undermined feudalism and then *somewhat later*, after this work of destruction had been substantially completed, prepared the ground for the growth of capitalism.[22] The transition from feudalism to capitalism is thus not a single uninterrupted process – similar to the transition from capitalism to socialism – but is made up of two quite distinct phases which present radically different problems and require to be analysed separately.

It might be thought that this characterisation of the transition from feudalism to capitalism is in conflict with the traditional Marxian view. But I think this is not so: all it does is to make explicit certain points which are implicit in this view.

'Although [Marx wrote] we come across the first beginnings of capitalist production as early as the 14th or 15th century, sporadically, in certain towns of the Mediterranean, the capitalistic era dates from the 16th century. Wherever it appears, the abolition of serfdom has long been effected, and the highest development of the middle ages, the existence of sovereign towns, has long been on the wane.'

And again:

'The circulation of commodities is the starting point of capital. Commodity production and developed commodity circulation, *trade*, form *the historical preconditions* under which it arises. World trade and the world market open up in the sixteenth century the modern life history of capital'.[23]

[22] It is not necessary to specify that the period is non- or post-feudal, since commodity production and feudalism are mutually exclusive concepts. On the other hand, capitalism is itself a form of commodity production, and for this reason the qualification 'pre-capitalist' must be explicitly made.

It could be argued that the best name for the system would be 'simple commodity production', since this is a well-established concept in Marxian theory. It seems to me, however, that to use the term in this way might lead to unnecessary confusion. Simple commodity production is usually defined as a system of independent producers owning their own means of production and satisfying their wants by means of mutual exchange. Such a theoretical construction is useful for a number of reasons: for example, it enables us to present the problem of exchange value in its simplest form; and it also is helpful in clarifying the nature of classes and their relations to the means of production. In pre-capitalist commodity production, however, the most important of the means of production – the land – was largely owned by a class of non-producers, and this fact is enough to differentiate the system sharply from the usual concept of simple commodity production.

[23] *Capital*, I, p. 787 and 163. I have translated this passage anew. The Moore and Aveling translation is inaccurate and omits the emphasis which appears in the original.

Such statements, I think, unmistakably imply a view of the transition from feudalism to capitalism such as I have suggested.[24]

We should be careful not to push this line of reasoning about the transition from feudalism to capitalism too far. In particular, it seems to me that it would be going too far to classify pre-capitalist commodity production as a social system *sui generis*, on a par with feudalism, capitalism and socialism. There was no really dominant relation of production to put its stamp on the system as a whole. There were still strong vestiges of serfdom and vigorous beginnings of wage-labour, but the forms of labour relation which were most common in the statistical sense were pretty clearly unstable and incapable of providing the basis of a viable social order. This holds especially of the relation between landlords and working tenants paying a money rent ('the overwhelming majority of the 16th century English countryside', according to Christopher Hill). Marx analysed this relation with great care in a chapter called 'The Genesis of Capitalist Ground Rent', and insisted that it could be properly understood only as a transitional form:

'The transformation of rent in kind into money rent, taking place first sporadically, then on a more or less national scale, requires a considerable development of commerce, of city industries, of the production of commodities in general, and with them of the circulation of money. . . . Money rent, as a converted form of rent in kind and as an antagonist of rent in kind is the last form and at the same time the form of the dissolution of the type of ground rent which we have considered so far, namely ground rent as the normal form of surplus value and of the unpaid surplus labour which flows to the owner of the means of production. . . . In its further development money rent must lead . . . either to the transformation of land into independent peasants' property, or

[24] I have, of course, selected these particular quotations from Marx for their conciseness and clarity. But obviously isolated quotations can neither prove nor disprove the point. The reader who wishes to make up his own mind about Marx's view of the transition from feudalism to capitalism will have to study carefully at least the following parts of *Capital*: I, Part viii; and III, ch. 20 and 47.

In some respects, the recently published manuscripts which Marx wrote during the winter of 1857–58 in preparation for the *Critique of Political Economy* are even more valuable in throwing light on his ideas about the nature of the transition from feudalism to capitalism: see *Grundrisse der Kritik der politischen Okonomie* (*Rohentwurf*), Marx Engels-Lenin Institute (Moscow, 1939), especially the section entitled 'Formen die der kapitalistischen Produktion vorhergehen' starting on I, p. 375. An adequate examination of this source, however, would require a long article by itself; and I can only say here that my own interpretation of Marx, which was fully formed before the *Grundrisse* became available to me, was confirmed by this new material.

into the form corresponding to the capitalist mode of production, that is to rent paid by the capitalist tenant.'[25]

Moreover, this is not the only type of unstable relation in the pre-capitalist commodity-producing economy. Dobb has shown in a very illuminating section of his chapter on the growth of the proletariat 'how unstable an economy of small producers can be in face of the disintegrating effects of production for the market, especially a distant market, unless it enjoys some special advantages which lends it strength or special measures are taken to give protection to its poorer and weaker members' (p. 254).

We are, I think, justified in concluding that while pre-capitalist commodity production was neither feudal nor capitalist, it was just as little a viable system in its own right. It was strong enough to undermine and disintegrate feudalism, but it was too weak to develop an independent structure of its own: all it could accomplish in a positive sense was to prepare the ground for the victorious advance of capitalism in the 17th and 18th centuries.

A Few Remarks on the Rise of Capitalism

In general, I agree fully with Dobb's analysis of the rise of capitalism. It seems to me that his treatment of this problem is exceptionally clear and illuminating: I would be inclined to rate it the high point of the whole volume. But there are two theses, clearly regarded by Dobb himself as important, which seem to me to require critical examination. The first concerns the origin of the industrial capitalist in the full sense of the term; the second concerns the process of original accumulation.[26]

Dobb cites Marx's chapter on 'Merchant Capital' (III, ch. 20) in support of the view that industrial capital develops in two main ways. The following is the key passage from Dobb:

'According to the first – "the really revolutionary way" – a section of the producers themselves accumulated capital and took to trade, and in course of time began to organise production on a capitalist basis free from the handicraft restrictions of the guilds. According to the second, a section of the existing merchant class began to "take possession directly

[25] *Capital*, III, ch. 47, p. 926 f. Changes have been made in the Untermann translation.

[26] Dobb follows the Moore and Aveling translation in speaking of 'primitive' accumulation. This is likely to be misleading, however, since the point is not that the process is primitive in the usual sense of the term (though it may be and usually is) but that it is not preceded by previous acts of accumulation. Hence 'original' or 'primary' is a better rendering of *ursprünglich* in this context.

of production"; thereby "serving historically as a mode of transition", but becoming eventually "an obstacle to a real capitalist mode of production and declin(ing) with the development of the latter"'.[27]

Dobb puts much stress on the first of these methods. On p. 128 he writes:

'While the growing interest shown by sections of merchant capital in controlling production – in developing what may be termed a deliberately contrived system of "exploitation through trade" – prepared the way for this final outcome [i.e., the subjection of production to genuine capitalist control], and may in a few cases have reached it, this final stage generally seems, as Marx pointed out, to have been associated with the rise from the ranks of the producers themselves of a capitalist element, half-manufacturer, half-merchant, which began to subordinate and to organise those very ranks from which it had so recently risen (p. 128)'.

Again:

'The opening of the 17th century witnessed the beginnings of an important shift in the centre of gravity: the rising predominance of a class of merchant-employers from the ranks of the craftsmen themselves among the yeomanry of the large companies – the process that Marx described as the "really revolutionary way" (p. 134)'.

And later, after a lengthy analysis of the failure of capitalist production despite early and promising beginnings, to develop in certain areas of the continent, Dobb says:

'When seen in the light of a comparative study of capitalist development, Marx's contention that at this stage the rise of a class of industrial capitalists from the ranks of the producers themselves is a condition of any revolutionary transformation of production begins to acquire a central importance (p. 161)'.

It is noteworthy, however, that Dobb admits that 'the details of this process are far from clear, and there is little evidence that bears directly upon it' (p. 134). In fact, so little evidence, even of an indirect character, seems to be available that one reviewer felt constrained to remark that 'it would have been desirable to find more evidence for the view, derived from Marx, that the really revolutionary transformation of pro-

[27] Dobb, p. 123. The internal quotes are from *Capital*, III, p. 393 f.

duction and the breaking of the control of merchant capital over production, was accomplished by men coming from the ranks of former craftsmen'.[28]

I think, however, that the real trouble here is not so much a lack of evidence (for my part, I doubt if evidence of the required kind exists) as a misreading of Marx. Let us reproduce the entire passage in which Marx speaks of the 'really revolutionary way':

'The transition from the feudal mode of production takes two roads. The producer becomes a merchant and capitalist, in contradiction from agricultural natural economy and the guild-encircled handicrafts of medieval town industry. This is the really revolutionary way. Or the merchant takes possession in a direct way of production. While this way serves historically as a mode of transition – instance the English clothier of the seventeenth century, who brings the weavers, although they remain independently at work, under his control by selling wool to them and buying cloth from them – nevertheless it cannot by itself do much for the overthrow of the old mode of production, but rather preserves it and uses it as its premise'.[29]

As can be readily seen, Marx does not say anything about capitalists rising from the ranks of the handicraft producers. It is, of course, quite true that the expression used by Marx – 'the producer becomes a merchant and capitalist' – might have that implication; but it might equally well mean that the producer, whatever his background, *starts out* as both a merchant and an employer of wage-labour. It seems to me that the whole context goes to show that the latter is the more reasonable interpretation. What Marx was contrasting, I believe, was the launching of full-fledged capitalist enterprises with the slow development of the putting-out system. There is no indication that he was concerned about producers' rising from the ranks. Moreover, when he does deal explicitly with this problem in the first volume of *Capital*, what he says is quite impossible to reconcile with Dobb's interpretation of the above-quoted passage.

'The genesis of the industrial capitalist [Marx wrote] did not proceed in such a gradual way as that of the farmer. Doubtless many small guildmasters, and yet more independent small artisans, or even wage-labourers, transformed themselves into small capitalists, and (by

[28] Perez Zagorin in *Science and Society*, XII, Spring, 1948, p. 280 f.
[29] *Capital*, III, p. 393.

gradually extending exploitation of wage-labour and corresponding accumulation) into full-blown capitalists . . . The snail's-pace of this method corresponded in no wise with the commercial requirements of the new world market that the great discoveries of the end of the fifteenth century created'.[30]

These are the opening remarks of a chapter entitled 'Genesis of the Industrial Capitalist'; most of the rest of the chapter is devoted to describing the methods of trade and plunder by which large amounts of capital were brought together much more rapidly than this 'snail's-pace'. And while Marx says very little about the actual methods by which these accumulations found their way into industry, it is hardly credible that he would have assigned an important role in the process to the producer risen from the ranks.

If we interpret Marx to mean that the 'really revolutionary way' was for those with disposable capital to launch full-fledged capitalist enterprises without going through the intermediate stages of the putting-out system, we shall, I think, have little difficulty in finding a wealth of evidence to support his contention. Nef has shown conclusively (of course without any reference at all to Marx) that what he calls the first industrial revolution in England (about 1540 to 1640) was very largely characterised by precisely this kind of investment in such 'new' industries as mining, metallurgy, brewing, sugar refining, soap, alum, glass, and salt-making.[31] And the proof that it was a 'really revolutionary way' was provided by the results of England's first industrial revolution: economic supremacy over all rival nations and the first bourgeois political revolution.

I turn now to the second of Dobb's theses on the rise of capitalism which seems to me to require critical examination. Here I can be briefer.

Dobb sees the process of original accumulation as involving two quite distinct phases (p. 177 ff.). First, the rising bourgeoisie acquires at bargain prices (or in the most favourable case for nothing: e.g., the church lands under Henry VIII) certain assets and claims to wealth. In this phase, wealth is not only transferred to the bourgeoisie; it is also concentrated in fewer hands. Second, and later, comes the realisation phase. Dobb writes that

'of no less importance than the first phase of the process of accumula-

[30] *Ibid.*, I, p. 822.

[31] J. U. Nef., *Industry and Government in France and England, 1540–1640* (Philadelphia, 1940), especially ch. 1 and 3.

tion was the second and completing phase, by which the objects of the original accumulation were realised or sold (at least in part) in order to make possible an actual investment in industrial production – a sale of the original objects of accumulation in order with the proceeds to acquire (or to bring into existence) cotton machinery, factory buildings, iron foundries, raw materials and labour-power (p. 183)'.

So far as I can see, Dobb offers no evidence at all of the existence of this realisation phase. Nor is this surprising because it seems to me equally clear that there are no reasons to suppose that such a phase must have existed or actually did exist. As Dobb himself makes perfectly plain, the assets acquired and concentrated in fewer hands during the acquisition phase were of various kinds, including land, debt-claims, and precious metals: in other words, frozen and liquid assets alike. He recognises, too, that this was the period during which the bourgeoisie developed banking and credit machinery for turning its frozen assets (especially the public debt) into liquid assets. Under the circumstances, it is impossible to see why the bourgeoisie should be under any compulsion to sell in order to realise capital for industrial investment. Further, it is impossible to see what *class* could buy assets from the bourgeoisie in order to supply it with liquid funds. Naturally, this does not mean that individual members of the bourgeoisie could not or did not sell assets to other members of the same class or to members of other classes in order to acquire funds for industrial investment, but there was surely no other class to which the bourgeoisie *as a whole* could sell assets in this period of capitalist development.

Actually Dobb, aside from asserting the necessity and importance of the realisation phase, makes very little of it. When it comes down to analysing the necessary pre-conditions for industrial investment, he shows that the required complement to acquisition on the part of the bourgeoisie was not realisation by the bourgeoisie, but the break-up of the old system of production and especially dispossession of enough landworkers to form a class willing to work for wages. This is certainly correct, and I can only regret that Dobb's reiterated statements about the importance of the realisation phase may serve to divert the attention of some readers from his excellent treatment of the essential problems of the period of original accumulation.

A Reply

Maurice Dobb

Paul Sweezy's article on the transition from feudalism to capitalism raises in a clear and stimulating manner a number of important issues, discussion of which can only be beneficial to an understanding both of historical development and of Marxism as a method of studying that development. May I state at the outset that I personally welcome his contribution to such discussion as a distinguished challenge to further thought and study? With a good deal of what he says I feel no disagreement. In some places where he dissents from what I have said, the difference between us is one of emphasis and of formulation. But in one or two places a more fundamental difference over method and analysis seems to emerge; and here I feel that his interpretation is misleading.

First, I am not quite clear whether Sweezy rejects my definition of feudalism or merely considers it to be incomplete. This definition, as he says, rests on a virtual identification of feudalism with serfdom – if by the latter is meant, not merely the performance of obligatory *services*, but exploitation of the producer by virtue of direct politico-legal compulsion.[1] If he means that feudalism thus defined covers something wider than the medieval form of European economy and embraces a wide variety of types which (in any fuller study of feudalism) deserve careful analysis, I readily agree. But in referring to a '*system* of production' he seems to be saying something other than this, and to be contrasting a *system* of production with a mode of production in Marx's

[1] Sweezy suggests that such a widening of the term is unsatisfactory since elements of direct politico-legal compulsion over labour may be found at widely separated periods of history, including modern times. Where such elements predominate, they would on this definition constitute the form of economy in question feudal; but if they are merely incidental and subordinate, their presence no more suffices to do so than does the incidental existence of hired wage-labour suffice to constitute a particular society capitalist. In most of the 'incongruous' cases which Sweezy has in mind, compulsory labour is purely incidental, not typical.

use of this term. What precisely a system of production is intended to cover I am not clear. But what follows indicates that the term is intended to include the relations between the producer and his market. There are even hints that these relations of exchange (by contrast with relations of production) are the focus of attention in Sweezy's interpretation of the historical process. (He regards 'the crucial feature of feudalism', for example, as being 'that it is a system of *production for use*'.)

If this is so, then I think we have a fundamental issue between us. The definition which I was using in my *Studies* was advisedly in terms of the relations of production characteristic of feudalism: namely the relations between the direct producer and his overlord. The coercive relationship, consisting in the direct extraction of the surplus labour of producers by the ruling class, was conditioned, of course, by a certain level of development of the productive forces. Methods of production were relatively primitive, and (so far as the producers' own subsistence, at least, was concerned) were of the type of which Marx spoke as the 'petty mode of production', in which the producer is in possession of his means of production as an individual producing unit. This I regard as the crucial characteristic; and when different economic forms have this characteristic in common, this common element which they share is of greater significance than other respects in which they may differ (e.g., in the relation of production to the market). Admittedly this production-relationship is itself capable of considerable variation, according to the form which the compulsory extraction of the surplus product takes: e.g., direct labour services or the appropriation of tribute either in kind or in money.[2] But the distinction between these does not correspond to that between 'western European feudalism', which Sweezy thinks that I should have distinguished and concentrated upon, and feudalism in eastern Europe (although in Asiatic feudalism the tributary relationship would seem to have predominated and to have

[2] See Marx's analysis of 'Labor Rent, Rent in Kind and Money Rent', *Capital*, III. I would particularly draw attention to the passage in the course of Marx's treatment of this subject in which he says: 'The specific economic form in which unpaid surplus labour is pumped out of the direct producers determines the relation of rulers and ruled, as it grows immediately out of production itself and reacts upon it as a determining element . . . It is always the direct relation of the owners of the conditions of production to the direct producers which reveals the innermost secret, the hidden foundation of the entire social construction . . . The form of this relation between rulers and ruled naturally corresponds always with a definite stage in the development of the methods of labour and of its productive social power. This does not prevent the same economic basis from showing infinite variations and gradations in its appearance, even though its principal conditions are everywhere the same', *Capital*, III, p. 919.

given this its distinctive impress). While there were important differences undoubtedly between conditions in western and eastern Europe, there were also striking similarities as regards 'the form in which unpaid surplus labour was pumped out of the direct producers'; and it is my belief that the desire to represent 'western European feudalism' as a distinctive *genus* and to endow it alone with the title of 'feudal' is a product of bourgeois historians and of their tendency to concentrate upon juridical characteristics and *differentia*.

Regarding the 'conservative and change-resisting character of western European feudalism', which needed some external force to dislodge it, and which I am accused of neglecting, I remain rather sceptical. True, of course, that, by contrast with capitalist economy, feudal society was extremely stable and inert. But this is not to say that feudalism had no tendency within it to change. To say so would be to make it an exception to the general Marxist law of development that economic society is moved by its own internal contradictions. Actually, the feudal period witnessed considerable changes in technique;[3] and the later centuries of feudalism showed marked differences from those of early feudalism. Moreover, it would seem to be not to western Europe but to the East that we have to look for the most stable forms: in particular, to Asiatic forms of tributary serfdom. And it is to be noted that it was of the form where surplus labour is appropriated *via* dues in kind – and of this form specifically – that Marx spoke as 'quite suitable for becoming the basis of stationary conditions of society, such as we see in Asia'.[4]

Sweezy qualifies his statement by saying that the feudal system is not necessarily static. All he claims is that such movement as occurs 'has no tendency to transform it'. But despite this qualification, the implication remains that under feudalism class struggle can play no revolutionary role. It occurs to me that there may be a confusion at the root of this denial of revolutionary and transforming tendencies. No one is suggesting that class struggle of peasants against lords gives rise, in any simple and direct way, to capitalism. What this does is to modify the dependence of the petty mode of production upon feudal overlordship and eventually to shake loose the small producer from feudal exploitation. It is then from the petty mode of production (in the degree to which it secures independence of action, and social differentiation in turn develops within it) that capitalism is born. This is a fundamental point to which we shall return.

3 Molly Gibbs, *Feudal Order*, London, 1949, p. 5–7, 92 f.

4 *Capital*, III, p. 924.

In the course of supporting his own thesis that an internally stable feudalism could only be disintegrated by the impact of an external force[5] – trade and markets – Sweezy represents my own view as being that the decline of feudalism was *solely* the work of internal forces and that the growth of trade had nothing to do with the process. He seems to see it as a question of *either* internal conflict *or* external forces. This strikes me as much too simplified, even mechanical, a presentation. I see it as an *interaction* of the two; although with primary emphasis, it is true, upon the internal contradictions; since these would, I believe, operate in any case (if on a quite different timescale), and since they determine the particular form and direction of the effects which external influences exert. I am by no means denying that the growth of market towns and of trade played an important role in accelerating the disintegration of the old mode of production. What I am asserting is that trade exercised its influence to the extent that it accentuated the internal conflicts within the old mode of production. For example, the growth of trade (as I pointed out in my *Studies* in several places, e.g., p. 60–2 and 253 f.) accelerated the process of social differentiation within the petty mode of production, creating a *kulak* class, on the one hand, and a semi-proletariat, on the other. Again, as Sweezy emphasies, towns acted as magnets to fugitive serfs. I am not much concerned to argue whether this flight of serfs was due more to the attraction of these urban magnets (and alternatively in some parts of Europe to the lure of free land) or to the repulsive force of feudal exploitation. Evidently it was a matter of both, in varying degrees at different times and places. But the specific effect which such flight had was due to the specific character of the relationship between serf and feudal exploiter.[6]

Hence I do not agree that I am called upon to 'show that the feudal ruling class's growing need for revenue and the flight of serfs from the land can both be explained in terms of forces operating inside the fuedal system', or 'that the rise of towns was a process internal to the feudal system', (although to some extent I believe that the latter is true, and that, precisely because feudalism was far from being a purely 'natural economy', it encouraged towns to cater for its need of long-distance trade). At the same time, I think that Sweezy is wrong in asserting that

[5] His reference to 'historical developments which in fact can only be explained as arising from causes external to the system' leaves us in no doubt that this is his view.

[6] Incidentally, I agree entirely with the important consideration which Sweezy stresses tnat it was not so much the magnitude of the flight to the towns which was significant, but that the threat of it (accompanied perhaps by no more than a small movement) might suffice to force the lords into making concessions, seriously weakening to feudalism.

there is necessarily correlation between feudal disintegration and 'nearness to centres of trade'. In my *Studies* I cited several pieces of evidence to rebut the simplified view which has been popularised by the vulgar theorists of 'money economy'. Of these I will repeat here only two. It was precisely in the backward north and west of England that serfdom in the form of direct labour services disappeared earliest, and in the more advanced south-east, with its town markets and trade routes, that labour services were most stubborn in their survival. Similarly, in many parts of eastern Europe intensification of serfdom in the 15th and 16th centuries was associated with the growth of trade, and the correlation was, not between nearness to markets and feudal disintegration (as Sweezy claims), but between nearness to markets and strengthening of serfdom (cf. my *Studies*, p. 38–42). These facts are mentioned by Sweezy. Yet this does not prevent him from maintaining that it was only 'on the periphery of the exchange economy' that feudal relations were proof against dissolution.

The fact that the 'system of production' on which Sweezy focuses attention is more concerned with the sphere of exchange than with relations of production is indicated by a rather surprising omission in his treatment. He nowhere pays more than incidental attention to what has always seemed to me a crucial consideration: namely, that the transition from coercive extraction of surplus labour by estate-owners to the use of free hired labour must have depended upon the existence of cheap labour for hire (i.e., of proletarian or semi-proletarian elements). This I believe to have been a more fundamental factor than proximity of markets in determining whether the old social relations survived or were dissolved. Of course, there was interaction between this factor and the growth of trade: in particular (as I have already mentioned) the effect of the latter upon the process of social differentiation within the petty mode of production. But this factor must, surely, have played a decisive role in determining the precise effect which trade had in different places and at different periods? Possibly Sweezy plays down this factor because he thinks it too obvious to stress; or possibly because he is thinking of the leasing of farms for a money rent as the immediate successor of labour-services. This latter consideration brings us to his question: 'What came after feudalism in Europe?'

I entirely agree with Sweezy in regarding economic society in western Europe between the 14th century and the end of the 16th as being complex and transitional, in the sense that the old was in process of rapid disintegration and new economic forms were simultaneously appearing. I also agree with him in thinking that during this period the petty mode of production was in process of emancipating itself from feudal exploitation, but was not yet subjected (at least in any significant degree) to capitalist relations of production, which were eventually to destroy it. Moreover, I regard the recognition of this fact as vital to any true understanding of the passage from feudalism to capitalism. But Sweezy goes further than this. He speaks of it as transitional in a sense which excludes the possibility of its still being feudal (even if a feudal economy at an advanced stage of dissolution). There seems to me to be point in doing this only if one wishes to speak of it as a distinct mode of production *sui generis*, which is neither feudal nor capitalist. This is to my mind an impossible procedure; and Sweezy agrees in not wishing to go so far as this. In the final picture, therefore, these two centuries are apparently left suspended uncomfortably in the firmament between heaven and earth. In the process of historical development they have to be classified as homeless hybrids. While this sort of answer might be adequate enough in a purely evolutionary view of historical development through successive systems or stages, I suggest that it will not do for a revolutionary view of historical development – a view of history as a succession of class systems, with social revolution (in the sense of the transfer of power from one class to another) as the crucial mechanism of historical transformation.

The crucial question which Sweezy has apparently failed to ask (or if he has, he would seem to have burked the answer to it) is this: what was the ruling class of this period? Since (as Sweezy himself recognises) there was not yet developed capitalist production, it cannot have been a capitalist class. If one answers that it was something intermediate between feudal and capitalist, in the shape of a bourgeoisie which had not yet invested its capital in the development of a bourgeois mode of production, then one is in the Pokrovsky-bog of 'merchant capitalism'. If a merchant bourgeoisie formed the ruling class, then the state must have been some kind of bourgeois state. And if the state was a bourgeois state already, not only in the sixteenth century but even at the beginning of the fifteenth, what constituted the essential issue of the seventeenth century civil war? It cannot (according to this view) have been *the* bourgeois revolution. We are left with some such supposition as the one advanced in a preliminary discussion of the matter some years ago: that it was a struggle against an attempted *counter*-revolution staged by Crown and Court against an *already existent* bourgeois state power.[7] Moreover, we are faced with the alternative of either denying that there was any crucial historical moment describable as the bourgeois revolution, or of seeking for this bourgeois revolution in some earlier century at or before the dawn of the Tudor age.

This is a matter which has occupied a good deal of discussion among Marxist historians in England in the last few years. The larger question of the nature of the absolute states of this epoch was also the subject of discussion among Soviet historians just before the war. If we reject the alternatives just mentioned, we are left with the view (which I believe to be the right one) that the ruling class was still feudal and that that state was still the political instrument of its rule. And if this is so, then this ruling class must have depended for its income on surviving *feudal* methods of exploiting the petty mode of production. True, since trade had come to occupy a leading place in the economy, this ruling class had itself an interest in trade (as also had many a medieval monastery in the heyday of feudalism), and took certain sections of the merchant bourgeoisie (specially the export merchants) into economic partnership and into political alliance with itself (whence arose many of the figures of the 'new Tudor aristocracy'). Hence, this late, dissolving form of feudal exploitation of the period of centralised state power had many differences from the feudal exploitation of earlier centuries; and admittedly in many places the feudal 'integument' was wearing very threadbare. True also, feudal exploitation of the petty mode of production only rarely took the classical form of direct labour services, and had assumed predominantly the form of money rent. But as long as political constraint and the pressures of manorial custom still ruled economic relationships (as continued to be the case over very large areas of the English countryside), and a free market in land was absent (as well as free labour mobility), the form of this exploitation cannot be said to have shed its feudal form – even if this was a degenerate and rapidly disintegrating form.

In this connection I would draw attention to the fact that in the passage about money rent which Sweezy quotes from Marx (*Capital*, III, ch. 47), the money rent of which Marx is here speaking is not yet capitalist ground rent, with the farmer as an independent tenant paying a contractual rent, but is still (by manifest implication) a form of *feudal* rent, even if a dissolving form ('money rent, as a converted form of rent in kind and as an antagonist of rent in kind is *the last form* and *at the same time the form of dissolution* of the type of ground rent which we have considered so far. . . .'). Earlier in the same section Marx says: 'the basis of

7 P. F., in the course of a discussion on Christopher Hill's booklet, *The English Revolution 1640*, in the *Labour Monthly* (1941).

this rent remains the same as that of the rent in kind, from which it starts. The direct producer still is the possessor of the land . . . and he has to perform for his landlord . . . forced surplus labour . . . and this forced surplus labour is now paid in money obtained by the sale of the surplus product' (p. 926).

On the two final points of Sweezy's criticism I will try to be brief. Of the outstanding role played at the dawn of capitalism by capitalists who had been spawned by the petty mode of production I suggest that there is abundant evidence,[8] whatever the proper interpretation may be of that crucial passage from Marx's discussion of the matter (and I still think it bears the interpretation customarily placed upon it). Some of this evidence I quoted in my *Studies* (ch. 4). This is doubtless a matter deserving of more research than it has had hitherto. But the importance of the rising small and middle bourgeoisie of this period has already been shown by Tawney, for one. There is accumulating evidence that the significance of *kulak* enterprise in the village can hardly be overestimated. There are signs of him at a quite early date, hiring the labour of the poorer 'cotter' and in the sixteenth century pioneering new and improved methods of enclosed farming on a fairly extensive scale. Historians of this period have recently pointed out that a distinctive feature of English development in the Tudor age was the ease with which these *kulak* yeomen farmers rose to become minor gentry, purchasing manors and joining the ranks of the squirearchy. It may well be (as Kosminsky has suggested) that they played a leading role even in the Peasants' Revolt in 1381. Undoubtedly they prospered greatly (as employers of labour) from the falling real wages of the Tudor Inflation; and smaller gentry and rising *kulaks* were organisers of the country cloth industry on an extensive scale. Evidently they were a most important driving force in the bourgeois revolution of the seventeenth century, providing in particular the sinews of Cromwell's New Model Army. Moreover, the fact that they were is, I believe, a key to understanding the class alignments of the bourgeois revolution: in particular the reason why merchant capital, far from always playing a progressive role, was often to be found allied with feudal reaction.

Similarly, in the urban craft gilds there were many entrepreneurs of a similar type, who took to trade and employed poorer craftsmen on the putting-out system. I have suggested (and if I remember rightly the

[8] The passage of mine which Sweezy quotes, referring to 'little evidence that bears directly upon it', relates to '*the details* of the process' and not to the existence of this type of capitalist or to the role which he played.

suggestion originally came from Unwin) that these developments were responsible for the movements to be observed among the gilds at the end of the sixteenth century and the beginning of the seventeenth: in particular for the rise of the new Stuart corporations. So far as one can see, it was they (certainly it was the country clothiers) who were firm supporters of the English revolution, and not the rich patentees, such as those of whom Nef has talked, many of whom were royalist since they still depended on privilege and derived their privilege from court influence. I cannot see how the importance of this line of development in generating the first, pre-industrial-revolution, stage of capitalism can possibly be denied.[9] Even at the time of the industrial revolution many of the new entrepreneurs were small men who had started as 'merchant-manufacturers' of the putting-out system. True, in some industries (e.g., iron, copper and brass), where larger capitals were needed, it was already different. But it was conditions of technique which determined whether the small capitalist, risen from the ranks, could or could not become a pioneer of the new mode of production; and until the technical changes associated with the industrial revolution (*some* of which, it is true, were already occurring two centuries before 1800) the small capitalist could still play a leading role.

With regard to the so-called 'realisation phase' in the accumulation process, I must acknowledge that Sweezy has laid his finger on a weak place in the analysis, about which I myself had doubts, and on which I was aware that the evidence was inadequate. Whether such a phase exists or not does not affect my main contention; since this was that *dispossession* of others is the essence of the accumulating process, and not merely the acquisition of particular categories of wealth by capitalists. This is not to deny, however, that the bourgeois-enrichment aspect of the matter had a place; in which case I believe that the distinguishing of the 'two phases' retains some importance. I suggest that it is a topic to which Marxist research might usefully be directed; and I continue to

[9] Sweezy quotes Marx's reference to such developments as proceeding 'at a snail's pace', compared with the full possibilities of expansion. But so was the development of capitalism 'at a snail's pace' (relatively to later developments) in the period of 'the infancy of capitalist production' of which Marx is here speaking. It was, surely, because of this that the transformation could only be completed after the new bourgeoisie had won political power, and (as Marx says later in the same chapter) had begun to 'employ the power of the State . . . to hasten, hothouse fashion, the process of transformation of the feudal mode of production into the capitalist mode, and to shorten the transition'. Then, but only then, could the snail's pace of earlier development be accelerated and the ground laid for the rapid growth of the industrial revolution.

think that 'the second phase' is a hypothesis which corresponds to something actual.

We can agree that it was not a case of the bourgeoisie realising assets, previously accumulated, to some *new class*. Indeed, there is no need for them to do so *as a class*, since, once a proletariat has been created, the only 'cost' to the bourgeoisie as a whole in the extension of capitalist production is the subsistence which they have to advance to workers (in the form of wag.) – a fact of which the classical economists were well aware. Ownership of land and country houses, etc., did not of itself assist them in providing this subsistence. Even if they could have sold their properties to third parties, this would not necessarily – leaving foreign trade apart – have augmented the subsistence fund for capitalist society as a whole. But what is the case for the class as a whole may not be the case for one section of it, which (as Sweezy implies) may be handicapped by lack of sufficient liquid funds to serve as working capital; and there may well be substantial meaning in speaking of one stratum of the bourgeoisie (imbued with a desire to buy labour power: i.e., to invest in production) selling real estate or bonds to other strata of the bourgeoisie which still have a taste for acquiring wealth in these forms. It is, of course, possible that all the investments needed to finance the industrial revolution came from the *current income* of the new captains of industry of the period: the Darbys, Dales, Wilkinsons, Wedgwoods and Radcliffes. In this case nothing remains to be said. Previous bourgeois enrichment in the forms we have mentioned can be ignored as a factor in the financing of industrial growth. This, however, seems *prima facie* unlikely. I am not aware that much work has been done on the sources from which such constructional projects as the early canals and railways in England were financed. We know that many of the new entrepreneurs were handicapped for lack of capital, and that much of the capital for the expanding cotton industry in the early 19th century came from textile merchants. That the credit system was not yet adequately developed to meet the needs of developing industry is shown by the mushroom growth of the unstable 'country banks' in the early 19th century precisely to fill this gap. It seems an hypothesis worthy of investigation that in the 18th century there was a good deal of selling of bonds and real estate to such persons as retired East Indian 'nabobs' by men who, then or subsequently, used the proceeds to invest in the expanding industry and commerce of the time; and that it was by some such route – by a process having two stages – that the wealth acquired from colonial loot fertilised the industrial revolution.

Even if there was no significant amount of transfer of assets, I think that my 'second phase' may not altogether lack justification. It may have significance (if, admittedly, a somewhat different one) as denoting a period in which there had been a shift for the bourgeoisie as a whole from an earlier preference for holding real estate or valuable objects or bonds to a preference for investing in means of production and labour-power. Even if no considerable volume of selling of the former actually took place, the shift may nevertheless have had a large influence on the prices of such assets and on economic and social activities.

A Contribution to the Discussion

Kohachiro Takahashi

Maurice Dobb's *Studies in the Development of Capitalism*, London, 1946, raises many important problems of method. It presents a concrete case of a problem in which we cannot but be deeply interested – the problem of how a new and higher stage of the science of economic history can take up into its own system and make use of the positive results of preceding economic and social historians. The criticism of Dobb's *Studies* by the able American economist Paul M. Sweezy[1] and Dobb's rejoinder,[2] by indicating more clearly the nature and location of the questions in dispute, give Japanese historians an opportunity (after having been isolated during the years of the last war) to evaluate the theoretical level of economic history in Europe and America today.

Dobb's *Studies*, while not confined to the development of English capitalism, pays inadequate attention to French and German writing, both certainly on no lower a plane than the English work. These sources must be studied not only to obtain a more comprehensive knowledge of comparative capitalist structures but also to establish more accurate historical laws. I shall confine my comments here and for the present to Western Europe; it would be premature to introduce into the present discussion the historical facts of feudal organisation in Japan and other Asiatic countries, or of the formation of capitalism there. The Sweezy-Dobb controversy, if participated in critically by historians with the same awareness of problems in every country, could lay the foundation for co-operative advances in these studies.

I

Both Dobb's *Studies* and Sweezy's criticism start with general conceptual definitions of feudalism and capitalism, which are not mere questions of terminology, but involve methods of historical analysis. Since Sweezy

[1] See above. 'A Critique'.
[2] 'Reply', *ibid.*

has not given a clear and explicit definition of feudalism, we do not know precisely what he considers to be its root. In any case, however, the transition from feudalism to capitalism relates to a change in the mode of production, and feudalism and capitalism must be stages of socio-economic structure, historical categories. A rational comprehension of feudalism presupposes a scientific understanding of capitalism as an historical category.[3] Dobb, rejecting the traditional concepts current among 'bourgeois' historians, looks for the essence of feudal economy in the relations between the direct producers (artisans and peasant cultivators) and their feudal lords. This approach characterised feudalism as a mode of production; it is central to Dobb's definition of feudalism, and in general coincides with the concept of serfdom. It is 'an obligation laid on the producer by force and independently of his own volition to fulfil certain economic demands of an overlord, whether these demands take the form of services to be performed or of dues to be paid in money or in kind . . . This coercive force may be that of military strength, possessed by the feudal superior, or of custom backed by some kind of judicial procedure, or the force of law'.[4] This description coincides in essence with the account given in Vol. III of *Capital* in the chapter on 'Genesis of Capitalist Ground Rent'.[5] This sort of feudal serfdom

'contrasts with Capitalism in that under the latter the labourer, in the first place, . . . is no longer an independent producer but is divorced from his means of production and from the possibility of providing his own subsistence, but in the second place . . . his relationship to the owner of the means of production who employs him is a purely contractual one . . . in the face of the law he is free both to choose his master and to change masters; and he is not under any obligation, other than that imposed by a contract of service, to contribute work or payment to a master'.[6]

Sweezy criticises Dobb's identification of feudalism with serfdom.

[3] Marx, *A Contribution to the Critique of Political Economy* (Chicago, 1904), 'Introduction', p. 300 f.

[4] Dobb, *Studies, op. cit.*, p. 35 f.

[5] Or again, 'In all previous [*i.e.*, pre-capitalist] forms the land-owner, not the capitalist, appears as the immediate appropriator of others' surplus labour. . . . Rent appears as the general form of surplus labour, unpaid labour. Here the appropriation of this surplus labour is not mediated by exchange, as with the capitalist, but its basis is the coercive rule of one part of society over the other part, hence direct slavery, serfdom, or a relation of political dependence'. Marx, *Theorien über den Mehrwert*, ed. Kautsky, Vol. III (Stuttgart, 1910), ch. VI, p. 451.

[6] Dobb, *Studies*, p. 36.

He cites a letter in which Engels says: 'it is certain that serfdom and bondage are not a peculiarly (*spezifisch*) medieval-feudal form, we find them everywhere or nearly everywhere where conquerors have the land cultivated for them by the old inhabitants'.[7] Sweezy denies that serfdom is a specific historical category.[8] He does not, however, indicate what it is that constitutes the special existence-form of labour power proper to feudalism as a mode of production.

My own opinion would be as follows: When we consider the ancient, the feudal and the modern bourgeois modes of production as the chief stages in economic history, the first thing to be taken into account must always be the social existence-form of labour power, which is the basic, the decisive factor in the various modes of production. Now certainly the basic forms (types) of labour are slavery, serfdom and free wage labour; and it is surely erroneous to divorce serfdom from feudalism as a general conception. The question of the transition from feudalism to capitalism is not merely one of a transformation in forms of economic and social institutions. The basic problem must be the change in the social existence-form of labour power.

Although the peasants' lack of freedom, as serfs, naturally showed variations and gradations according to region or stage of feudal economic development, serfdom is the characteristic existence-form of labour power in the feudal mode of production, or as Dobb puts it, 'exploitation of the producer by virtue of direct politico-legal compulsion'.[9] Sweezy, having divorced serfdom from feudalism and neglected the characteristically feudal existence-form of labour power, had to seek the essence of feudalism elsewhere. In feudal society, in his opinion, 'markets are for the most part local and . . . long-distance trade, while not necessarily absent, plays no determining role in the purposes or methods of production. The crucial feature of feudalism in this sense is that it is a system of *production for use*'. Sweezy does not assert that market- or commodity-economy did not exist in feudal society. He does say that '. . . commodity production and feudalism are mutually exclusive concepts'.[10] But it is too simple to present the essence of feudalism as 'a system of production for use' as contradictory to 'production for the market'. Exchange-value (commodities) and money (different from

[7] Marx-Engels, *Selected Correspondence* (New York, n.d.), p. 411 f., cited in Sweezy, above p. 33.

[8] 'Critique', above, pp. 33–35.

[9] 'Reply', above, p. 57. Cf. Marx, *Capital*, Vol. III (Chicago, 1909), p. 918.

[10] 'Critique', above, p. 35 and p. 50, no. 22.

'capital') lead an 'antediluvian' existence,[11] as it were, could exist and ripen in various kinds of historical social structures. In these early stages almost all of the products of labour go to satisfying the needs of the producers themselves and do not become commodities, and so exchange-value does not entirely control the social production-process; still some commodity production and circulation does take place. Therefore, the question to ask as to a given social structure is not whether commodities and money are present, but rather how those commodities are produced, how that money serves as a medium in production. The products of the ancient Roman latifundia entered into circulation as slave-produced commodities, and the feudal land-owners' accumulations of the products of forced labour or of feudal dues in kind entered into circulation as serf-produced commodities. Again there are the simple commodities produced by the independent self-sufficient peasants or artisans, and the capitalist commodities based on wage labour, and so forth. But it is not the same with capital or capitalism as a historical category. Even on a feudal basis, the products of labour could take the commodity form, for the means of production were combined with the direct producers.[12] For this reason, a 'system of production for the market' cannot define specific historical productive relations (nor, therefore, class relations). Sweezy clearly misses the point when, in the passage relating to the definition of feudalism, he hardly mentions feudal ground-rent, the concentrated embodiment of the antagonistic seigneur-peasant relationship and lays principal stress on 'system of production for use' or 'system of production for the market', *i.e.* on the relations obtaining between producers and their markets, on exchange relationships rather than productive relationships. His position seems to be a sort of circulationism.

We should prefer to start from the following theses: The contradiction between feudalism and capitalism is not the contradiction between 'system of production for use' and 'system of production for the market', but that between feudal land-property – serfdom and an industrial capital – wage-labour system. The first terms of each pair are modes of exploitation and property relationship, the latter terms are existence-forms of labour power and hence of its social reproduction. It is possible to simplify this as the contradiction of feudal land property and industrial capital.[13] In feudalism, since the immediate producers appear in combination with the means of production, and hence labour power cannot take the form of a commodity, the appropriation of surplus labour by the feudal lords takes place directly, by extra-economic coercion without the mediation of the economic laws of commodity exchange. In capitalism, not merely are the products of labour turned into commodities, but labour power itself becomes a commodity. In this stage of development the system of coercion disappears and the law of value holds true over the entire extent of the economy. The fundamental processes of the passage from feudalism to capitalism are, therefore: the change in the social form of existence of labour power consisting in the separation of the means of production from the direct producers; the change in the social mode of reproduction of labour power (which comes to the same thing); and the polarisation of the direct producers, or the dissociation of the peasantry.

Dobb's analysis started directly from feudal land property and serfdom themselves. But for example, when we are analysing the concept of 'capital', we cannot start directly from capital itself. As the well-known opening passage of *Capital* says, 'the wealth of those societies in which the capitalist mode of production prevails, presents itself as an immense accumulation of commodities', and the single commodities appear as the elementary form of this wealth. Thus, just as the study of *Capital* starts with analysis of the commodity, and goes on to show the development of the categories Commodity → Money → Capital, so likewise when analysing feudal land property obviously the method cannot be restricted to a mere historical narration, but must go on to deal with the nature of the laws of feudal society. That is, starting from the simplest and most abstract categories and advancing systematically, we finally reach the most concrete and complex category, feudal landownership. Then, taking the inverse logical path, the initial categories now reappear as containing a wealth of specifications and relationships.[14] What will be the elementary form, cell, or unit of a society based on the feudal mode of production? What categories will occupy the first place

[11] *Capital*, Vol. 1 (Chicago, 1906), p. 182; Vol. III (Chicago, 1909), p. 696.

[12] *Capital*, Vol. 1, p. 394.

[13] c.f. *Capital*, Vol. 1, p. 182. Also Vol. II (Chicago, 1907), p. 63: 'Industrial capital is the only form of existence of capital, in which not only the appropriation of surplus value or surplus product, but also its creation is a function of capital. Therefore it gives to production its capitalist character. Its existence includes that of class antagonisms between capitalists and labourers. To the extent that it assumes control over social production, the technique and social organisation of the labour process are revolutionised and with them the economic and historical type of society. The other classes of capital, which appear before industrial capital amid past or declining conditions of social production, are not only subordinated to it and suffer changes in the mechanism of their functions corresponding to it, but move on it as a basis, live and die, stand and fall with this basis'.

[14] *A Contribution to the Critique of Political Economy* (Chicago, 1904), p. 294 f.

in the analysis of feudal land property? Tentatively the elementary unit should be set as the *Hufe* (virgate, *manse*); then the *Gemeinde* (village community, *communauté rurale*) should be taken as the intermediate step; and we should end by developing in orderly fashion the highest category of feudal land property (*Grundherrschaft*, manor, *seigneurie*).[15]

Of course this sort of logical development of the categories virgate → community → manor is not the historical process itself. However, it is precisely the study of the logical structure of feudal land-property, starting from its elementary form, which makes clear the historical law of the rise, development and decline of feudal society, something which 'bourgeois' historical science has not yet obtained, but the first volume of *Capital* suggests. On this account, questions of basic method arise in connection with the excellent analysis of feudal society which Sweezy and Dobb, as we should naturally expect, have given us.

[15] The *Hufe* (*virgate*) is a total peasant share (*Werteinheit*, Lamprecht calls it) composed of a *Hof* (a plot of ground with a house on it), a certain primary parcel of arable land (*Flur*) and a part in the common land (*Allmende*); or, roughly, 'land enough to support the peasant and his family' (Waitz). It is the natural object by which the peasant maintains himself (or, labour power reproduces itself). Its economic realisation, in that sense the *Hufe's* general form, is the community or the communal collective regulations: the *Flurzwang* or *contrainte communautaire* (G. Lefebvre), *servitudes collectives*, (Marc Bloch) which go with the *Dreifelderwirtschaft* and the open-field system, *Gemengelage* or *vaine pâture collective*. The collective regulations constitute an apparatus of compulsion by which the labour process is mediated. However, the inevitable expansion of productivity arising out of the private property inherent in the *Hufe* led, and could not but lead, to men's 'rule over men and land' (Wittich). The relationships of domination and dependence into which this sort of *Hufe* community branched off constituted the feudal lord's private property, *i.e.*, the manor, or feudal land property. In this way we have the sequence of categorical development, *Hufe* → *Gemeinde* → *Grundherrschaft*. Conversely, as this sort of domination by the feudal lord took over the village community and the *Hufe*, and the rules of seigneurial land property penetrated them, *Hufe* and village community as 'natural' objects and their mutual relations were changed into a historical (specifically, the fuedal) form and relationships. Now, under feudal land property, the *Hufe* appears as a peasant holding (*Besitz*, tenure) and the communal regulations of customs are turned into instruments of seigneurial domination. They become historical conditions for realising fuedal rent and making sure of labour power; the peasant is tied to his land (appropriation). At the same time, the peasant's labour process becomes the process of rent formation; the unity of the two will constitute the feudal productive process. In general, coercion (communal regulations and the forced exaction of fuedal dues by the lord) is the mediating factor in feudal reproduction, just as in capitalist society the circulation process of capital appears as the mediating factor in capitalist reproduction. The collapse of feudal society therefore is the disappearance of this system of coercion. On the other hand, since these feudal compulsions operate within a framework in which the direct producer is linked with the means of production, the dissolution of these compulsions (the prerequisite for modern private property and the bourgeois freedom of labour) produces the conditions for the separation of the means of production from the direct producers (expropriation). For details, see my *Skimin kakumei no kozo (Structure of the Bourgeois Revolution)* (Tokyo, 1950), p. 77–85.

2

Sweezy looked for the crucial feature of feudalism in a 'system of production for use', and so had to explain the decline of feudalism in the same way. He is certainly not unaware of the existence of the feudal mode of production in Eastern Europe and Asia; why then did he restrict his consideration of the question to Western Europe alone? Is he going along with the bourgeois legal historians in describing the feudal system as *Lehnswesen*? For example, J. Calmette's *La société féodale*, in the popular Collection Armand Colin,[16] states on its first page that feudalism is peculiar to the middle ages in Western Europe, and denies the reality of a Japanese feudalism. Or was Sweezy's treatment motivated by the historical fact that modern capitalism arose and grew to maturity in Western Europe? He says that 'western European feudalism . . . was a system with a very strong bias in favour of maintaining given methods and relations of production' and refers to 'this inherently conservative and change-resisting character of western European feudalism'.[17] It means little, however, to point out that feudalism was conservative with respect to its categorical opposite, modern capitalism. Compared with the feudalism of Eastern Europe or the Orient, Western European feudalism does not appear as more conservative: quite the contrary. The decisive factor in checking the autonomous growth of modern capitalist society in Eastern Europe and Asia was precisely the stability of the internal structure of feudal land property in those countries. The fact that modern capitalism and bourgeois society may be said to have taken on their classic form in Western Europe indicates rather an inherent fragility and instability of feudal land property there. Sweezy's meaning is perhaps that Western European feudalism, being intrinsically conservative and change-resisting, could not collapse because of any force internal to feudalism; the collapse began only because of some external force. Since for Sweezy feudalism was 'a system of production for use', the force coming from outside such a system to destroy it was 'production for the market' ('an exchange economy') or 'trade'. About half of his whole essay in criticism of Dobb is devoted to a detailed discussion on this point.

Now in the 14th and 15th centuries the devastation of village communities, the decrease in the rural population, and the consequent

[16] Paris, 1932. Other French historians, notably Marc Bloch and Robert Boutruche, think otherwise, however, and are deeply interested in Japanese feudalism. Marx already in ch. 24 of the first volume of *Capital* speaks of the 'purely feudal organisation' in Japan.

[17] Above, p. 36.

shortage of money on the part of feudal lords were general, and gave rise in England, France and Germany to the *crise des fortunes seigneuriales.*[18] The exchange- or money-economy which began to make strides during the late middle ages led to the ruin of a large part of the feudal nobility whose basis was the traditional 'natural' economy.[19] The so-called medieval emancipation of the serfs was based chiefly on the seigneurs' need for money – usually for war or for the increasing luxury of the feudal nobility.[20]

On Sweezy's hypothesis, the feudal ruling class' constantly increasing demand for money in this 'crisis' of feudalism arose from the ever greater luxury of the feudal nobility, a conception similar to that presented in the first chapter on the *Hof*[21] of Sombart's *Luxus und Kapitalismus.* The excessive exploitation of the peasants by their lords, to which Dobb would ascribe the source of the collapse of feudalism, was really, in Sweezy's view, an effect of the lords' need for cash. With the resultant flight of the peasants there came the establishment of the cities, which produced the money economy. Thus, according to Sweezy, Dobb 'mistakes for immanent trends certain historical developments [of feudalism] which in fact can only be explained as arising from causes external to the system'.[22] The 'external' force which brought about the collapse of feudalism was 'trade, which cannot be regarded as a form of feudal economy', especially long-distance trade, not the local or inter-local market.[23]

'We ought', Sweezy says, 'to try to uncover the process by which trade engendered a *system* of production for the market, and then to trace the impact of this process on the pre-existent feudal system of production for use'. Thus he saw 'how long-distance trade could be a creative force, bringing into existence a system of production for exchange alongside

[18] Marc Bloch, *Caractères originaux de l'histoire rurale française* (Oslo, 1931), p. 117–19; H. Maybaum, *Die Entstehung der Gutswirtschaft im Mecklenburg* (Stuttgart, 1926), p. 109–13; and the recent excellent work of R. Boutruche, *La crise d'une société* (Paris, 1947), II.

[19] Cf., eg., R. Boutruche, 'Aux origines d'une crise nobiliaire', *Annales d'histoire sociale*, Vol. I, No. 3, Paris, 1939, p. 272 f.

[20] Marc Bloch, *Rois et serfs*, Paris, 1920, p. 59 f., p. 174 f., etc.; A. Dopsch, *Naturalwirtschaft und Geldwirtschaft in der Weltgeschichte*, Wien, 1930, p. 178.

[21] Sombart, *Luxus und Kapitalismus*, 2nd ed., München, 1922, Ch. I.

[22] Above, p. 40.

[23] From the point of view of the social division of labour I should like to stress rather the local or inter-local exchange, or internal market; on this subject we must take into consideration Hilton's valuable suggestions in his *Economic Development of Some Leicester Estates in the 14th and 15th Centuries.* Dobb was able to grasp both the rise of industrial capital and the formation of the 'internal market' in an indivisible relation; see *Studies*, p. 161 f. On this point cf. the method of *Capital*, Vol. I, ch. xxx.

the old feudal system of production for use'. While Sweezy is well aware of the many historical facts showing that an 'exchange economy is compatible with slavery, serfdom, independent self-employed labour and wage-labour', he does not properly appreciate one of the strong points of Dobb's theory, concerning the feudal reaction and what Engels calls the second serfdom in Eastern Europe. Sweezy, following Pirenne, looks for the explanation 'in the geography of the second serfdom, in the fact that the phenomenon becomes increasingly marked and severe as we move eastward away from the centre of the new exchange economy'.[24] Dobb, however, using various recent studies, brings out the fact that:

'It was precisely in the backward north and west of England that serfdom in the form of direct labour services disappeared earliest, and in the more advanced south-east, with its town markets and trade routes, that labour services were most stubborn in their survival. Similarly, in . . . eastern Europe intensification of serfdom in the fifteenth and sixteenth centuries was associated with the growth of trade, and the correlation was, not between nearness to markets and feudal disintegration . . ., but between nearness to markets and strengthening of serfdom'.[25]

The essential cause therefore is not trade or the market itself; the structure of the market is conditioned by the internal organisation of the productive system. Kosminsky has formulated this point even more clearly than Dobb. 'Production for exchange' on the large feudal estates and church lands of Southern and Eastern England, which had the structure of the 'classical manor', evoked the obvious response of the growth of labour services and the intensification of serfdom; whereas in Northern and Western England, with their small and medium-sized secular estates, the obvious response called forth was the formation of money rents and the decline of serfdom. Actually, as the exchange- or money-economy developed, 'feudalism dissolved soonest and most easily in those areas and on those estates [the 'non manorial estates'] where it had been least successful in establishing itself', while in those

[24] Above, p. 45.

[25] 'Reply', above p. 61, *Studies*, p. 34–42, 51–59. Chapters 20 and 36 of Vol. III of *Capital* tend to bear Dodd out; see p. 384 f., 389, 391 f. '. . . in the 16th and 17th centuries the great revolutions, which took place in commerce with the geographical discoveries and rapidly increased the development of merchants' capital, form one of the principal elements in the transition from feudal to capitalist production. . . . However, the modern mode of production, in its first period, the manufacturing period, developed only in places, where the conditions for it had been previously developed during medieval times', p. 391 f.

places (on the 'classical manors') which successfully set up and maintained domination over the unfree serf population in the process of 'adapting the system of labour services to the growing demands of the market' it could lead to an intensification of the feudal exploitation of the peasantry, and in many cases did. Thus, it is precisely the *Rittergut* or *Gutswirtschaft* production for the market that took form in Eastern Germany (the fullest embodiment of Kosminsky's and Postan's 'feudal reaction') that typifies the 'second serfdom' to which Sweezy and Dobb refer. The essential point is that 'the development of exchange in the peasant economy, whether it served the local market directly, or more distant markets through merchant middlemen, led to the development of money rent. The development of exchange in the lords' economy, on the other hand, led to the growth of labour services'.[26]

Sweezy is right in regarding the 'crisis' at the end of the middle ages as a product of the disintegrating action of trade on the system of production for use. He falls into error when he is so absorbed in trade, especially the development of long-distance trade, as to ascribe to it the collapse of feudalism itself. Certainly the disintegrative action of trade, in England at least – and in general too, as Dobb points out in reply to Sweezy's criticism[27] – accelerated the process of differentiation among the petty producers, tending to create a class of yeoman kulaks on the one hand and a local semi-proletariat on the other, with the final result of the collapse of feudalism and the establishment of capitalist production. R. H. Tawney[28] showed the presence in 16th century England of such a capitalist disintegrative process – the trend toward 'the tripartite division into landlord, capitalist farmer and landless agricultural labourer' which is characteristic of modern English agriculture. However, this division had its origin within the structure of already existing English feudal society, and there is no reason to ascribe it to trade as such. In

[26] E. A. Kosminsky, 'Services and Money Rents in the 13th Century', *Economic History Review*, Vol. V, London, 1935, No. 2, p. 42–45. Hence, 'The rise of money economy has not always been the great emancipating force which nineteenth-century historians believed it to have been . . . the expansion of markets and the growth of production is as likely to lead to the increase of labour services as to their decline. Hence the paradox of their increase in Eastern Germany, at the time when the production of grain for foreign markets was expanding most rapidly, and hence also the paradox of their increase in England, too, at the time and in the places of the highest development of agricultural production for the market during the middle ages (viz., the 13th century).' M. Postan, 'The Chronology of Labour Service', *Transactions of the Royal Historical Society, 4th series*, Vol. XX, London, 1937, p. 192 f., p. 186.

[27] 'Reply', above, p. 60; cf. *Studies*, p. 60.

[28] *Agrarian Problem in the Sixteenth Century*, London, 1912.

taking up this point, Dobb's reply to Sweezy is inadequate and makes unnecessary concessions. He should have pointed out more concretely how in Western Europe too the destruction of the class of small peasant producers by trade did not always result in the formation of capitalist production but also in bringing about the feudal reaction. In France, for example, the 'crisis' had the effect of restoring feudalism, not of finally destroying it.[29] In France at that time, the dissolution by trade of the class of small peasant producers did not establish a capitalist wage-labour system, but initiated usurious land-proprietorship, *Laboureurs-fermiers* and *Labourers-marchands* on the one hand and semi-serfs on the other.[30] The latter were the prototype of those *métayers* whom Arthur Young, in his *Travels in France*, describes as victims of 'a miserable system that perpetuates poverty'; but at the time we are speaking of they were neither in the category of the proletariat nor in the stage of *métayage* which marks the transition from feudal dues to capitalist rent.[31] Both Sweezy and Dobb treat of the disintegrative action of trade on feudalism and the 'feudal reaction' without going beyond feudal land property with its labour services, whereas they should have considered rents in kind too; the latter would be the more important question for France and Japan.[32]

Sweezy does not take the break-up of a given social structure as the result of self-movement of its productive forces; instead he looks

[29] In this crisis 'though the lords may have changed frequently, the framework of the feudal hierarchy appeared as it had been during the previous century', Y. Bezard, *La vie rurale dans le sud la région parisienne* (Paris, 1929), p. 54. 'The seigneurial regime was untouched. Even more: it will not be long in acquiring a new vigour. But seigneurial property, to a great extent, has changed hands', Bloch, *Caractères originaux*, *op. cit.*, p. 129.

[30] Raveau gives a vivid picture confirming this fact, *L'agriculture et les classes paysannes au XVIe siècle* (Paris, 1926), p. 249 f. In Poitou, the development of the exchange-money economy divorced the peasants from the land, but did not make them into a proletariat. When the peasants sold their holdings, they were not driven off the land, but were bound to it by the new proprietors to cultivate it on half-shares (*à demi-fruits*). The new *métayers* could only subsist by selling the following harvest ahead of time or by getting advances in grain or money from the stocks of the new proprietors. The new debts compelled the peasants to sacrifice the next harvest too, and they were caught in a vicious circle from which they could not escape. 'They were riveted down to their holdings; the merchants created a new serfdom by means of their capital', *Ibid.*, p. 80; and of p. 82, 93, 121, 268–71.

[31] The written *métayage* contracts of the old regime bind the peasant renters to personal, that is feudal obligations of *fidélité, obéissance, soumission*, J. Donat, *Une communauté rurale a la fin de l'ancien régime*, Paris, 1926, p. 245. *Métayage* gave rise to 'veritable bonds of personal dependence between bourgeois and peasant', Bloch, *Caractères originaux, op. cit.*, p. 143. And G. Lefebvre, the authority on agrarian and peasant questions at the time of the French Revolution, points out the existence in *métayage* of an aristocratic tradition of relations of *protection et obéissance* – that is, of feudal subordination – between landed proprietor and *métayer* in the old regime. Lefebvre, *Questions agraires au temps de la Terreur*, Paris, 1932, p. 94.

for an external force. If we say that historical development takes place according to external forces, the question remains, however, how these external forces arose, and where they came from. In the last analysis these forces which manifest themselves externally must be explained internally to history. The dialectics of history cannot go forward without self-movements (the contradictions of inner structure). Internal movements and external influences of course react on each other; and Dobb points out how enormous an influence external circumstances can exert; still, 'the internal contradictions . . . determine the particular form and direction of the effects which external influencies exert'.[33] Sweezy's insistence that the collapse of Western European feudalism was due to the impact of external causes only – trade and the market, especially the external one – follows from his very method of historical analysis.[34]

3

One very important point of Dobb's is his emphasis on the fact that capitalism grew out of a petty mode of production, which attained its independence and at the same time developed social differentiation from within itself. Dobb's thesis presents the historical question in two phases: first, this petty production gradually establishes itself solidly as the basis of feudal society; then this small-scale production, as the result of the development of productivity, escapes from feudal restrictions, arrives at its own disintegration, and thereby creates the capitalist relationships.[35]

[32] This point is the more important one in Asia, where natural rents (rents in kind) predominate. The form of dues in kind 'is quite suitable for becoming the basis of stationary conditions of society, such as we see in Asia. . . . This rent may assume dimensions which seriously threaten the reproduction of the conditions of labour, of the means of production. It may render an expansion of production more or less impossible, and grind the direct producers down to the physical minimum of means of subsistence. This is particularly the case, when this form is met and exploited by a conquering industrial nation, as India is by the English', *Capital*, Vol. III, p. 924 f. See 'Hoken shakai kaitai e no taio ni tsuite' ('On the Opposition to the Break-Up of Feudalism') in my *Kindai shakai seiritsu shiron (Historical Essay on the Formation of Modern Society)*, Tokyo, 1951, p. 113 f.

[33] 'Reply', above, p. 60.

[34] The historical conception of the decline of a society as self-disintegration as the result of this sort of internal self-development, is confirmed even by 'bourgeois' historians; *e.g.*, with respect to the decline of classical antiquity, Eduard Meyer emphasized that the decline of the Roman Empire did not come about because of the invasions of barbarian tribes from without, but that the invasions took place only at a time when the Empire had already decayed internally: E. Meyer, *Kleine Schriften*, Vol. I, 2nd ed., Berlin, 1924, p. 145 f., 160. Also Max Weber, 'Die sozialen Gründe des Untergangs der antiken Welt', 1896, in *Gesammelte Aufsätze sur Soz. u. WG*, Tübingen, 1924, p. 290 f., 293–97. Cf. *Capital*, Vol. III, p. 390 f.

(A.) However, the firm establishment of the petty mode of production as the basis of feudalism occurs in the dissolution process of the 'classical' manorial system (the labour rent stage of feudal landed property), the system of direct exploitation of the seigneurial demesne on the classical manor system, namely weekly forced labour by the serfs (week-work). The way in which the emancipation of the serfs went along with this process is shown in a general way at least by modern historians. The process can be seen in the commutation of services in 14th and 15th century England, with a complete change from labour rent directly to money rent, signifying actually the disappearance of serfdom; or again in Southwestern Germany and especially France, where the first stage in the abolition of labour services was the establishment of fixed rents in kind which gradually were changed into money rents. From the 12th and 13th century on, in France and Southwest Germany, the lords' demesne lands (*domaine proche, Salland*), which had hitherto been cultivated by the serfs' forced labour (*Frondienst, corvée*), was parcelled out to the peasants and entrusted to them for cultivation. The peasants no longer rendered forced labour services to the lord, but turned over to him a fixed proportion of the crop as dues (*campi pars, champart, terrage, agrier*).[36] Although this process was a necessary concomitant of a partially established money rent, yet the basic part of the feudal rent was now no longer labour services, but a 'rent' (*redevance, Abgabe*), as historians call it. This sort of feudal land property, arising as a result of the collapse of the manorial system (or *Villikationssystem*), was feudal land property under small-scale peasant management, or what German historians term *Rentengrundherrschaft* or *reine Grundherrschaft*.[37]

This change in the structure of feudal land property accompanying the decline of the manorial system brought a change in the form of rent: in England to money rent, in France and Germany to rent in kind; but it did not produce any basic change in the nature of feudal rent. The peasants had previously contributed surplus labour directly in the form of

[35] *Capital*, Vol. 1, p. 367, *Ibid.*, Vol. III, p. 393. See 'Shoki shihon shugi no keizai kozo' ('Economic Structure of Early Capitalism') in my *Kindai shihon shugi no seiritsu (Formation of Modern Capitalism)*, Tokyo, 1950, p. 3 f.

[36] Bloch, *Caractères originaux, op. cit.*, p. 100 f.; Oliver Martin, *Histoire de la prévôté de vicomte de Paris*, Vol. I, Paris, 1922, p. 420 f.

[37] Max Weber, *Wirtschaftsgeschichte*, Tübingen, 1923, p. 101; G. v. Below, *Ges. der deutschen Landwirtschaft in Mittelalter*, Jena, 1937, p. 73–76. Cf. among Japanese studies of Western European medieval history Senroku Uehara's '*Grundherrschaft* in Klosterburg Monastery', 1920, in his collection *Doitsu chusei no shakai to keizai (German Medieval Society and Economy)*.

work, and now paid it in realised forms – products or their money price. The change came to nothing more than this. In both cases the rent appears as the 'normal form' of surplus labour, and does not have the nature of a part of the 'profit', realised by the producers and paid in the form of capitalist rent. Although a 'profit' actually does arise, the rent constitutes a 'normal limit' to this profit formation. In both cases the feudal landlords, in virtue of that ownership, use 'extra-economic coercion' directly, without the intervention of the laws of commodity exchange, to take the surplus labour from the peasant producers (*tenanciers, Besitzer*) who actually occupy the land, the means of production. However, the method of exacting rent, the form of extra-economic coercion, is changing. At the time of the classical manorial system, the labour of the peasants on the demesne was organised under the direct supervision and stimulation of the lord or his representative (*villicus, bailiff, maire, sergent*). On the *reine Grundherrschaft*, however, the entire process of agricultural production was now carried out on the peasants' own parcels, and their necessary labour for themselves and their surplus labour for the lord were no longer separate in space and time. The direct producers were able to arrange their entire labour time pretty much as they wished. The emancipation of the peasants in medieval France and Southwest Germany, that is, the change from the status of serfs (*Leibeigene*) to sokemen or yeomen (*Hörige, vilains francs*) took place on a large scale in the 13th–15th centuries. Thus the method of exacting rent changed from various sorts of personal and arbitrary obligations to certain *real* (*dinglich*) relations of things, and the feudal payment-exaction relations between lords and peasants became contractually fixed. These contractual relations were, to be sure, not like those of modern bourgeois society, where free commodity owners mutually bind themselves as mutually independent personalities, legally on a single plane; they took the form rather of customary law (rent in kind itself was often called *coutumes, Gewohnheitsrecht*, and the peasants who paid it *coutumiers*). Thus for the first time it is possible for us to speak of 'peasant agriculture on a small scale' and the independent handicrafts, which together formed 'the basis of the feudal mode of production'.[38]

As rent in kind gives way to money rent, these small-scale peasant farms, the petty mode of production in agriculture, become more and

[38] See *Capital*, Vol. I, p. 367, note; and cf. my 'Iwayuru nodo kaiho ni tsuite' ('On so-called Serf Emancipation') in *Shigaku zasshi (Zeitschrift für Geschichtswissenschaft)*, Vol. 51, 1940, No. 11–12; and my *Kindai shakai seiritsu shiron (Historical Essay on the Formation of Modern Society)*, p. 36–51.

more clearly independent, and at the same time their self-disintegration too goes on more rapidly and freely. As money rent establishes itself, not only do the old traditional personal relations between lord and peasant change into the more objective impersonal money relations, but, as with the 'rent of assize', the part of the surplus labour which is set as fixed money rent becomes relatively smaller, with the advance of labour productivity and the consequent fall in money-value. To this extent surplus labour forms what has been called an 'embryonic profit', something going to the peasants (direct producers) over and above the amount necessary for subsistence, which the peasants themselves could transform into commodities. As for the money rent, its value became so low that in effect the peasants were released from the obligation of paying it.[39]

The original peasant holdings had been turned into free peasant property. The peasants formerly on the old tenures set for themselves the rate at which they redeemed the feudal rents, freed themselves from the regulations of feudal land property, and became proprietors of their lands. The formation of this sort of independent self-sustaining peasants – historically, the typical representative is the English yeomanry – resulted from the disintegration process of feudal land property and established the social conditions for money rent. Looking at the process from another angle, we can say that when money rent had been established generally and on a national scale, the peasants (the direct producers), in order merely to maintain and reproduce such a state of affairs, did to be sure satisfy the major part of their direct requirements for sustenance by the activities of a natural economy (production and consumption); but a part of their labour power and of the product of their labour, at the very least a part corresponding to the previous feudal rent, always had to be turned into commodities and realised in money by the peasants themselves. In other words, the peasants were in the position of commodity producers who simply had to put themselves always in contact with the market,[40] and whose position as commodity producers brought about the inevitable social differentiation of that condition, the petty

[39] 'Sometimes the freeholders shook themselves loose from all payments and services altogether . . . the connection of the freeholders with the manor was a matter rather of form and sentiment than of substance', Tawney, *Agrarian Problem in the Sixteenth Century, op. cit.*, p. 29–31, 118. Up to the sixteenth century their relations with respect to their manorial lords were mainly formal. The situation was the same in parts of France. For example, in Poitou during the 16th century, many deeds of sale end by saying, 'The seller could not say of what lord and under what dues the places which are the object of the present sale are held', Raveau, *op. cit.*, p. 70, 102 f., 264, 288.

mode of production.[41]

(B.) Now there was an interval of two centuries between the passage from labour services to money rents and the disappearance of serfdom, in the 14th century, and the initial point of the true capitalist era in the 16th century (in England, the 200 years from Edward III to Elizabeth). Let us examine the way in which Sweezy and Dobb handle this interval, the recognition of which, in Dobb's words, is 'vital to any true understanding of the passage from feudalism to capitalism'.[42]

Sweezy holds that serfdom came to an end in the 14th century. This is correct, for labour services actually had been replaced by money rents by that time. Although he warns us that this change is not identical with the end of feudalism itself, still he treats them alike when he deals with the two centuries between the termination of feudalism and the inception of capitalism, and to this extent he is wrong. For, although the peasants had been freed from direct serfdom (labour services), they were still burdened with and regulated by the money rent which was the expression of feudal land property; and although the money rent contained a smaller and smaller part of their surplus labour, the peasants did not shake off the servile category. Sweezy's conception of money rent as essentially a transitional form between feudal rents and capitalist rent corresponds to his methodology. In the words of the passage Dobb refers to, the basis of money rent was breaking up, but 'remains the same as that of the rent in kind [in England, labour services], from which it starts'.[43] That is, the direct producers were, as before, peasant landholders (*Besitzer*); the difference is only that they now paid their surplus labour changed into money form to their landlords, in accordance with extra-economic coercion, 'political constraint and the pressures of

[40] Where a definite [viz., contractual] social productivity of labour has not evolved or, what comes to the same thing, when the peasants do not have a corresponding social position as commodity producers, the money rent is imposed and exacted from above, and cannot completely replace the traditional rents in kind. Not only do both forms appear side by side, as for example in the old regime in France; but very often history presents the spectacle of a reversion to rents in kind (the reappearance of labour services in the *Ostelbe* in Germany, or of rent in kind in France). When money rent was imposed on the peasants in such circumstances, despite their unripeness in various respects as commodity producers, it did not work toward peasant emancipation, but toward their impoverishment.

[41] Tawney's *Agrarian Problem in the Sixteenth Century, op. cit.*, gives many instances of this breaking up of the peasant class. The virgate system *(Hufenverfassung)*, the comparatively uniform standard system of peasant holdings as seen in the 13th century manor, now disappears for good. It gets to the point where, to cite Tawney (*op. cit.*, p. 59 f.), 'Indeed there is not much sense in talking about virgates and half-virgates at all'.

[42] 'Reply', above, p. 62.

[43] *Capital*, Vol. III, p. 926. Cf., 'Reply', above, p. 64.

manorial custom', as Dobb put it.[44] Money rent, in its 'pure' form, is only a variant of rent in kind, or labour services, and in essence 'absorbs' profit in the same 'embryonic' way as does rent in nature.[45] Out of this economic condition there arose both the peasants that were to do away with feudal rent altogether and the industrial capitalists that were to remove limits to industrial profit, both necessarily allied in the bourgeois revolution against the landed aristocracy and the monopolistic merchants.

Why then did Dobb find it necessary to assert that 'the disintegration of the feudal mode of production had already reached an advanced stage before the capitalist mode of production developed, and that this disintegration did not proceed in any close association with the growth of the new mode of production within the womb of the old', and that therefore this period 'seems to have been neither feudal nor yet capitalist so far as its mode of production was concerned'?[46] He does see beyond the usual view that with the establishment of money rent, and hence the disappearance of serfdom, the end of feudalism had come. Now, the overwhelming majority of peasants in 16th century England paid money rents. The prosperous freehold farmers no longer paid feudal dues and had risen to the status of independent free producers (Tawney's 'prosperous rural middle class'). These 'kulak yeomen farmers' employ their poorer neighbours both in agriculture and in industry, although still on a small scale (Tawney's 'Lilliputian capitalists'). Since Dobb is fully aware of these facts, his meaning is probably that although the class of independent semi-capitalist farmers was expanding during this interval, labour itself as a whole did not yet come intrinsically into subordination to capital.

However, it is not the case that after the peasant class had been emancipated from the feudal mode of production, then this free and independent peasantry disintegrated or polarised. Historically the peasant class had already split to a certain extent at the time of serfdom. Serfs were not emancipated under the same economic conditions; and in England, in the rural districts, the peasantry as commodity producers matured especially early; accordingly their emancipation itself sprang also from the self-disintegration of the peasant class. Thus Dobb had

[44] 'Reply', above, p. 63.

[45] 'To the extent that profit arises in fact as a separate portion of the surplus labour by the side of the rent, money rent as well as rent in its preceding forms still is the normal barrier of such embryonic profit', *Capital*, Vol. III, p. 927.

[46] *Studies*, p. 19 f.

to correct his formulation in the *Studies* by now saying that these centuries were 'transitional, in the sense that the old was in process of rapid disintegration and new economic forms were simultaneously appearing'.[47]

Sweezy on the other hand, remains too much of a prisoner of Dobb's earlier formulation, 'neither feudal nor yet capitalist'. For Sweezy, 'the transition from feudalism to capitalism is not a single uninterrupted process . . . but is made up of two quite distinct phases which present radically different problems and require to be analysed separately'. He entitles the 'neither feudal nor capitalist' system which prevailed in Western Europe during the 15th and 16th centuries 'pre-capitalist commodity production'. The 'first undermined feudalism and then *somewhat later*, after this work of destruction had been substantially completed, prepared the ground for the growth of capitalism'.

Sweezy deli erately rejects the term of 'simple commodity production' here, although he notes that in value theory it is a term which 'enables us to present the problem of exchange value in its simplest form'. He thinks the term historically inappropriate, since simple commodity production is 'a system of independent producers owning their own means of production and satisfying their wants by means of mutual exchange', while 'in pre-capitalist commodity production . . . the most important of the means of production – the land – was largely owned by a class of non-producers'.[48] To the extent that the peasants' land was still burdened with feudal rents, even though in money form, the peasant was not an owner of land, in the modern sense, and it is improper to call them independent producers. However, actually in England at that time an upper group of freeholders and customary tenants had been transformed from the status of feudal tenants to that of free independent self-subsistent peasant proprietors.

An even more fundamental matter is Sweezy's unhistorical method in introducing the notion of modern property rights, precisely in treating of feudal land property and tenure. Feudal or seigneurial land property, on our premises, is a form of domination forming the basis for the lord's possession (forcible grasp); the lord's property was *Obereigentum, propriété eminente*, and the peasants were *Untereigentümer* or holders (*Besitzer*) of their lands; the peasants' possession (*domaine utile*) was their actual ownership. In view of all this, the legal concepts of private property in modern bourgeois society are inapplicable.[49] Rather, it is

[47] 'Reply', above, pp. 61–62.

[48] Above, p. 50.

precisely the economic content which is important here,[50] namely the combination of the peasants as direct producers with their means of production (land, etc.); capitalism is premised on the separation of the peasants from the land. This is the key to the peasant-bourgeois development of that period. The prosperity arising out of the labour of this sort of producers, subsequent to the disintegration of feudalism but not yet deprived of their means of production, was a *Volksreichtum* and was the effectual social base of the absolute monarchy.[51]

Sweezy falls into contradiction when he calls this period neither feudal nor capitalist, using the transitional category of 'pre-capitalist commodity production', and at the same time denies the possibility that the peasant basic producers might be 'independent producers'. This contradiction he tries to overcome by describing the money rent paid by these peasants as a transitional form (from feudal rent to capitalist rent). Marx discerns such transitional forms in the *Metäriesystem* or *Parzelleneigentum* of the *kleinbäuerlicher Pächter*,[52] but not in money rent itself. Sweezy's position may be that absolutism was in its essence already no longer feudal. Chapter IV of Dobb's *Studies* and his 'Reply' give an adequate reply on this point and its connection with the bourgeois revolution. In any case, the introduction of the category of 'pre-capitalist commodity production' in this connection is not only unnecessary, but obscures the fact that feudal society and modern capitalist society were ruled by different historical laws. In capitalist society the means of production, as capital, are separated from labour, and the characteristic law of development is that productivity develops (broadening organic composition of capital; formation of an average rate of

[49] This is a well-known criticism of *propriété paysanne* in historical circles. For an early phase of the controversy, see Minzes, *Beitrag zur Geschichte der National-güterveräusserung im Laufe der französischen Revolution*, Jena, 1892. Criticising him later, G. Lefebvre proves that peasants with *une tenure héréditaire*, although still liable to feudal dues, were *paysans propriétaires*, 'Les recherches relatives à la répartition de la propriété et de l'exploitation foncières, à la fin de l'ancien régime', *Revue d'histoire moderne*, No. 14, 1928, p. 103 f., 108 f. Further see in Raveau, *op. cit.*, p. 126 and M. Bloch, *Annales d'histoire économique et sociale*, Vol. I, 1929, p. 100, further proof that peasant *tenanciers féodaux* were *véritables propriétaires*.

[50] 'The private property of the labourer in his means of production is the foundation of petty industry, whether agricultural, manufacturing or both; petty industry, again, is an essential condition for the development of social production and of the free individuality of the labourer himself. Of course, this petty mode of production exists also under slavery, serfdom, and other states of dependence. But it flourishes, it lets loose its whole energy, it attains its adequate classical form, only where the labourer is the private owner of his own means of labour set in action by himself', *Capital*, Vol. I, p. 834 f.

[51] *Ibid.*, Vol. I, p. 789.

[52] *Ibid.*, Vol. III, ch. xlvii, sec. 5; Vol. I, p. 814 f.

profit; tendency of the rate of profit to fall; crises) as if it were the productivity of capital. In feudal society, on the other hand, the means of production are combined with the producer, and productivity develops (collapse of the manorial system and development of small-scale peasant agriculture; formation of money rents; tendency of the rent rate to fall; *crise seigneuriale*) as the productivity of the direct producer himself; and therefore the law of development in feudalism can only lead in the direction of the liberation and the independence of the peasants themselves. It is clear again that absolutism was nothing but a system of concentrated force for counteracting the crisis of feudalism arising out of this inevitable development.[53] These, I think, are the 'laws and tendencies', to use Sweezy's expression, of feudal society, as the method of Volume III of *Capital* suggests.[54]

4

We come finally to the relations between the formation of industrial capital and the 'bourgeois' revolution. The basic economic process of the bourgeois revolution was the abolition of feudal productive relations, in accordance with the development of industrial capital; and we held that this constitutes the *logical* content of the 'passage from feudalism to capitalism', and that a rational analysis of the historical character of feudalism would first be possible *post festum*, when we take the bourgeois revolution as the starting point. It is therefore most important to explain the development of productive forces which historically made inevitable the bourgeois movement which abolished the traditional feudal productive relations; and the social forms of existence of industrial capital at that time. One of Dobb's most valuable contributions to historical science is that he sought the genesis of industrial capitalists not among the *haute bourgeoisie* but in what was taking form within the class of the petty-commodity-producers themselves in the process of freeing themselves from feudal land property; that is, he looked for their origin in what was being born from the internal economy of the body of small producers; and therefore that he set a high value on the role played by this class of small- and medium-scale commodity-producers as the chief agents of productivity in the early

[53] On the structural crisis of economic society in the 18th century, see the admirable analysis of C.-E. Labrousse *La crise de l'économie française à la fin de l'ancien régime et au début de la révolution*, Paris, 1944, esp. p. vii–lxxv.

[54] See my 'Hoken shakai no kiso mujun' ('Basic Contradictions of Feudal Society'), 1949, and my *Shimin kakumei no kozo (Structure of the Bourgeois Revolution)*, p. 60–62.

stage of capitalism. According to Dobb, the representatives of capitalist productive relations at that time were to be found in the independent self-sustaining peasant class and the small and middle-scale craftsmen. In particular, the kulak yeoman farmers improved their farms and farming by degrees and purchased the labour power of their poorer neighbours, the cotters; not only did they keep expanding the scale of their productive operations, initiating the country cloth industry (manufacture as the early form of capitalist production) but entrepreneurs of the same type appeared in the town crafts as well.[55] 'Cromwell's New Model Army and the Independents, who were the real driving force of the [English bourgeois] revolution drew their main strength from the provincial manufacturing centres and . . . from sections of the squirearchy and the small and middling type of yeoman farmer.' These elements were steadfast supporters of the English revolution; the chartered merchants and monopolists belonged to the Royalist party, to a great extent; and 'merchant capital, far from always playing a progressive role, was often to be found allied with feudal reaction [absolutism]'.[56] To return to the terms of my thesis, the English revolution in the 17th century which destroyed feudal reaction (absolutism) thus marked the first step toward the subordination of merchant capital to industrial capital.

This way of posing the problem and of historical analysis appeared in Japan independently of Dobb, and earlier and more consciously, in the creative and original historical theories of Hisao Otsuka.[57] I should say therefore that Dobb's opinion can be taken as confirming the methodological level of the science of economic history in Japan; to Sweezy, perhaps, it is less convincing. Instead of making a concrete analysis of the social genesis and existence-form of industrial capital at that time, all Sweezy does with respect to the classical passage[58] in Volume III of *Capital* on the 'two ways' of transition from the feudal mode of production is to make some critical remarks *en passant* on Dobb's opinions and documentation. Now this Chapter XX (like ch. XXXVI) is a 'historical' one which comes at the end of a number of chapters dealing with merchant capital and interest-bearing capital. Its analysis treats of the nature or laws of early merchant or usury capital, which had an independent existence only in pre-capitalist society; and the process by which, in the course of the development of capitalist production, this merchant capital is subordinated to industrial capital. It is not

[55] *Studies*, p. 125 f., 128 f., 134 f., 142 f., 150 f., etc.; 'Reply', above, p. 64.

a question of a merely formal or nominal change, that is of the merchant turning industrialist. Therefore, in discussing the theory of the 'two ways', viz. (1) 'the producer becomes a merchant and capitalist' – 'this is the really revolutionary way' –; and (2) 'the merchant takes possession in a direct way of production', the merchant becomes an industrialist, 'preserves it [the old mode of production] and uses it as its premise', but becomes eventually 'an obstacle to a real capitalist mode of production and declin(ing) with the development of the latter':[59] all of this

[56] *Studies*, p. 171; 'Reply', p. 64 above. Dobb's insight that those who carried out the bourgeois revolution, who were the real vehicles of the industrial capital (capitalist production) of that time, were to be found in the rising small and middle bourgeoisie, and that the centre of attention must be focussed on the contradiction between them and the merchant and usurer capitalists *(Haute bourgeoisie)*, had been reached forty years before him by G. Unwin, *Industrial Organization in the 16th and 17th Centuries*, 1904, and Max Weber, *Die Protestantische Ethik und der Geist von Kapitalismus*, 1904–5. It is surprising that Dobb, in discussing the 'capitalist spirit' (*Studies*, p. 5, 9), overlooks this remarkable insight of Weber's. Weber brings out clearly two clashing social systems in that heroic period of English history. The 'capitalist spirit' which appeared in the form of Puritanism was the way of life, the form of consciousness best suited to the class of yeomen and small and middle industrialists of that time, and is not to be found in the mentality of 'hunger for money', 'greed for gain', common to monopolist merchants and usurers of all times and countries. 'In general, at the threshold of modern times, it was not only, and not even mainly, the capitalist entrepreneurs of the trading patriciate, but much rather the up and coming layers of the industrial middle class which were the vehicles of the attitude that we have here labeled "spirit of capitalism",' Weber, *Gesammelte Aufsätze zur Religionssoziologie*, Vol. 1, Tübingen, 1920, p. 49 f.; and cf. *ibid*., p. 195 f. On this point even Tawney has not broken away from Brentano's thesis in *Die Anfänge des modernen Kapitalismus* (München, 1916), that the capitalist spirit arose together with profit-seeking commerce. For example, in Tawney, *Religion and the Rise of Capitalism*, London, 1926, p. 319: 'There was plenty of the "capitalist spirit" in fifteenth-century Venice and Florence, or in South Germany and Flanders, for the simple reason that these areas were the greatest commercial and financial centres of the age, though all were, at least nominally, Catholic.' Pirenne, often cited by both Dobb and especially Sweezy, and undoubtedly one of the foremost authorities, published a sketch dealing with 'the evolution of capitalism through a thousand years of history', entitled 'The Stages in the Social History of Capitalism', *American Historical Review*, Vol. XIX, 1914, p. 494–515. He pointed out the shift in capitalists from one age to another: modern capitalists did not come from medieval capitalists, but rather from their destruction; essentially, however, Pirenne regarded commodity production and money circulation itself as the mark of capitalism, and, so far as he was concerned, feudal capitalism and modern capitalism 'have only a difference of quantity, not a difference of quality, a simple difference of intensity, not a difference of nature', *op. cit*., p. 487. For him too, the *spiritus capitalisticus* is the greed for gain born in the 11th century, along with trade.

[57] Hisao Otsuka, *Kindai Ōshu keizai shi josetsu (Introduction to the Economic History of Modern Europe)*, Tokyo, 1944. The kernel of the argument of this work is clearly formulated even earlier in the same author's essay, 'Noson no orimoto to toshi no orimoto' ('Country and Town Clothiers') in *Shakai keizai shigaku (Social and Economic History)*, 1938, Vol. VIII, No. 3–4.

[58] *Capital*, Vol. III, p. 393.

[59] Above, pp. 52–53.

should be understood as a whole, in history as well as in theory. A little earlier the text runs, 'In the pre-capitalist stages of society, commerce rules industry. The reverse is true of modern society', and the question of 'the subordination of merchants' capital to industrial capital' is raised. And after the passage in dispute there come the statements, 'The producer is himself a merchant. The merchants' capital performs no longer anything but the process of circulation . . . Now commerce becomes the servant of industrial production.'[60]

Sweezy's analysis[61] is that the second way, merchant to manufacturer or industrialist, proceeds by the roundabout path of the 'putting-out system', while in the first way 'the producer, whatever his background [presumably the social background], *starts out* as both a merchant and an employer of wage-labour', or 'becomes a full-fledged capitalist entrepreneur without going through the intermediate stages of the putting-out system'. This seems rather a superficial interpretation. In Sweezy the problem is envisaged as a mere comparison of forms of management, and the social character – the contradiction – of the two is lost sight of.

Sweezy's reference to the putting-out system as Way No. II is undoubtedly correct. A little further on in the same chapter in *Capital*, the way of 'merchant → industrialist (manufacturer)' is explained; in it the merchant capitalist subordinates the petty producers (the town craftsman and especially the village producer) to himself and operates the putting-out system for his own benefit, making loans in advance to the workers. In addition, however, the way of 'producer → merchant (capitalist)' is exemplified, 'the master weaver, instead of receiving his wool in instalments from the merchant and working for him with his journeymen, buys wool or yarn himself and sells his cloth to the merchant. The elements of production pass into his process of production as commodities bought by himself. And instead of producing for the individual merchant, or for definite customers, the master cloth-weaver produces for the commercial world. The producer is himself a merchant.'[62] Here the petty commodity producers are rising toward independence and the status of industrial capitalists from being under the control of merchant capital in the putting-out system. Thus, the whole reference to the original text points not merely to the existence of the two ways, but to their opposition and clash. The substance of the path

[60] *Capital*, Vol. III, p. 389, 392, 395 f.
[61] Above, pp. 54–55.
[62] *Capital*, Vol. III, p. 395.

of 'producer → merchant' is that of a 'revolutionary' process of subordination of the earlier merchant capital to industrial capital (capitalist production).[63]

With respect to Way No. I, Sweezy, without going so far as altogether to deny the existence of cases of the transformation of petty commodity producers into industrial capitalists, regards them as of no importance in the social genesis of industrial capitalists. He rather takes as the general case the transition directly to industrial capitalists without passing through the detour of the putting-out system. He almost certainly has in mind the centralised manufacturers (*fabriques réunies*), usually pointed out by economic historians, from the facts adduced in J. U. Nef's study of practices in mining and metallurgy.[64] Historically, this sort of centralised manufactures, set up either under the protection and favour of the absolute monarchies as *manufactures royales* (*d'etat privilégiées*) or as institutions for forced labour, existed in many countries.[65] However, in essence this is not genuine manufacture as the initial form of capitalist production (industrial capital); but a mere cohesion point or node of the putting-out system of merchant capital, as our works have given evidence; and hence this was the same as Way No. II in character. Is this 'revolutionary', when it was unable to bring about the development of genuine capitalist production? In Western Europe, on the contrary, it was outstripped by the rise of the class of petty producers and their economic expansion, and finally succumbed by degrees. Monopolistic enterprises of this sort, Dobb has pointed out in the case of England, were of a 'conservative' nature and allied with the state power of the absolute monarchy; and therefore in the end they were destroyed

[63] Again, as for the 'producer becoming a merchant', a chapter preceding this, which analyses commercial profit, states: 'In the process of scientific analysis, the formation of an average rate of profit appears to take its departure from the industrial capitals and their competition, and only later on does it seem to be corrected, supplemented, and modified by the intervention of merchant's capital. But in the course of historical events, the process is reversed. . . . The commercial profit originally determines the industrial profit. Not until the capitalist mode of production has asserted itself and the producer himself has become a merchant, is the commercial profit reduced to that aliquot part of the total surplus-value, which falls to the share of the merchant's capital as an aliquot part of the total capital engaged in the social process of reproduction', *Capital*, Vol. III, p. 337 f. Similarly the development of capitalist production in agriculture reduced rent from the position of being the normal form of surplus labour (feudal rent or services) to the position of being an 'offshoot' of profit (the part over and above the average rate of profit).

[64] *Industry and Government in France and England, 1540–1640*.

[65] J. Koulischer, 'La grande industrie aux XVIIe et XVIII siècles. France, Allemagne, Russie', *Annales d'histoire écon et soc.*, 1931, No. 9; cf. Dobb, *Studies*, p. 138 f., p. 142 f.; 'Reply', above, p. 64.

and disappeared in the bourgeois revolution.[66] Such an evolution was characteristic in the formation of capitalism in Western Europe, especially in England. On the other hand enormous monopolistic enterprises of this nature played important parts in the establishment of capitalism in Eastern Europe and Japan; but this is not taken up by Sweezy.

Dobb too, however, in dealing with the problem of the 'two ways', sees the 'producer → merchant' way as the '"putting-out", or *Verlag*-system, organised by merchant-manufacturers' or by 'entrepreneurs . . . who took to trade and employed poorer craftsmen on the putting-out system';[67] here he has clearly fallen into a contradiction. In the historical form of the putting-out system the 'merchant-manufacturers' realise their profit by concentrating the purchase of raw materials and the sale of the products exclusively in their own hands, advancing the raw materials to the small producers as the work to be finished; this cutting-off of the small producers from the market, this monopoly of the market by the putters-out, clearly had the effect of blocking the road on which the direct producers were independently rising as commodity producers, and becoming capitalists.[68] Although these *marchands-entrepreneurs* were often called *fabricants* they were not genuinely 'progressive' industrial capitalists. They 'controlled' production only from the outside, and in order to continue their domination, as merchant capitalists, they maintained the traditional conditions of production unchanged; they were conservative in character. This then is not Way No. I, but certainly within Way No. II.

Why then does Dobb take the putting-out system and the putting-out merchants' capital as Way No. I? Perhaps at the base of this opinion lie facts of economic history which are peculiar to England. Dobb identifies the putting-out system with the 'domestic system' (*industrie à domicile, Hausindustrie*). 'On the whole . . . in seventeenth-century England the domestic industry, rather than either the factory or the manufacturing

[66] This was the case in France too. Tarlé's studies on industry under the *ancien régime* lead him to stress once more the 'enormously important fact' that the strenuous battle for a broader and freer national production – the propulsive force of French capitalism – was not waged by *la grande industrie* nor by the prosperous *industriels des villes* (the putters-out), but by the *petits producteurs des campagnes*, E. Tarlé, *L'industrie dans les campagnes en France à la fin de l'ancien régime*, Paris, 1910, p. 53. Labrousse's brilliant work points out the widening economic and social schism and antagonism between the privileged feudal minority and the ensemble of the nation, *Esquisse du mouvement de sprix at des revenus en France au xvii siécle*, (2 vols., Paris, 1933), vol. II, p. 615, 626, 419–21, 639, 535–44.

[67] *Studies*, p. 138; 'Reply', above p. 64.

workshop, remained the most typical form of production.'[69] The domestic system in England (a different thing from the German *Hausindustrie*, which is very often identical in content with the *Verlagssystem*) very often denotes independent small and middle industries rather than the putting-out system in the strict and original sense.[70] Moreover, it is worthy of note in English economic history that the conduct of the putting-out system by merchant capital appeared lenient, and that the class of small producers who received advances of raw materials from

[68] The putting-out system although it is commodity production, is not capitalist production. The landlord who directly runs the manor by means of the forced labour of the serfs, or the feudal landholder who exacts rent in kind from them, may indeed convert the produce into commodities but are still not capitalists. The putting-out system presupposes the possession of the means of production by the direct immediate producers; it does not presuppose wage-labour. Similarly the system of feudal land property is premised on the holding of the land by the peasants. The feudal lord, diverging from the *Hufe* peasants, put an end to their independence; he got hold of the village community and its collective constraints on the basis of which the mutual relations of the *Hufe* peasants had been organised, and reorganised them within the framework of feudal land property relations and domination. In a similar way, the putting-out merchants emerged from among the independent craftsmen and put an end to their independence, got control of the town craft guilds and their collective constraints on the basis of which the mutual relations of the independent craftsmen had been organised, and reorganised them under the control of merchant capital. The sequence of categorical development – craft → guild → putting-out system (merchant capital) is the – formal or fictitious – projection of the basic logical structure of feudal land property, virgate → community → manor (see above, note 15). Cf. *Contribution to a Critique of Political Economy, op. cit.*, p. 302. The separation of the independent craftsmen, who were at once producers and merchants, from their commercial functions of buying the raw materials and selling the products, and the concentration of these functions in the hands of the merchants, were the conditions for the establishment of the merchant capitalist putting-out system. And in the same way it was 'extra-economic constraints' on the part of the merchant putters-out that insured the cutting-off of the producers from the market, that is the negation of their independence as commodity producers. The craftsmen, losing their independence, submitted to the rule of the merchant putters-out. However, in the productive process itself there was as yet no change; rather, the guild and craft conditions of production and labour were maintained as its premises. The change was confined to the process of circulation. At the base of the petty craftsmen's industries, the process of production was unified by the putting-out merchants and came under their control. Thus the putting-out system as a mode of production does not differ essentially from feudal handicrafts. See further Weber, *Wirtschaftsgeschichte, op. cit.*, p. 147.

[69] *Studies*, p. 142 f.

[70] P. Mantoux, *The Industrial Revolution in the 18th Century*, London, 1937, p. 61. Toynbee too points out this state of affairs in English industry before the Industrial Revolution: 'the class of capitalist employers was as yet but in its infancy. A large part of our goods were still produced on the domestic system. Manufactures were little concentrated in towns, and only partially separated from agriculture. The 'manufacturer' was, literally, the man who worked with his own hands in his own cottage. . . . An important feature in the industrial organisation of the time was the existence of a number of small master-manufacturers, who were entirely independent, having capital and land of their own, for they combined the culture of small freehold pasture-farms with their handicraft', *Lectures on the 18th Century in England*, London, 1884, p. 52 f.

the merchants were able to establish their independence from the control of the putting-out system with relative ease. Conditions of this sort were especially conspicuous in 18th-century Lancashire; according to the study of Wadsworth and Mann, within the lax framework of the putting-out system, weavers could easily rise to be putters-out and the latter to be manufacturers.[71] Dobb may have had some such sort of economic and social situation in mind. His account[72] suggests this: 'many of the new entrepreneurs were small men who had started as "merchant-manufacturers" of the putting-out system'. The real content, therefore, of the 'merchant-manufacturers' whom Dobb has chosen as Way No. I is not the monopolist oligarchy of putting-out merchant capitalists in the strict sense, who were an obstacle to the development of capitalist production, as we see in the case of the *Verlegerkompagnie*, whose control was abolished with the bourgeois revolution, but is rather the class of small- and middle-scale industrial and commercial capitalists who threaded their way to independence in the interstices of the merchant capitalist 'control' and became the merchant-manufacturers. It is here that Dobb looks for the historical genesis of 'manufacture' as the first stage of capitalist production, and not in what historians call the 'factory' or 'manufactory'. This is undoubtedly one of Dobb's contributions to historical science.[73] But he should have given a more precise development to this comment on the genesis of industrial capital in the light of the internal organisation peculiar to English agriculture.

Although Dobb made a concrete and substantial analysis of the 'two ways' and was able to get insight into the historical character of the 'classical' bourgeois revolution, on an international scale his various theses call for re-examination. As for Western Europe, in both England and France that revolution had as its basis the class of free and independent peasants and the class of small- and middle-scale commodity producers. The revolution was a strenuous struggle for the state power between a group of the middle class (the Independents in the English Revolution, the Montagnards in the French), and a group of the *haute bourgeoisie* originating in the feudal land aristocracy, the merchant and

[71] Wadsworth and Mann, *The Cotton Trade and Industrial Lancashire, 1600–1780*, Manchester, 1931, p. 277; and cf. p. 70–5, 241–48, 273–77.

[72] 'Reply', above, p. 64.

[73] On this point see Hisao Otsuka, 'Toiya seido no kindai teki keitai' ('Modern forms of the putting-out system'), 1942, in his *Kindai shihonshugi no keifu (Ancestry of Modern Capitalism)*, Tokyo, 1951, p. 183 f. See too Kulischer's resumé of the results of socio-economic history, *Allgemeine Wirtschaftsgeschichte*, Vol. II, Munich and Berlin, 1929, p. 162 f.

financial monopolists (in the English Revolution the Royalists and after them the Presbyterians, in the French Revolution the Monarchiens, then the Feuillants, finally the Girondins); in the process of both revolutions, the former routed the latter.[74] Dobb has pointed this out in the case of England.

However, in Prussia and Japan it was quite the contrary. The classical bourgeois revolutions of Western Europe aimed at freeing producers from the system of 'constraints' (feudal land property and guild regulations) and making them free and independent commodity producers;[75] in the economic process it was inevitable that they should be dissociated, and this differentiation (into capital and wage-labour) forms the internal market for industrial capital. It need hardly be said that what constituted the social background for the completion of the bourgeois revolution of this type was the structural disintegration of feudal land property peculiar to Western Europe. On the contrary, in Prussia and Japan, the erection of capitalism under the control and patronage of the feudal absolute state was in the cards from the very first.[76]

Certainly, the way in which capitalism took form in every country was closely tied up with previous social structures, i.e., the internal intensity and organisation of feudal economy there. In England and France, feudal

[74] Compare Weber's 'conflict of the two ways of capitalist activity'. He finds that the sources of the period, when speaking of the adherents of the various Puritan sects, describe part of them as propertyless (proletarians) and part as belonging to the stratum of small capitalists. 'It was precisely from this stratum of *small* capitalists, and *not* from the great financiers: monopolists, government contractors, lenders to the state, colonialists, promotors, etc., that what was *characteristic* of Occidental capitalism came: bourgeois-private economic organization of industrial labour (see *e.g.* Unwin, *Industrial Organization in the 16th and 17th Centuries*, p. 196 f.); and 'To the "organic" organization of society, in that fiscal-monopolistic direction it took in Anglicanism under the Stuarts, namely in Laud's conceptions: – to this league of church and state with the "monopolists" on the basis of a Christian social substructure, Puritanism, whose representatives were always passionate opponents of this sort of government-privileged merchant-, putting-out, and colonial capitalism, opposed the individualistic *drives* of rational legal gain by means of individual virtue and initiative, which were decisively engaged in building up industries, without and in part despite and against the power of the state, while all the government-favoured monopoly industries in England soon vanished', *Protestantische Ethik, loc. cit.*, p. 195, note; p. 201 f.

[75] The Independents in the Puritan Revolution were of this sort, and so were the Montagnards in the French Revolution, as the last authority on the subject points out: 'Their social ideal was a democracy of small autonomous proprietors, of peasants and independent artisans working and trading freely', G. Lefebvre, *Questions agraires au temps de la Terreur* Strasbourg, 1932, p. 133.

[76] Cf. 'Kindai teki shinka no futatsu no taiko teki taikei ni tsuite' ('On Two Contrary Systems of Modern Progress'), 1942, in my *Kindai shakai seiritsu shiron (Historical Essay on the Formation of Modern Society)*, p. 151 f.

land property and serfdom either disintegrated in the process of the economic development, or were wiped out structurally and categorically in the bourgeois revolution. G. Lefebvre emphasised the part of the *revolution paysanne* in the French Revolution.[77] These revolutions in Western Europe, by the independence and the ascent of the petty commodity producers and their differentiation, set free from among them the forces making – as it were *economically* – for the development of capitalist production; while in Prussia and Japan this 'emancipation' was carried out in the opposite sense. The organisation of feudal land property remained intact and the classes of free and independent peasants and middle-class burghers were undeveloped. The bourgeois 'reforms', like the *Bauernbefreiung* and the *Chiso-kaisei* (agrarian reforms in the Meiji Restoration), contain such contrary elements as the legal sanctioning of the position of the Junker's land property and parasite land proprietorship of semi-feudal character. Since capitalism had to be erected on this kind of soil, on a basis of fusion rather than conflict with absolutism, the formation of capitalism took place in the opposite way to Western Europe, predominantly as a process of transformation of putting-out merchant capital into industrial capital. The socio-economic conditions for the establishment of modern democracy were not present; on the contrary capitalism had to make its way within an oligarchic system – the 'organic' social structure – designed to suppress bourgeois liberalism. Thus it was not the internal development itself of those societies that brought about the necessity of a 'bourgeois' revolution; the need for reforms rather came about as the result of external circumstances. It can be said that in connection with varying world and historical conditions the phase of establishing capitalism takes different basic lines: in Western Europe, Way No. I (producer → merchant), in Eastern Europe and Asia, Way No. II (merchant → manufacturer). There is a deep inner relationship between the agrarian question and industrial capital, which determines the characteristic structures of capitalism in the various countries.[78] For our part, what the author of *Capital* wrote about his fatherland in 1867, in the preface to the first edition, still holds true, despite the different stage of world history: 'Alongside of modern evils, a whole series of inherited evils oppress us, arising

[77] On the 'peasant revolution', see G. Lefebvre, 'La Revolution et les paysans', *Cahiers de la rev. fr.*, 1934, No. 1.

[78] This problem was raised early in Japan: see Seitora Yamada's original *Nihon shihon shugi bunseki (Analysis of Japanese Capitalism)*, 1934, in particular the preface which contains in compact form a multitude of historical insights.

from the passive survival of antiquated modes of production, with their inevitable train of social and political anachronisms'.[79] Thus the question of 'two ways', so far as we are concerned, is not merely of historical interest, but is connected with actual practical themes. *Hic Rhodus, hic salta!*

[79] *Capital*, Vol. I, p. 13.

A Further Comment

Maurice Dobb

With Professor H. K. Takahashi's stimulating article on 'The Transition from Feudalism to Capitalism', which makes such an important contribution to deepening and extending our appreciation of the important questions at issue, I find myself in general agreement; and there is very little that I wish or am competent to add to what he has said. In particular, I find his development of the notion of the 'two ways' and his use of it to illuminate the contrast between the way of the bourgeois revolution and that of Prussia and Japan specially enlightening. With reference to what he has said in criticism of myself I would like merely to make three comments.

He is, of course, quite justified in saying that my book paid 'inadequate attention to French and German writing'; he might have added with even more justice that I had almost entirely ignored the experience of southern Europe, Italy and Spain in particular. I can only explain that this was done advisedly, and that my book was entitled *Studies in the Development of Capitalism* to indicate its selective and partial character. No pretence was made of writing, even in outline, a comprehensive history of Capitalism. The method adopted can, I think, be described as consisting of a treatment of certain crucial phases and aspects in the development of Capitalism, primarily in terms of England as the classic case, with occasional references to continental parallels (as with developments in the guilds or the putting-out system) or contrasts (as with the feudal reaction in Eastern Europe or the creation of a proletariat) to illuminate the particular issues that I was trying to clarify. To have developed these parallels and contrasts as they deserved, and to have made from them anything like a complete comparative study of the origin and growth of Capitalism under diverse conditions would have required a range of knowledge of the historical literature of Europe to which I could lay no claim. Even a much more encyclopaedic mind than mine would probably have had to wait upon a decade or so of 'cooperative advances in these studies' to which Professor Takahashi refers.

Secondly, in asserting that in my book I spoke of the period from the 14th to the 16th century in England as 'neither feudal nor yet capitalist', I think that Professor Takahashi has been misled into accepting my posing of a problem as my own conclusion about it. If he will look at the passage on page 19 of my book again, I think he will see that I am here asking a question (there is in fact a question-mark at the end of the sentence) – formulating a difficulty which has presented itself to so many students of this period. On the very next page I state that, despite the disintegration of Feudalism and the appearance of 'a mode of production which had won its independence from Feudalism: petty production . . . which was not yet capitalist although containing within itself the embryo of capitalist relations', one still could not speak of the end of Feudalism ('But unless one is to identify the end of Feudalism with the process of commutation . . . one cannot yet speak of the end of the medieval system, still less of the dethronement of the medieval ruling class' – p. 20). Admittedly the sparseness of my references to agriculture (which he criticises) left my conclusion much less supported than it might have been. But here I believe that, despite the illumination shed by Tawney and some others, much field-work remains to be done by specialists in this period – specialists who are guided by the method of Marxism. Again, I am very ready to admit that earlier viewpoints of my own, embodied in earlier drafts, may have left their trace in the final version and have been responsible for the presentation being less clear than it should have been. But it was certainly not my intention to endorse the view that the period between Edward II and Elizabeth was 'neither feudal nor yet capitalist'; and the statement that this period was 'transitional', of which Professor Takahashi speaks as a 'correction' introduced only in my 'Reply', was in fact made on page 20 of the book.

I should continue to defend, however, my other and distinct statement that 'the disintegration of the feudal mode of production had already reached an advanced stage before the capitalist mode of production developed, and that this disintegration did not proceed in any close association with the growth of the new mode of production within the womb of the old'. It does not imply that these transitional centuries were 'neither feudal nor yet capitalist', but rather the contrary; and I believe that it provides a key to the difficulty which has led so many to adopt something akin to the Sweezy-view of this period. I regarded it as a statement in general and preliminary form of the thesis which I gather that Professor Takahashi fully accepts: namely, that the disintegration of Feudalism (and hence its final and declining stage) came *not* as the result of the assault upon it of an incipient 'Capitalism' in the guise of 'merchant capital' wedded to 'money economy', as has been commonly supposed, but as a result of the revolt of the petty producers against feudal exploitation. This partial independence of the petty producers resulted in an acceleration of their own disintegration (even if this was not the start of the process) by accelerating the process of social differentiation among them; and out of this process (but *only* after its maturing during a transitional period of feudalism-in-decline) the capitalist mode of production was born. Precisely *because* this process of social differentiation within the petty mode of production had to mature before capitalist production was born, an interval was necessary between the start of the decline of serfdom and the rise of Capitalism. In Professor Takahashi's own words: 'As rent in kind gives way to money rent, these small-scale peasant farms, the petty mode of production in agriculture, become more and more clearly independent, and at the same time their self-distintegration too goes on more rapidly and freely'. The only disagreement between us here seems to be a possible difference of emphasis on the degree of this 'self-disintegration' at an earlier period and a later period.

Thirdly, as regards the 'two ways' and my references to the putting-out system, Professor Takahashi's interpretation is correct when he speaks of me as including the putting-out system of the English petty domestic-industry type as belonging to Way No. I. I thought, however, that I had made clear in my chapter on 'The Rise of Industrial Capital' that I regarded the putting-out system, not as a homogeneous economic form, but rather as a generic name for a complex phenomenon embracing several different types. One, the pure *Verleger*-type of industry organised by merchants of companies like the Haberdashers, Drapers, Clothworkers, Leathersellers, I treated as merchant-into-manufacturer Way No. II (see p. 129–34 of my *Studies*); and immediately went on to contrast with it that movement of which the rise of a class of merchant-manufacturer employers from among the ranks of craftsmen composing the (subordinate) 'Yeomanry' of the Livery Companies and the challenge of the new Stuart corporations formed from these elements (of which Unwin wrote) were the expression (p. 134–8). On whether this organised-from-below form of putting-out system is a peculiarly English phenomenon, or whether it has continental parallels, I should hesitate to venture a dogmatic opinion. Here I can do no more than suggest that preoccupation with the search for the large-scale capitalist *entrepreneur* may possibly have blinded continental historians to the role played by the small and *parvenu* type of merchant-manufacturer, and that the true picture of the *Verlags-system* may not, even in Germany, be quite such a systematic and tidy one as German economic historians have represented it. Again one must appeal to those 'cooperative advances' in the study of such questions in various countries, of which Professor Takahashi speaks.

A Rejoinder

Paul Sweezy

The problems that troubled me most when I first took up Dobb's *Studies in the Development of Capitalism* (New York, 1947), were, very briefly these: There existed throughout most of Western Europe in the early Middle Ages a feudal system such as Dobb well describes on pp. 36–37. This mode of production went through a process of development which culminated in crisis and collapse, and it was succeeded by capitalism. Formally, the analogy with the life history of capitalism – development, general crisis, transition to socialism – is very close. Now, I have a pretty good idea about the nature of the prime mover in the capitalist case, why the process of development which it generates leads to crisis, and why socialism is necessarily the successor form of society. But I was not at all clear about any of these factors in the feudal case when I sat down to Dobb's book. I was looking for the answers.

The greatest tribute I can pay to Dobb's book is that when I had finished studying it I felt much clearer in my own mind about all these questions. This was partly because he succeeded in convincing me and partly because he stimulated me to look into other sources and to do some fresh thinking on my own. My original article in *Science and Society* was in the nature of a report on the tentative answers I had reached. (I think, incidentally, that I should have made this plainer. Dobb of course formulated his problems in his own way, and he was interested in much that bears only indirectly if at all on the questions to which I was seeking answers. Some of my 'criticisms,' therefore, were really not criticisms at all; they should have been presented as supplementary suggestions and hypotheses.)

In his 'Reply', Dobb indicates various points of disagreement with my answers, and Takahashi, if I understand him rightly, rejects them very nearly *in toto*. But I know little more about what Dobb's answers are (to *my* questions, of course) than I did after finishing the book, and I know next to nothing about what Takahashi's are. I should therefore like to use the opportunity afforded by this rejoinder to restate my questions and answers as concisely as possible and in a form which may perhaps invite alternative formulations from Dobb and Takahashi.[1]

First Question. What was the prime mover behind the development of Western European feudalism?[2]

In the case of capitalism, we can answer this question positively and unambiguously. The prime mover is the accumulation of capital which is inherent in the very structure of the capitalist appropriation process. Is there anything analogous in the case of feudalism?

Dobb's theory finds an analogue in the feudal lords' growing need for revenue. In his view, 'it was the inefficiency of Feudalism as a system of production, coupled with the growing needs of the ruling class for revenue, that was primarily responsible for its decline; since this need for additional revenue promoted an increase in the pressure on the producer to the point where this pressure became literally unendurable.' (*Studies*, p. 42.) As a result, 'in the end it led to an exhaustion, or actual disappearance, of the labour-force by which the system was nourished.' (p. 43.) The question is whether the lords' growing need for revenue – the *fact* of which is not in dispute – can be shown to be inherent in the structure of the feudal mode of production. I gave reasons for doubting that any such relation exists ('Critique', above, pp. 37–39), and I showed how the lords' growing need for revenue could readily be explained as a by-product of the growth of trade and urban life.

Dobb is rather impatient with my emphasis on this subject. According to him, I seem to feel that the development of feudalism is

'a question of *either* internal conflict or *external* forces. This strikes me as much too simplified, even mechanical, a presentation. I see it as an *interaction* of the two; although with primary emphasis, it is true, upon the internal contradictions; since these would, I believe, operate in any case (if on a quite different time-scale), and since they determine the parti-

[1] In what follows, I refer to Dobb's book as *Studies*, to my review-article as 'Critique', to Dobb's reply as 'Reply', and to Takahashi's article as 'Contribution'.

[2] I insist on speaking of *Western European* feudalism, because what ultimately happened in Western Europe was manifestly very different from what happened in other parts of the world where the feudal mode of production has prevailed. The extent to which this may be due to variations among different feudal systems, and the extent to which it may be due to 'external' factors are, of course, very important questions. Since, however, I do not pretend to be able to answer them, the only sensible thing for me to do is to confine my attention to Western Europe. By doing so, I do not want to imply that I think other feudalisms are subject to different laws of development; I want to evade the question altogether.

cular form and direction of the effects which external influence exert ('Reply', above, p. 60).'

Historically, of course, Dobb is entirely right. It *was* an interaction of internal and external factors that determined the course of feudal development, and I never intended to deny it. But the same can be said of the historical development of capitalism, a fact which does not keep us from seeking and finding the prime mover within the system. I cannot agree, therefore, that Dobb is justified in describing my formulation of the question with regard to feudalism as 'mechanical'. It is a theoretical question, and I continue to believe that it is crucial to the whole analysis of feudalism.

The second half of the foregoing quotation clearly indicates that Dobb does in fact take a position on this question, despite his reluctance to formulate either the question or the answer in a clear-cut fashion. And the position is precisely the one which I attributed to him on the basis of the book, namely, that feudalism does contain an internal prime mover. Since he adduces no new arguments in support, however, I can only remain unconvinced.

So far as I can see, Takahashi contributes little to the clarification of this issue. His interesting analysis of the *elements* of feudalism ('Contribution', above, pp. 70–73) does not lead him to any formulation of the laws and tendencies' of the system, and when he does address himself specifically to this question, the result is not very enlightening, at least to me. In feudal society, he writes,

> 'the means of production are combined with the producer, and productivity develops (collapse of the manorial system and development of small-scale peasant agriculture; formation of money rents; tendency of the rent rate to fall; *crise seigneuriale*) as the productivity of the direct producer himself; and therefore the law of development in feudalism can only lead in the direction of the liberation and independence of the peasants themselves (*Ibid.*, above p. 87).'

Here rising productivity is treated as the crucial factor, but it is certainly not self-evident that rising productivity is an inherent characteristic of feudalism. In fact, there is a good deal of historical and contemporary evidence that suggests precisely the opposite hypothesis. Here again, as in the case of Dobb's growing need of the lords for revenue, I think we have to do with the influence of forces external to the feudal system.

On this whole question of external forces, Takahashi takes me severely to task:

'Sweezy does not take the break-up of a given social structure as the result of self-movement of its productive forces; instead he looks for an "external force". If we say that historical development takes place according to external forces, the question remains, however, how these external forces arose, and where they came from ("Contribution", above, pp. 78–79).'

The latter point, of course, is a valid one which I never intended to deny. Historical forces which are external with respect to one set of social relations are internal with respect to a more comprehensive set of social relations. And so it was in the case of Western European feudalism. The expansion of trade, with the concomitant growth of towns and markets, was external to the feudal mode of production,[3] but it was internal as far as the whole European-Mediterranean economy was concerned.

A thorough study of Western European feudalism – which Dobb of course never claimed to offer – would have to analyse it in the context of this larger European-Mediterranean economy. How this can be done has been brilliantly demonstrated by Pirenne who argued, first, that the origins of feudalism in Western Europe are to be sought in the isolation (by the Arab expansion of the seventh century) of that relatively backward region from the real economic centres of the ancient world; and second, that the later development of feudalism was decisively shaped by the re-establishment of these broken commercialties.[4] Viewed in this way, the growth of trade from the tenth century on was obviously no mysterious external force, such as Takahashi quite mistakenly accuses me of 'looking for'. But when attention is narrowly centred on feudalism as such – as Dobb was quite justified in doing – it seems to me not only legitimate but theoretically essential to treat the growth of trade as an external force.

3 I am unable to understand Dobb's reasoning when he says that 'to some extent' he believes that the growth of towns was an internal feudal process ('Reply', above, p. 60). Surely the fact cited by Dobb in this connection that feudalism 'encouraged towns to cater for its need of long-distance trade' does not prove the point. One would have to show that the feudal ruling class took the initiative in building the towns and successfully integrated them into the feudal system of property and labour relations. Undoubtedly this did happen in the case of some towns, but it seems to me that Pirenne has conclusively shown that the decisive trading centres typically grew up in an entirely different way. But what particularly indicates the non-feudal character of the towns was the general absence of serfdom.

4 In addition to Henri Pirenne's *Economic and Social History of Medieval Europe*, London, 1936, see also his *Mohammed and Charlemagne*, New York, 1939, the posthumously published work which gives the author's fullest treatment of the twin problems of the end of antiquity and the rise of feudalism in Western Europe.

The answer to the first question, then, seems to me to be this: the feudal system contains no internal prime mover and when it undergoes genuine development – as distinct from mere oscillations and crises which do not affect its basic structure – the driving force is to be sought outside the system. (I suspect that this applies pretty generally to feudal systems, and not only to Western Europe, but this is an issue which is beyond the scope of the present discussion).

Second Question. Why did the development of feudalism in Western Europe lead to crisis and ultimate collapse?

Having determined that an external prime mover is behind the developmental process, we must of course conclude that the answer to this question is to be sought in the impact of this external force on the structure of feudalism. As Dobb rightly insists, in other words, the process is one of interaction, and I take it that Takahashi would not disagree. There are therefore no basic differences here. My chief criticism of both Dobb and Takahashi in this connection is that in their anxiety to minimise the importance of trade as a factor in the decline of feudalism they avoid a direct analysis of this interactive process. Both of them, for example, tend to treat the substitution of money rents for labour services or payments in kind as largely a matter of form and to lose sight of the fact that this change can occur on any considerable scale only on the basis of developed commodity production.

My own effort to deal with the interactive process and its outcome was given in my original article ('Critique', above pp. 41–45). It doubtless contains many weaknesses – for example, in the treatment of the so-called 'second serfdom', which Dobb criticises – but I still think it has the merit of being an explicit theoretical analysis. I would like to see others improve upon it.

Third Question. Why was feudalism succeeded by capitalism?

If one agrees with Dobb, as I do, that the period from the fourteenth century to the end of the sixteenth century was one in which feudalism was in full decay and yet in which there were no more than the first beginnings of capitalism, this is a genuinely puzzling question. One cannot say that feudalism had created productive forces which could be maintained and further developed only under capitalism – as, for example, one definitely can say that capitalism has created productive forces that can only be maintained and further developed under socialism. True, the decline of feudalism was accompanied (I would say 'caused') by the generalization of commodity production, and, as Marx repeatedly emphasised, 'commodity production and developed commodity circulation, trade, form the historical preconditions under which it [capital] arises.' (*Capital*, I, p. 163.) But historical preconditions do not in themselves provide a sufficient explanation. After all, the ancient world was characterised by highly developed commodity production without ever giving birth to capitalism; and the clear beginnings of capitalism in Italy and Flanders during the late Middle Ages proved abortive. Why, then, did capitalism finally catch on and really get going in the late sixteenth century, especially in England?

Dobb throws a good deal of light on this question, though I'm sure that he would be the last to claim to have given the definitive answer. Much of his emphasis is placed upon what Marx called 'the really revolutionary way' for industrial capitalists to develop, which Dobb interprets to mean the rise of small men from the ranks of petty producers. In my original article, I criticised this interpretation of Marx, but Dobb's reply and further reflection have led me to conclude that, while it is not the only possible interpretation, it is nevertheless a legitimate one which points in a fruitful direction. What is required now, it seems to me, is a great deal more factual research on the origins of the industrial bourgeoisie. This kind of research should do more than anything else to unlock the secret of the definitive rise of capitalism from the late sixteenth century.

I am not at all clear about Takahashi's position on this question. He criticises Dobb for going too far in describing the fifteenth and sixteenth centuries as transitional. Presumably, his meaning is that feudalism survived essentially intact until the rise of capitalism overthrew it and there is therefore no disjunction between the processes of feudal decline and capitalist rise such as both Dobb and I assert. Be that as it may, there is no doubt that Takahashi agrees with Dobb as to the revolutionary significance of the rise of small producers from the ranks; and I assume that he would also agree with me as to the urgency of more factual research on the nature and extent of this phenomenon.

One final point in this connection. Developing Dobb's suggestion that the fifteenth and sixteenth centuries seem to have been 'neither feudal nor yet capitalist' (*Studies*, p. 19), I proposed that the period be given the name of precapitalist commodity production. Dobb rejects this proposal, preferring to consider the society of that period as one of feudalism 'in an advanced stage of dissolution'. ('Reply', above, p. 62). He says:

'The crucial question which Sweezy has apparently failed to ask . . . is this: what was the ruling class of this period? . . . . it cannot have been a capitalist class. . . . If a merchant bourgeoisie formed the ruling class, then the state must have been some kind of bourgeois state. And if the was a bourgeois state already . . . what constituted the essential issue of the seventeenth century civil war? It cannot (according to this view) have been *the* bourgeois revolution. We are left with some such supposition as . . . that it was a struggle against an attempted *counter*-revolution staged by crown and court against an already existent bourgeois state power. . . . If we reject the alternatives just mentioned, we are left with the view (which I believe to be the right one) that the ruling class was still feudal and that the state was still the political instrument of its rule. ("Reply", above, pp. 62–63).'

I recognise that these are questions that British Marxists have been earnestly debating for some years now, and it is perhaps rash of me to express any opinion on them at all. Let me, therefore, put my comment in the form of a query. Why isn't there another possibility which Dobb does not mention, namely, that in the period in question there was not one ruling class but several, based on different forms of property and engaged in more or less continuous struggle for preferment and ultimately supremacy?

If we adopt this hypothesis, we can then interpret the state of the period in accordance with the well-known passage from Engels:

'At certain periods it occurs exceptionally that the struggling classes balance each other so nearly that the public power gains a certain degree of independence by posing as the mediator between them. The absolute monarchy of the seventeenth and eighteenth centuries was in such a position, balancing the nobles and the burghers against one another.'[5]

In this interpretation, the civil war was *the* bourgeois revolution in the straightforward sense that it enabled the capitalist class to master the state and achieve definitive ascendancy over the other classes.

[5] *Origin of the Family*, Chicago, 1902, Kerr ed., p. 209. Engels clearly was thinking of the continent; for England the dates were earlier.

A Comment

Rodney Hilton

Paul Sweezy puts a number of questions which historians ought to try to answer. As an acute Marxist student of capitalist society, Sweezy naturally is interested in Marxist investigations of analogous problems in pre-capitalist society. The most important question he puts is undoubtedly No. 1, about the 'prime mover' in feudalism. By this I presume he means what were the internal contradictions of the feudal mode of production which made for its development and eventual replacement. At least that is what, as a Marxist, he should mean, though his own suggestion that feudalism had no 'prime mover', that is no internal dialectic, is in fact non-Marxist.

Before trying to tackle this question, some matters of fact should be considered. Marxism is a method which demands concrete data for the solution of historical problems, even if the answer in the end can be put in abstract terms (as in some chapters of *Capital*). The nearest approach to concrete data on which Sweezy seems to work are the theorising of H. Pirenne. Since these are not to be accepted by Marxists, and in fact have been challenged by a lot of non-Marxist specialists, we must, before dealing with Sweezy's problems, dispose of Pirenne.[1]

Pirenne's most important theories for our purpose concern the decline of trade during the Dark Ages and the origin of towns. He considered that the barbarian kingdoms (especially the Merovingian Frankish kingdom) which succeeded the Western Empire did not interrupt the flow of East-West Mediterranean trade and that as a consequence the local trade of Western Europe was not diminished. Towns still flourished, gold currency was used, and much of the Roman administrative and fiscal system remained. It was only when (in

[1] Pirenne's positive contribution to understanding medieval economic history was of course very great and demands respect. We should also be grateful for the stimulating way in which he poses hypotheses, even though (perhaps *because*) we do not agree with them.

the seventh and eighth centuries) the Islamic invaders cut the Mediterranean trade routes, that not only international but local trade dried up. The result was the domination of the large serf-worked estate and almost universal production for immediate consumption. Not until the restoration of trade between the Eastern and Western ends of the Mediterranean did commodity production in Western Europe begin again. This commodity production was stimulated first of all by international trade. These first traders at the end of the Dark Ages, the founders or re-founders of the medieval towns were composed of the flotsam of society, as it were, in Sweezy's sense, 'external' to feudal society. Once they had got trade and town life going again, local markets developed. In other words international trade in luxuries was according to Pirenne the determining factor both in the seventh century decline in commodity production and in its eleventh century revival.

Without going into too great detail we can say that on most essential points this interpretation cannot now be accepted. The decline in commodity production, which may have reached its lowest point in Carolingian times, started not merely long before the Arab invasions, but long before the collapse of the Roman Empire as a political system. From at least as early as the crisis of the third century town life had been contracting, and self-sufficient serf-worked estates had begun to dominate the social structure of the Empire. East-West trade was also contracting, not only for political reasons, but because payments from the West in gold were less and less possible. The reason for this was a drainage of gold to the East which started probably at least as early as the first century, and which was not replaced either by the process of warfare or of trade, since Western exports were much less in value than imports from the East.

The Arabs in fact did not have to cut very much. But in any case, Pirenne was wrong in seeing the Arabs as the enemies of East-West trade. Naturally there was some dislocation, but the Arabs favoured the continuance of such trading relations as were economically feasible, as scholars have shown in detail. A French historian, in fact, has put forward the very plausible view that the Arabs positively encouraged East-West trade by the 'dethésaurisation' of gold hoards in those parts of the Byzantine and Sassanid Empires which they overran.[2]

So the low level of production for the market in the Dark Ages was largely the continuation of an economic development which had begun

[2] M. Lombard, 'L'Or musulman du VIIe au XIe siècle', *Annales*, 1947.

within the political and social framework of the Empire. That does not mean that we should simply see the Carolingian era as one of complete economic and social retrogression. Important, though insufficiently explored, developments in economic, social and political life took place, without which the future expansive development of the feudal mode of production could not have happened. In fact by the end of the tenth century there were important signs of the development of commodity production. Local markets began to expand into towns. Town life developed, as a consequence of the development of economic and social forces, *within* feudal society, *not*, as Pirenne thought, as a result of the external impact of itinerant traders like Godric of Finchale. This fact has now been sufficiently demonstrated by the careful study of individual towns in France, Germany and Italy. Pirenne's interpretation of the revival of trade and the changes in the economy of European feudalism (on which so much of Sweezy's own theories rest) must be abandoned.[3]

What was the cause of social development under feudalism? I am inclined to think that in studying this problem we should not limit ourselves to feudalism, but deal with pre-capitalist society as a whole, or at any rate pre-capitalist *class* society. Sweezy sees capital accumulation as the prime mover in capitalist society because it is inherent in the processes of capitalist production. Now of course there is no process of accumulation in pre-capitalist societies such as inevitably flows from the exploitation of wage labour by competing capitalists. But surely we must see the growth of the surplus product over subsistence requirements as the necessary condition for the development of class society between the break-up of primitive communism and the beginning of capitalism. The growth of this surplus product depended of course on the development of the forces of production – the tools and labour skill of artisans and agriculturalists. The development of the forces of production must depend in turn on the size *and use* of the surplus product. In other words improved techniques even in very primitive economies depend on the application to them of the results of accumulation – not accumulated capital, of course, but accumulated surplus product. This is obvious. It does not in itself explain why in any given pre-capitalist society the dialectical interaction of the forces of production and the accumulated surplus product should result first in the expansion, then in the decline of the mode of production (slavery or feudalism). But then

3 Research summarized in 'The Origins of the Medieval Town Patriciate', by A. B. Hibbert, *Past and Present*, 1953, no. 3, p. 15–27; and *Les Villes de Flandre et d'Italie sous le gouvernement des patriciens: XIe–XVe siècles*, by J. Lestocquoy.

this could not be understood without taking into account also the prevailing relations of production: after all, the process of capitalist accumulation cannot be understood if one leaves out of the calculation the relation between capitalists and workers.

For example, production relations obviously must be taken into account if one is to answer one of Sweezy's questions, *i.e.*, why did not capitalism develop from the commodity production of the ancient world? Marx, and the Marxists who have read (as surely Paul Sweezy has) their *Capital*, Vol. III, would answer that commodity production in itself is not enough to disturb the 'solidity and internal articulation' of a mode of production. In the case of slavery the reason for the non-appearance of capitalism is that those sectors of the economy where commodity production was most advanced tended to be those where slaves were most exploited. But the exploitation of slaves restricted technical development so that once the slave supply began to decline the fundamental technical backwardness of a slave economy was revealed. Far from keeping the slave separate from the means of production – necessary pre-condition of capitalism – the slave owners solved (or tried to solve) the economic problems of late ancient society by settling their slaves on peasant holdings; in fact by creating the production relations characteristic of feudal society.

However it is not my intention to examine the problem of the 'prime mover' for all pre-capitalist modes of production.

Feudalism is our problem. The ingredients of our answer seem to me essentially to be the following. The principal feature of the mode of production in feudal society is that owners of the means of production, the landed proprietors, are constantly striving to appropriate for their own use the whole of the surplus produced by the direct producers. Before we ask why they do this we must briefly show that in different ways this is what in fact they did try to do. At different stages of the development of European feudalism the character of the direct producers changes, as do other aspects of the economic system, and consequently the specific character of the landowners' exploitation changes. In some parts of early feudal Europe the free peasant communities with considerable relics of forms of tribal organization persist. In such cases (especially for instance in England before the Danish invasions) the military aristocracy – also semi-tribal in character – is faced with the complex problem of transforming the peasants' tribute once paid freely to their tribal king, now alienated to the noble by the king, into feudal rent, and at the same time of reinforcing this rent-receiving position by promoting the colonization of uncultivated land by slaves, semi-free clients, etc. At the same time, in some villages not subordinated to members of the king's retinue, the break-up of the tribal community throws up some peasant families with more power and possessions than their fellows, who 'thrive' to the status of rent-receiving nobles. On the other hand, in other parts of Europe (*e.g.*, Italy, Western and Southern Gaul) the Roman nobility have been undergoing the process of transformation into feudal nobles since the third century. Their slave-run latifundia have been turned into serf-worked estates, the servile peasants being partly former slaves and partly depressed free landowners. This type of exploitation was partly taken over by Teutonic military infiltrators (*hospites*) such as Burgundians and Visigoths who fused with the old Roman nobility. Their type of exploitation could however vary according to the completeness with which their Roman predecessors had integrated the pre-Roman tribal communities into the Imperial slave system.

By the ninth century – the period referred to by German and French historians as the high middle ages – the feudal economy of Europe was dominated by large estates composed of *villae* whose territory, divided into demesne and peasant land, had the function of supplying foodstuffs and manufactured goods to the lord. Feudal rent was mostly in labour, partly in kind, to an insignificant extent in money. The big estates did not of course cover even the greater part of the territory of feudal Europe, but they were the *decisive* elements in the economy. The rôle of surviving peasant allods, or the estates of small nobles, was not be become significant until the feudal mode of production began to break down, as Kosminsky has shown for England. Between the ninth and the thirteenth centuries enserfment went apace, but by the time the *legal* position of the exploited was worsened and made uniform, the development of commodity production brought about changes in the form of rent, so that rents in kind and in money had largely replaced labour rent by the end of the thirteenth century (except for England), producing in its turn an amelioration of legal status. For various reasons connected with the development of commodity production (of which the fragmentation of holdings and the development of peasant resistance to exploitation were most important), the direct appropriation of rent assessed on peasant holdings relaxed, but the total demand for feudal rent by the lords as a whole was maintained through the exploitation of seigniorial privileges and the development of private and public taxation. In short we may say that the ruling class in one way or the other, either through its private franchises or through the agency of the state, was striving to maximise feudal rent, that is the forcibly appropriated surplus of the direct producer, all the time. But of course, its success was not always equal to its efforts, and in the examination of its failure we come to the reasons for the decline of the feudal mode of production.

But, Sweezy will ask, *why* did the feudal rulers strive to get as near the whole of the direct producers' surplus as possible? What is the analogy here to the capitalists' need to accumulate and to cheapen production in order to compete on the market? And what were the economic and social consequences making for movement in feudal society, of this drive for rent?

The feudal rulers did not of course increase feudal rent in order to place the product of a peasant holding or of enforced peasant labour, on the market, although one of the incidental ways of realising rent in kind or demesne produce may have been by selling it. Fundamentally they strove to increase feudal rent in order to maintain and improve their position as rulers, against their innumerable rivals as well as against their exploited underlings. The maintenance of class power in existing hands, and its extension if possible, is the driving force in feudal economy and feudal politics. For this reason rent had to be maximised. In the ninth century the Carolingian magnate maintained his enormous retinue of supporters by feeding them directly from the produce of his *villae*. When the huge but ephemeral Empire of the Carolingians disintegrated, and gave place to smaller and more manageable feudal kingdoms, duchies and counties, the supporters of the leading kings and nobles were enfeoffed with land in return for military service, so that permanent retinues, unwieldly and difficult to maintain, could be reduced. But, enfeoffments of knights, while taking an administrative burden off their feudal chiefs, by no means relieved the peasants, who were exploited still harder. The struggle for power and the struggle for land are of course intertwined, but the consequence was the multiplication of demands by an increasing population of greater and lesser lords for various forms of feudal rent. The extending scope of state powers still further intensified the burden on the peasantry, as did the increasing demands of the ecclesiastical landlords.

Finally we must remember that the development of the home and foreign market, perhaps from as early as the 10th century, was another important factor which drove the feudal lords to make increased rent demands. The specialisation of industrial production in towns, whose burgesses strove successfully for economic and political privileges, caused the terms of trade between town and country to tip to the latter's disadvantage. In so far as he was involved in buying and selling, the lord bought dear and sold cheap. And the increasing need of landlords for 'consumption loans' as their luxury and armaments expenses increased, put them in debt to the money-lenders. Ultimately it was only an increase in feudal rent that could close the gap between the feudal lords' income and expenditure.

In order convincingly to demonstrate that the struggle for rent was the 'prime mover' in feudal society, a more detailed examination of the facts than can be made here would be necessary. But perhaps some of the possible fields of study might be indicated. The conflicts between the Capetian monarchy and the leading French feudatories in the eleventh and twelfth centuries are a commonplace of political history. The growth of the feudal state (whether the monarchical state of the Capetians or the ducal and comital states of the greater vassals of Normandy, Flanders, Anjou, etc.) has consequently been the preserve of 'political' historians. But the real picture does not emerge until the process of colonisation of new land and of intensified exploitation of the peasantry, in other words, the process of maximisation of rent is seen as the basis of the better documented political struggle. Something of the process can be discerned in the account of his estate administration by Suger, Abbot of St. Denis, but the story would have to be put together bit by bit, mainly from charter material. The same sort of problem could be studied in the Germany of Frederick Barbarossa and Henry the Lion,[4] not to speak of England in the twelfth and thirteenth centuries, where every fundamental issue of feudal society – the struggle for rent between lords and peasants and rival lords, the growth of law as an instrument for rent maximisation, the growth of the state as the engine of oppression – is better documented than in any other European country.

The exaction of feudal rent by the landlords varied in its incidence, because the specific economic circumstances varied for a whole number of reasons during the feudal epoch, and above all because those from whom rent was demanded were by no means social or economic equals, nor continued to have the same characteristics over any considerable period of time. The demand for rent in its widest sense was clearly the important factor in determining the movement of the feudal economy. The obligation on the part of the peasant to hand over his surplus

[4] An essay on 'The State of the Dukes of Zähringen' by T. Mayer in *Medieval Germany*, II, ed. G. Barraclough, suggests lines of development which a Marxist historian could pursue further.

could have either the effect of depressing him completely or of stimulating him to increase his production on his holding. For as Marx points out, though feudal rent represents the surplus product of the peasant, the necessary routine of any organised economic system produces regularity, so that rents were fixed over long periods. Therefore in many cases (in particular the case of the richer peasants) rent could constitute only a *part* of the surplus. The peasants would strive to increase the portion of the surplus kept by them and could either do this by enforcing an absolute or relative reduction of rent, or by increasing the productivity of the holding, or by enlarging the holding without a corresponding increase in rent. Such strivings would lead to peasant revolts and to the cultivation of new land. The lords would of course want to increase the amount of surplus coming to them, and in addition would try to bring fresh land under their control, either already settled by rent-paying tenants (not only direct rent from land but rent disguised as the fiscal benefits of justice), or as yet uncultivated and ready for settlement. Hence, the general expansion of cultivation which was going on certainly until the end of the thirteenth century, and which was a major contribution of the feudal order, was a product of the rent struggle.

The economic progress which was inseparable from the early rent struggle and the political stabilisation of feudalism was characterised by an increase in the total social surplus of production over subsistence needs. This, not the so-called revival of the international trade in silks and spices, was the basis for the development of commodity production. That is to say that in the period of predominantly natural economy more and more of the surplus could be devoted to exchange. The expansion therefore of medieval market centres and towns from the tenth or eleventh century was based fundamentally on the expansion of simple commodity production. The spectacular developments in international trade, the industrialisation of Flanders, Brabant, Liège, Lombardy and Tuscany, the growth of big commercial centres like Venice, Genoa, Bruges, Paris, London are chronologically secondary to the development of the forces of production in agriculture, stimulated in the process of the struggle for feudal rent.

The interaction of these various factors – all *internal* to feudal Europe – produced profound changes in the situation. The development of production for the market sharpened and diversified the existing stratification of the peasant producers. The rich peasants became richer and the poor, poorer. But they become a different kind of rich and a different kind of poor especially after the thirteenth century. The well endowed peasant family of earlier days was wealthy in the goods produced for its own consumption, but with the development of the market such wealthy peasants put more and more of their surplus up for sale. They take more land into their holdings; they employ more wage labour – and that labour is more and more the labour of the totally landless rather than of smallholders. They also object to the syphoning off of their surplus rent, and their antagonism to the landlord is reinforced by the despair of the other sections of the peasants for whom the demand for rent is not merely a restriction on economic expansion, but a depression of bare subsistence standards. The struggle for rent sharpens and in the fourteenth century reaches the acute stage of general revolt.

As far as the landlords are concerned this is a period of the crisis of their particular form of economic enterprise. Rents fall and incomes have to be recouped by the intensification of the fiscal exploitation by state taxation, warfare and plunder, frequently self-defeating because of deliberate currency inflation. The most efficient producers for the market, least encumbered with administrative overheads, traditional standards of luxury expenditure, and unproductive hangers-on, were of course the rich peasants and such members of the lesser nobility as disdained to imitate the style of their superiors. The successful competition of these elements was based on forms of exploitation which anticipate capitalist farming. Feudal rent is no longer a stimulus to increased and improved production (it can still be a drag on the middle peasant), but in general by the fifteenth century the stimulus of the market is becoming the main factor in developing production – the production of the new elements in the economy. For the economic basis of those who still held the commanding positions in the state was being undermined, in spite of desperate attempts (as by absolute monarchs) to use their control of the state to maintain the essentials of feudal power.

A Comment

Christopher Hill

Mr. Sweezy asks us to consider the possibility that in fifteenth and sixteenth century England 'There was not one ruling class but several, based on different forms of property and engaged in more or less continuous struggle for preferment and ultimately supremacy.' In support of this view he quotes a passage from Engels's *Origin of the Family*:

'At certain periods it occurs exceptionally that the struggling classes balance each other so nearly that the public power gains a certain degree of independence by posing as the mediator between them.'

The continuation of the passage makes it clear that Engels is considering only *two* 'struggling classes', not '*several* ruling classes'. Is it not indeed a logical absurdity to speak of 'several ruling classes' over a period of centuries? A ruling class must possess state power: otherwise how does it rule? Dual state power may exist for a very brief period during a revolution, as in Russia for some months in 1917. But such a situation is inherently unstable, almost a condition of civil war: it must lead to the victory of one class or the other. It has never lasted for a longer period, and state power has never, I suggest, been shared between 'several' would-be ruling classes. We have only to conceive of two or more ruling classes and two or more state machines, existing side by side for 200 years, to realise that this is a theoretical impossibility: the most cursory study of English history during the centuries in question will convince us that the theoretical impossibility did not exist in practice either.

This is not merely logic-chopping. For if we substitute Engels's 'struggling classes' for Mr. Sweezy's 'several ruling classes', then Mr. Dobb's questions still require an answer. What was the *ruling* class of this period? How are we to characterise the state?

These questions have been discussed at great length by Soviet and English Marxist historians. I can quote only their conclusions, not the arguments which led to them. Thus Z. Mosina, summing up Soviet discussions on absolutism which took place in March and April 1940, was able to say without fear of contradiction: 'The view of the absolute monarchy as a feudal landowners' state of the nobility has, as it were, been assimilated by all Soviet historians.' She included the Tudor and early Stuart monarchy in England as a form of absolutism, as Mr. Sweezy does, although she added that it presented specific problems.[1] These specific problems were debated in some detail by English Marxist historians in 1940 and again in 1946–47. Their final agreed conclusion was:

'The Tudor and early Stuart state was essentially an executive institution of the feudal class more highly organised than ever before. . . . Only after the revolution of 1640–49 does the state in England begin to be subordinated to the capitalists. . . . The revolution of 1640 replaced the rule of one class by another.'[2]

How does this fit with Engels's formulation, which Mr. Sweezy quotes, and which was frequently cited in the Soviet and English discussions? The important thing to notice is the extreme caution of Engels's statement, its many qualifications. (If he had known the use which would be made of it, he would no doubt have qualified it still further.) I quote from the latest translation, italicising those words which seem to me to require special emphasis:

'*By way of exception*, however, *periods occur* in which the warring classes balance each other *so nearly* that the state power, as *ostensible* mediator, acquires, *for the moment*, a *certain degree* of independence of both. Such was the absolute monarchy of the seventeenth and eighteenth centuries, which held the balance between the nobility and the class of burghers; such was the Bonapartism of the First, and still more of the Second French Empire, which played off the proletariat against the bourgeoisie and the bourgeoisie against the proletariat.'[3]

Would Mr. Sweezy argue from this passage that the proletariat was

[1] Z. Mosina, 'The Discussion of the Problem of Absolutism', in *Istorik Marksist*, No. 6, 1940, p. 69, 74.

[2] 'State and Revolution in Tudor and Stuart England', in *Communist Review*, July, 1948, p. 212 f.

[3] '*Origin of the Family*', in Marx and Engels, *Selected Works*, Lawrence and Wishart, 1950, II, p. 290. Note the word 'burghers', the word which Marx and Engels use for the urban *estate* in feudal society, before it has transformed itself into the modern *class* of the 'bourgeoisie', ready to challenge state power.

'a' ruling class in France between 1852 and 1870? Or that the Bonapartist state power *really* (as opposed to ostensibly) mediated independently between bourgeoisie and proletariat? Engels' concise formulation in this passage should be read in conjunction with his fuller exposition in *Anti-Dühring*, published six years earlier:

'This mighty revolution in the economic conditions of society [the fifteenth and sixteenth century economic revolution] was not followed by any immediate corresponding change in its political structure. The state order remained feudal, while society became more and more bourgeois.[4]

During the whole of this struggle ["the struggle of the bourgeoisie against the feudal nobility"] political force was on the side of the nobility, except for a period when the crown used the burghers against the nobility, in order that the two "estates" might keep each other in check; but from the moment when the burghers, *still politically powerless*, began to grow dangerous owing to their increasing economic power, the crown resumed its alliance with the nobility, and by so doing called forth the bourgeois revolution, first in England and then in France.'[5]

Thus it seems to me that Mr. Sweezy's hypothesis of two or more ruling classes in fifteenth and sixteenth century England is logically untenable; and that it certainly cannot be supported by anything Engels said. Engels's remark should not be dragged from its context, and should be interpreted in the light of what he and Marx said on other occasions.[6] When that is done it clearly squares with the conclusions of the Soviet and English Marxist historians, that the absolute monarchy is a form of feudal state.

Space does not permit of an argument based on historical evidence, in addition to these more formal logical arguments. But I believe that the facts confirm logic. Detailed consideration of the way in which the Tudor monarchy held the balance between nobility and burghers would not suggest that its mediation was ever more than ostensible, nor that its independence of the feudal ruling class was more than relative. The confusion which makes Mr. Sweezy (and others) wish to avoid calling the absolute monarchy a feudal state is, I believe, three-

[4] *Anti-Dühring*, Martin Lawrence, p. 120 f.

[5] *Ibid.*, pp. 186–7; my italics. Note that in Engels's view the 'burghers' were 'still politically powerless' at the time when Mr. Sweezy sees them as a ruling class.

[6] I tried to summarise their views in 'The English civil war interpreted by Marx and Engels', in *Science and Society*, Winter, 1948, p. 130–56.

fold. First, a hangover of the narrow bougeois-academic definition of 'feudal' as a military term, ignoring its social basis; secondly, the equating of a feudal state with a state in which serfdom predominates. One of the most valuable features, in my view, of Mr. Dobb's work on this period has been his refutation of this equation, and his demonstration that the partial emancipation of the petty mode of production does not in itself change the economic base of society (and still less the political superstructure), although it does prepare the conditions for the development of capitalism. If feudalism is abolished with serfdom, then France in 1788 was not a feudal state; and there never has been a bourgeois revolution in the sense of a revolution which overthrew the feudal state. Thirdly, there is the idea that a feudal state must be decentralised. In fact it was precisely the emancipation of the petty mode of production, resulting from the general crisis of feudal society, which led the feudal ruling class, from the mid-fourteenth century, to strengthen the central state power, in order (i) to repress peasant revolt, (ii) to use taxation to pump out the surplus retained by the richer peasantry and (iii) to control the movements of the labour force by *national* regulation, since the local organs of feudal power no longer sufficed. The absolute monarchy was a different form of feudal monarchy from the feudal-estates monarchy which preceded it; but the ruling class remained the same, just as a republic, a constitutional monarchy and a fascist dictatorship can all be forms of the rule of the bourgeoisie.

Some Observations

Georges Lefebvre

I have read the book by Dobb, and the debate that ensued between himself and Sweezy, together with the interventions of Takahashi, Hilton and Hill, all with great interest. So far as I can see, inadquate attention has been paid to this debate in France (the only reference to it I can cite is J. Néré's review of Dobb's book in the *Revue Historique*, January–March 1950). I am not a medievalist, and in any case my knowledge of the rural economy of the Middle Ages is confined to France, whereas Dobb and Sweezy concentrate on England. So I am not really qualified to take a position on the fundamental issue of the debate. But since Dobb and Sweezy seem to have made their observations as an economist or sociologist, my reflections will perhaps shed some light on the perspective of a historian.

I

Firstly, in so far as the organisation of production was the central problem of the debate, the 'feudal system' as such was not at issue, and the use of the word 'feudalism' was not appropriate to the discussion. For the specific characteristic of a feudal regime was the hierarchical relationship between a lord and his vassals rather than in the way a lord distributed fiefs to these vassals. Nor is the term 'seigneurial system' very helpful, for the seigneurial authority of a lord over the peasants of his domain was the result of a fragmentation of central political power, whereby the sovereign's rights passed into the control of the lords. The correct formulation for the purposes of the discussion is *manorial system* – although this system was a very ancient one, and was not strictly present in the later centuries of the Middle Ages.

Secondly, it should be said that any identification of the manorial system with serfdom must depend on how serfdom is initially defined. According to Marc Bloch, the relationship between the serf and his master derived originally from a type of personal dependency, exemplified by the particular institution known in France as *chevage;* it was only later that the serf came to be bound to the soil, *adstrictus ad glebam*. But this sort of interpretation is not universally accepted, and any adoption of one definition of serfdom ather than another would have to involve the specification of the individual countries concerned. On the other hand, it cannot be maintained that the social structure of the countryside, during the period under discussion, could be accounted for exclusively in terms of serfdom, in so far as various categories of freeholders, enfranchised villeins and allodial proprietors continued to exist.

Thirdly, since Dobb's fundamental thesis attributes the economic and social transformation of the manorial system to internal contradictions within it, I think it is important to draw attention to one such contradiction that he did not mention. When production is based on the exploitation of a labourer who is coercively held in a condition of servitude, the difficulty for the master is to supervise his work to assure its efficiency. The mass of labourers, who were slaves or subject to *corvée* labour, were rarely able to evade the control of an overseer – but who was to oversee the overseers? I remember as a student hearing lecturers, who were not familiar with Marx or Hegel, referring to this difficulty as one of the causes of the colonate in the Roman epoch, and citing as evidence a letter in which Pliny the Younger reports that instead of employing his slaves for the direct cultivation of his estate, he found it more expedient to grant them holdings with a labour obligation attached to them. From the Carolingian epoch onwards, such *servi casati* were not rare: the *Polyptychus Irminonis* mentions tenants, at least some of whom must have been in a servile condition.

Finally, I deem it necessary to recall the multiplicity of factors in history. Marx discovered the commanding importance of the economy, or to be more precise, the mode of production. Attached to this innovation, a work of genius for the time, he was not concerned to extend his enquiry to include other factors, though he would never have dreamed of excluding their influence; and since history is the work of Man, he was amused when he was accused of not taking human nature into account. For, after all, if the economy is the dominant factor in history, it is because man must be fed before all else: he produces because he is hungry. I do not want to multiply examples here; I shall therefore content myself with emphasising the importance of demography in medieval history – which Dobb himself concedes. If the lord stepped up his demands, as Dobb maintains, this was due in part to the fact that his progeniture multiplied the number of claimants to his revenue; if the peasants fled, this was due in part to the fact that their numbers were becoming too great to be supported by their lands. In this respect, there seems to me to be more to Sweezy's position than Dobb (although not denying the importance of the revival of commerce) is prepared to admit. If lords became more demanding, this was in large part because urban trade made available new objects to improve their style of life; while peasants fled the land because the development of towns attracted them with the chance of refuge and gainful employment.

2

We can now say a few words about the discussion of the 'two ways' to capitalist production. A merchant creates a manufactory, either in the strict sense of the term (what we in France call a *usine*) or in its wider sense, i.e. by the use of what the English call the *putting-out system*. He thereby becomes an industrialist, but since production remains subordinate to commerce, in this respect the structure of the economy remains unchanged. This is 'Way No. 2'. On the other hand, if an artisan ceases to produce for local consumption, and starts to supply the national or international market, the producer thereby becomes a merchant as well. That is 'Way No. 1': it is revolutionary because commerce is subordinate to production.

I agree with this account. The latter path produced what I would willingly call a technological revolution, and in my opinion it was indeed this with which Marx was preoccupied. But if capitalism is defined by a quest for *profit* levied on the products of wage-labour, the problem of its development appears to me to be highly complex. In particular, 'Way No. 2' could lead to capitalism just as easily as 'Way No. 1', and I do not believe that Marx was aware of this.

If an artisan proceeds along 'Way No. 1', he does more than subordinate commerce to production; to supply the market, in the widest sense of the term, he must engage wage-labour from which to realise a profit. This is what makes him a capitalist.

But if a merchant establishes a manufactory, he does exactly the same thing; he too is a capitalist. It may be objected perhaps that he diverges from the artisan if his manufactory is organised by a putting-out process, because the cottage worker remains an independent producer, and the merchant bargains with him over the price of his product like a consumer, and realises a profit only from its ulterior sale. The objection would be valid if the artisan continued at the same time to supply the local market and retained a certain freedom to choose his own clients – a state of affairs that would prevent him from being wholly subject to the will of the merchant. But it is obvious that, sooner or later, the putting-out system tends to exclude this hypothesis, since the merchant's orders, by their relative quantity and regularity, will eventually monopolise the artisan's activity. Furthermore, when the merchant provides work and raw materials, he not merely subordinates pre-existing artisans: he creates new artisans from rural masses, whose endemic unemployment puts them at his mercy. In either case the merchant is transformed into a capitalist, as Marx defines one; it is this development which explains the emergence of urban class struggles in Italy and Flanders in the fourteenth and fifteenth centuries.

These observations do not contradict Dobb's account of the opposition between the merchant and the producer turned capitalist – an opposition he claims was one of the characteristic features of the first English Revolution. The merchant community and the State furnished each other with mutual assistance: the former as creditor and supplier of public contracts (particularly for the army), the latter as distributor of privileges, prizes and monopolies. Besides, rulers favoured commerce and manufacture in the interests of taxation as well as preservation of the country's monetary stock: mercantilism and colonial exploitation, erected into systems, profited the merchant. Thus the latter had no thought of overturning the social and political order; it was predictable that he would take the part of the king if the monarchy was threatened. On the other hand, the symbiosis between the State and the merchants was a grievance to those early capitalist producers who did not enjoy the same advantages as the privileged merchants, and had to rely on their own resources.

Nevertheless, it is impossible to deny that the collusion between commerce and the State promoted the development of capitalism, even if we judge that Sombart overestimated its influence in this respect. Manufactures could never have developed so easily without the State to protect them from competition from more advanced economies. The public contracts they received provided them with major advantages and exerted a greater influence on their technical development than could be foreseen at the time. Orders for court luxuries were much less important than supplies to public services, especially the armed forces, for the latter demanded mass production. Handicrafts could not adapt themselves to this type of production and could not match its quantity, regularity, rapidity, and above all, uniformity of output, that were so essential for armaments. It was only the merchant who created a manufactory proper, or organised a putting-out system, who could meet the demands of the State, by concentrating and rationalising production. In this way merchants played a part in the historical mission of capitalism: the establishment of mass production by means of a rationalisation and mechanisation of the work-process rendered possible by a concentration of units of manufacture.

In these conditions, I believe we can summarise the situation in the following way. The merchant created manufactures; his interests coincided with those of State, and of the great landowners who were enclosing estates and evicting tenants, to transform agriculture. After them, peasants who had amassed savings and artisans who participated in primitive accumulation also strove to renew agriculture or establish manufactories. Since the State ignored them, they were jealous of merchants and aristocrats alike, and sought political influence to do away with privileges and monopolies, and to obtain public contracts themselves. So it was natural that at the time of the first English Revolution, they should have thrown in their lot with Parliament. The French Revolution of 1789 had a similar aspect to it. I should add, however, that the recourse to the State that these groups condemned so roundly in the merchants did not remain a foreign practice to them: once the advocates of free enterprise gained power, they made just as effective use of the State as the privileged merchants before them.

3

I should like to conclude with a few remarks on method. The principal task of the sociologist and economist, such as are Dobb and Sweezy, is to investigate economies and societies of the present. They may then compare them to disengage general categories. It is natural in this respect that the comparative method should lead them to extend their exploration to the economies and societies of the past. Thereafter, they must become historians.

Having reached this last stage, Dobb and Sweezy developed their hypotheses, not by way of research into original sources, but by borrowing previous findings from historians. There is no objection to this. Historians themselves occasionally have recourse to the same expedient. Only, they do not stop there. For once a hypothesis is formulated, theoretical intelligence must move outwards and interrogate the external world anew, to verify whether evidence confirms or invalidates its hypotheses.

I believe that the debate provoked by Dobb's book has now reached this point. It would seem futile and even dangerous to pursue it further in abstract terms. For how can we conform to the principles of experimental reason without recourse to historical scholarship and its rules? Thus the historian will formulate a plan of research; he will compose a questionnaire in which he indicates where he will start his enquiry. Dobb and Sweezy have performed the service of formulating the problems. Now it is up to the historians to answer them!

A Survey of the Debate

Giuliano Procacci

The most controversial problem in the polemic between Dobb and Sweezy concerns the validity of Pirenne's theses on the role played by commerce, in its various forms, in the development and decay of feudal society. The Belgian historian's views on this matter are well-known: he believed that the flow of trade which had developed under the Roman Empire in the Mediterranean basin was interrupted in the seventh century, when the Arab conquerors and the Frankish Empire, Mahommed and Charlemagne, ended this traditional geographical unity. The economic revival of Europe in the eleventh century was then, he thought, caused precisely by the re-emergence of international commerce once again. This was now largely the work of such *déracinés* as Godric of Finchale, who were the first to stimulate a renewal of trade and exchange in a society still fragmented into hermetic compartments of isolated economic activity. 'Im Anfang', as Hauser said later in reference to the origins of capitalism, 'war der Handel'. It is obvious that if commerce had a chronological and causal priority in the genesis and growth of feudal society, then we must conclude that trade, and that particular species of capital which it created, was the driving force in the development of the feudal society to which it had given birth. So, too, the decline of feudal society, and its supersession by capitalist society, must have been a direct function of the fortunes of commerce and of commercial capital.

The arguments adopted by Sweezy in his criticism of Dobb's book are fairly close to Pirenne's theses. But in order not to distort his thought, let us allow Sweezy to speak in his own words: 'We see thus how long-distance trade could be a creative force, bringing into existence a *system* of production for exchange alongside the old feudal system of production for use. Once juxtaposed, these two systems naturally began to act upon each other.'[1] 'Western European feudalism', according to Sweezy,

[1] P. M. Sweezy, 'A Critique', p. 42.

'in spite of chronic instability and insecurity, was a system with a very strong bias in favour of maintaining given methods and relations of production.'[2] Thus the dissolvent of this static system had to be external; and it was precisely commerce which, promoting the growth of towns and the establishment of the first industries, and attracting serfs into towns, had the long-run effect of making a 'coexistence' between feudalism and a *system* of production for exchange impossible. It thus in the end virtually liquidated feudalism in the countries of Western Europe. Sweezy is well aware that capitalist production, in so far as it was a higher and more complex form of commodity production, was something very different from the commodity production that developed during the feudal era. Therefore he found himself confronted with a difficulty: what is the correct definition of the historical period which extends approximately from the fifteenth to the sixteenth centuries, during which feudalism was dead or dying but when no real elements or signs of the capitalist mode of production were yet present? Sweezy gets out of this difficulty by postulating a distinct historical phase, in which 'the predominant elements were neither feudal nor capitalist',[3] and which he proposes to classify as 'precapitalist commodity production'. In this respect he criticizes Dobb's judgment that this period was still mainly feudal in character.

From a purely abstract point of view, the logical defects of Sweezy's treatment of the problem are obvious. If we try to interpret the problem of the transition from feudalism to capitalism in the light of Marxism, as the American economist seeks to do, we cannot ignore the dialectical method which is the very essence of Marxism. Yet to assert that feudalism was an immobile historical formation, not itself capable of internal development but merely susceptible to external influence, is precisely to pose the problem in terms of random contingency and not in terms of dialectical interaction. Dobb justly comments in his Reply that 'to say so [i.e. that feudalism has no tendency within it to change] would be to make it an exception to the general Marxist law of development that economic society is moved by its own internal contradictions'.[4] By the same token, to hypostasize an intermediate and autonomous period between feudalism and capitalism (however one wants to 'label' it) is to abandon any historical account of the process of formation of the new within the old, or in Marx's terms, to describe the 'birth pangs'

[2] *Ibid.*, p. 36.

[3] *Ibid.*, p. 49.

[4] Dobb, 'A Reply', p. 59.

accompanying the emergence of a new society from the womb of the old. Methodological considerations similar to those advanced by Dobb have also been formulated by Hilton and Takahashi.

But these logical defects imply parallel defects in historical interpretation. Here we may recall the factual objections raised in successive interventions to Sweezy's criticisms. Both Dobb and Hilton reiterated that the growth and decay of feudalism came about as a result of elements operating within it. Dobb stressed the fact -- as he had already done in his *Studies* – that in certain areas which were peripheral to the great highways and trade-routes, the disintegration of typically feudal social relations (for example serfdom) occurred earlier than in areas which were directly on these trade-routes: thus in the most backward Northern and Western regions of England, serfdom disappeared earlier than in the more advanced South-East. So, too, the 'second serfdom' in Eastern Europe coincided with a period of commercial expansion. This is not to say – and Dobb underlines the point – that the growth of commerce and commodity production did not play a considerable part in the evolution and supersession of feudal society; but it was, to repeat a passage from Marx quoted by Dobb in his *Studies*, a coefficient subordinate to the 'solidity and internal articulation' of the mode of production itself.

Hilton's contribution to the polemic on the transition from feudalism to capitalism is intended precisely to describe this internal articulation. He develops some of the points made in the *Studies*, and attempts to penetrate the inner workings of feudal society. For him, the fundamental law of this society was the tendency on the part of the exploiting class to realise the maximum rent from the labour of the direct producers: this then conflicted with the necessities of social growth and provoked contradictions within the exploiting class itself. Hilton's analysis thereafter proceeds to particulars which we cannot consider here. However, one cannot avoid the impression, reading Hilton or for that matter parts of Dobb's book, that while these authors are convincing in their refutation of Pirenne's thesis, repeated by Sweezy, that commerce was the *prime mover* (Hilton's expression) of feudal society, they are less convincing in their historical reconstruction of the internal dialectic of feudalism, for they often seem more defensive and critical than constructive and positive in their arguments. It is, of course, true that difficulties of interpretation are more acute in this field because of the scarcity of available research; Sweezy is on relatively safe ground when he points out that Dobb himself admits how difficult it would be to prove his thesis that the prime mover of the feudal mode of production was *internal* to it.

It seems to me that this difficulty becomes most evident when we consider the way in which the problem – central to the debate – of the origins of medieval towns was treated. It was precisely in relation to this that Sweezy commented: 'Dobb's theory of the internal causation of the breakdown of feudalism could still be rescued if it could be shown that the rise of the towns was a process internal to the feudal system. But as I read Dobb, he would not maintain this. He takes an eclectic position on the question of the origin of the mediaeval towns but recognises that their growth was generally in proportion to their importance as trading centres. Since trade can in no sense be regarded as a form of feudal economy, it follows that Dobb could hardly argue that the rise of urban life was a consequence of internal feudal causes.'[5]

While, as we have seen, the American economist's assumption of a mutually exclusive relationship between commerce and feudalism cannot be accepted without careful scrutiny, his remarks on Dobb's uncertainty over the problem of the origins of towns are not without value. In effect, *Studies in the Development of Capitalism* confines itself to an exposition of various theories that relate to the question, and an adoption of the most probable elements from one or the other. But the problem of the origins of towns within the framework (or outside the framework) of feudal society is nowhere confronted in the systematic and conscious fashion that it merits, so that the reader may often feel he encounters these towns without knowing anything of their antecedent formation or genesis.

In his Reply, Dobb does not fail to take account of Sweezy's criticisms on this score. However his formulations seem to me to betray some uncertainty. He does not agree that he can be credited with the thesis 'that the rise of towns was a process internal to the feudal system'. But he adds in parentheses: 'Although to some extent I believe that the latter is true, and that, precisely because feudalism was far from being a purely "natural economy", it encouraged towns to cater for its need of long-distance trade.'[6] Perhaps the lack of clarity with which Dobb expresses himself reflects the fact that he has not devoted sufficient attention to the problem. Yet it is evident that if the problem of the relationship between town and country, as the historical form of the relationship between production and commerce, is not resolved in an

5 'A Critique', p. 40.

6 'A Reply', p. 60.

organic fashion, it is difficult to refute Pirenne's theory that commerce was a corrosive external influence on feudal society, and his related account of the 'capitalism' of mediaeval towns. Until those towns which were the centres of commerce are integrated into feudal society itself, and are considered (in Dobb's phrase) a result of the 'internal' development of that society, the temptation to locate the 'prime mover' of feudalism outside it will be too powerful, indeed too legitimate as well.

However, in Dobb's work this necessary integration remains more implicit than explicit. But other trends of historiographic research, also operating within a Marxist framework, have gone further. I refer in particular to those Soviet historians who see medieval towns, and the commodity production they stimulated as elements in the historical development of the feudal mode of production itself. This question has recently been discussed in the review *Voprosy Istorii*. The author of one article, F. Ya. Polyansky, maintains in effect that 'the creation of the town constituted one form of the political and economic expansion of the feudal regime';[7] he situates this assertion within the general view that commodity production was functional to feudalism, was an integral element within it, and not something external and antagonistic to it.[8] It follows that those manifestations of precocious capitalism genuinely present in the industry of a few medieval towns, particularly in Italy and Flanders, have no more than an 'episodic' character for Polyansky.[9]

However, if we wish to confine ourselves to Anglo-Saxon historiography, there is no lack of indications that this is the direction in which contemporary scholarship is moving. In February 1953, only one month after the appearance of the essay in *Voprosy Istorii* we have cited, the English review *Past and Present* published an article by A. B. Hibbert on the origins of the medieval town patriciates. In this, Hibbert discussed Pirenne's account of the role of commerce in the origins and growth of medieval urbanism, which he characterized as the view that 'there is a natural incompatibility between a feudal state and a state which permits the growth of commerce and industry'.[10] To this, he opposed his own conviction that 'both theory and facts suggest that in the early middle ages commerce, far from being a solvent of feudal society, was in fact a natural product of that society, and that up to a point the feudal rulers

[7] F. Ya. Polyansky, 'O Tovarnom Proizvodstve v Uslovyakh Feodalizma', in *Voprosy Istorii*, 1953, no. 1, pp. 52 et seq.

[8] *Ibid.*, p. 54.

[9] *Ibid.*, p. 55.

[10] A. B. Hibbert, 'The Origins of the Medieval Town Patriciate', in *Past and Present*, February, 1953, p. 16.

favoured its development'.[11] The precondition of the flowering of mercantile activity and commodity production was the development of the agrarian sector of the economy. The latter was, of course, 'internal' to the feudal mode of production, and a 'basic premise for any urban development'.[12]

Hibbert documents this thesis by recalling the fact that many medieval urban centres had 'seigneurial' origins – to modify a term that has been the object of a local historiographic polemic in Italy. He instances in this connection the towns of Genoa, Milan, Lincoln, certain Polish towns, Bergen, Cambridge, Arras, and the city of Dinant that Pirenne studied. For confirmation, besides certain well-known monographs on communes, Hibbert further cites Lestocquoy's study of Flemish and Italian towns[13] and Sapori's paper to the International Congress of History in 1950. However these appeared after the publication of Dobb's *Studies*, and neither Sweezy nor Dobb were able to take them into account at the time of their debate. But it is worth emphasising that there are indications that later research has confirmed the very tentative comments made by Dobb on the origin of medieval towns, in his Reply.

Nevertheless, it seems to me that, while on the specific topic of the role of commerce and mercantile capital in feudal society and hence the character of medieval towns, the position of the English historian is more adequate, it remains to some extent only a working hypothesis. The discussion between Sweezy and the English Marxists has all the marks of a duel between unequally armed combatants for, to the support of his thesis, the former can summon a whole mass of well-studied material, a whole current of research; whereas all the latter can rely on is a new and deeper awareness of the problem and an effort to interpret heterogeneous sources which are frequently inspired by the opposite point of view. The only way of emerging from this impasse is to give the contenders equal weapons, that is, to encourage research in keeping with this plausible explanatory hypothesis. Here, all parties to the discussion are agreed. Hilton emphasizes the need for this with particular lucidity in a perceptive article published in *Past and Present* in February 1952. Hilton states that 'Pirenne, in his studies of the growth of medieval towns and in his more general works, has had a consider-

[11] *Ibid.*, p. 17.

[12] *Ibid.*, p. 17.

[13] *Ibid.*, p. 27. The volume by Lestocquoy, *Aux Origines de la Bourgoisie: les Villes de Flandre et d'Italie sous le Gouvernement des Patriciens*, was published in Paris, 1953.

able influence on the teaching and study of medieval economic history. He emphasised that the growth of international trade played a key role in the transformation of feudal society. Many current assertions about medieval capitalism are derived from his work, and his conclusions have been supported by a number of subsequent studies.'[14] But this line of thought, promoted by the powerful personality of Pirenne, has proved to be inadequate – according to Hilton – to modern hypotheses on the role of commerce and mercantile capitalism. He concludes that historical research should therefore now be reoriented towards other sectors, which he specifies as agrarian history, the history of technology, and the history of the connection between the economic base and the political-juridical superstructures.

The second main problem raised by Sweezy was whether the fifteenth and sixteenth centuries should be classified as a capitalist or feudal epoch or Sweezy's 'pre-capitalist commodity period'. Here the reply by Dobb and the English Marxists was, in my opinion, more substantial. In this field they were able to draw on a considerable heritage of research and debate. In 1940, on the occasion of the third centenary of the English Revolution, the publication of a well-known study by Hill[15] gave rise to numerous discussions, which were resumed again in 1946–47 when this work was republished. The review *Labour Monthly* was the forum of the 1940–41 polemics, which included, amongst many interventions, an important statement by Dobb.[16] The problem at issue concerned the nature of the English Revolution. Was it a bourgeois revolution whose goal was the definitive installation of a capitalist mode of production for which necessary pre-conditions already existed, after maturing in the course of the sixteenth century and earlier? Alternatively, was it a move by a bourgeoisie *already* in power to forestall a feudal-aristocratic reaction? Most of the participants in the discussion opted the first interpretation, which was that proposed by Hill in his essay.

[14] R. H. Hilton, 'Capitalism, What's in a Name?'. See p. 146.

[15] C. Hill, *The English Revolution 1640. Three Essays*, London, 1949, second edition. The volume consists of three essays of which the first, by Hill, concerns the revolution in general, the second, by M. James, deals with materialist interpretations of revolutionary society in England by contemporaries, and the third, by E. Rickword, is on Milton.

[16] See the review of Hill's essay by P. F. in *Labour Monthly*, October, 1940, p. 558; the reply by D. Garman and counter-reply by P.F., *ibid.*, December, 1940; pp. 651 et seq.; the interventions by D. Torr and by Dobb, *ibid.*, February, 1941, pp. 88 et seq. A clear and comprehensive summary of the discussions is contained in the article 'State and Revolution in Tudor and Stuart England' in *Communist Review*, July, 1948, pp. 207 et seq., published by the History Group of the British Communist Party.

By its incitement to greater concreteness and avoidance of abstract or rigid dogmatism, Dobb's intervention was of particular authority. He pointed out that for the purposes of the discussion it was essential to establish which mode of production prevailed in England on the eve of the revolution. The term 'merchant capitalism', employed by all the participants in the debate, paid particular attention to the domain of exchange at the expense of that of production, and was therefore not suitable for defining a mode of production as such. Dobb was inclined to resolve the problem by classifying Tudor and Stuart England as feudal, while at the same time noting that, within this feudal society, those elements which were eventually to characterize bourgeois-capitalist society were in an advanced stage of development. Dobb was later to accentuate this interpretation in his *Studies*, in which he stresses the conservative role played by the mercantile classes in the various phases of the English Revolution.[17] One can understand how the experience of this discussion and the research it involved must have allowed the English Marxist historians to respond more confidently to Sweezy's criticisms in this respect. In fact both Dobb and Hill referred to the earlier debates we have just noted.

Dobb declares that he agrees with Sweezy in seeing European society between the fourteenth and sixteenth centuries as a complex historical formation in a state of transition, in the sense that the old economic forms were disintegrating, while new forms were emerging. However, this type of dynamic situation does not represent a distinct phase of history; it does not constitute a mode of production *sui generis*. All it implies is that the new emerged out of the old. A mode of production implies relations of production; these in turn presuppose classes with different social positions: serfs and feudal lords, 'free' workers and capitalists. Now what relations of production and what classes correspond to the particular mode of production postulated by Sweezy – pre-capitalist commodity production? This was the question that both Dobb and Hill put to the American. 'If a merchant bourgeoisie formed the ruling class, then the state must have been some kind of bourgeois state', Dobb comments. 'And if the state was a bourgeois state already, not only in the sixteenth century but even at the beginning of the fifteenth, what constituted the essential issue of the seventeenth century civil war?' Once we reject the hypothesis that the English Revolution was a form

[17] Dobb, *Studies in the Development of Capitalism*, Chapter IV. For this aspect of Dobb's theory, see the critical observations contained in B. Trentin's review of Dobb's book in *Società*, no. 3, 1952.

of bourgeois repression directed against a feudal counter-revolution, as inconsistent with the facts, 'we are left with the view (which I believe to be the right one) that the ruling class was still feudal and that the state was still the political instrument of its rule'.[18] Nor was there any validity in the idea later advanced by Sweezy that in sixteenth and seventeenth century England there was a certain balance of opposing class forces, with the result that 'several' classes shared and disputed power. Hill effectively proved that this hypothesis was not merely theoretically dubious, but empirically unfounded so far as the seventeenth century was concerned. In sum, the English historians tend to shift forward the *terminus ad quem* of feudalism, understood as a mode of production, right up to the eve of the bourgeois revolutions – in other words, up to the seventeenth century in the case of England, and even later in the case of continental Europe. It is well-known that this is also the periodization generally adopted by Soviet historiography.[19]

Certainly such a classification risks appearing somewhat surprising if it is applied abstractly and exclusively. In fact, all it claims is that until a particular point in time the *prevalent* mode of production in any given country was feudal; this prevalence does not exclude the possibility of there being capitalist 'germs' or 'forms' (we shall see the importance of these terms below) within the old mode of production. On this the English historians are more or less in agreement with Sweezy. Takahashi, who in turn corrected some of the errors in Dobb's formulations, concurs here as well. Therefore we may conclude that the fifteenth and sixteenth centuries (and later centuries as well, if we are considering countries other than England) do not appear as a phase in their own right, as a distinct intermediate 'era' between feudalism and capitalism, but as a historical period characterised by the emergence and development of capitalist forms (for example, the first manufactures) within the framework of a surviving feudal mode of production.

The problem of the origins of capitalism within feudal society has several aspects to it. The studies with which we are concerned here consider the problem of the rationalisation of agriculture (the English enclosures); the problem of the formation of the first labour market, after the social differentiation of the peasantry, from among the traditional agricultural population (the Poor Law of Elizabethan England); the problem of the shift in the relationship between town and country.

[18] Dobb, 'A Reply', p. 63.

[19] See the volume *Zur Periodisierung des Feudalismus und Kapitalismus in der geschichtlichen Entwicklung der UdSSR. Diskussionbeitrage*, Berlin, 1952.

But the most important problem of all obviously concerns the origins of the first capitalist manufactures, which brought into being new relations of production – those between the capitalist entrepreneur and the 'free' workers he hired. Did manufactures develop on the basis of the pre-existing guild system of medieval industry, or was it a new creation? Were its promoters the merchant classes tied to feudal society, of were they different men and new social strata? These were the general terms of the discussion. In particular the polemic came to be focussed on the currect historical interpretation of a well-known passage from Volume III of *Capital*, which in the interests of clarity it is worth while reproducing here: 'The transition from the feudal mode of production is two-fold. The producer becomes merchant and capitalist, in contrast to the natural agricultural economy and the guild-bound handicrafts of the mediaeval urban industries. This is the really revolutionary path. Or else, the merchant established direct sway over production. However much this serves historically as a stepping stone – witness the English seventeenth-century clothier, who brings the weavers, independent as they are, under his control by selling their wool to them and buying their cloth – it cannot by itself contribute to the overthrow of the old mode of production, but tends rather to preserve and retain it as its pre-condition.'[20]

These are the 'two ways' in which capitalist relations of production are established. Dobb, in his *Studies*, sought to differentiate these two phases historically. So far as Way No. 1 is concerned (from producer to capitalist), he located it in the formation during the sixteenth and seventeenth centuries of agricultural and industrial units of production based on a system of wage labour. These enterprises generally had a rather limited character and were created by new men coming directly from the ranks of the producers (well-to-do peasants, artisans). These strata formed the most advanced sector of the bourgeoisie: it was they who had most to gain from defeating the feudal mode of production. Cromwell's New Model Army was recruited largely from their ranks. As for Way No. 2 (from merchant to capitalist), this was the historical process by which the merchants and mercantile classes which developed within feudal society took in hand the control and direction of the process of industrial production in its existing forms.

Thus while in the first case there emerged a relationship between entrepreneur and 'free' worker, in the second case, a merchant-capitalist

[20] Marx, *Capital*, Vol. III, p. 334.

frequently confronted a producer who had not yet been separated from his means of production. In the first case, the producer-capitalist produced for the market and was therefore interested in its enlargement and in decreasing costs of production, thereby emancipating himself from subjection to commercial capital and indeed tending to subordinate the latter to industrial capital. In the second case the merchant-capitalist produced only as much as his trading business could accommodate, subordinating his productive activity to his interests as a merchant, and therefore commercial capital continued to predominate over industrial capital. In the first case the capitalist's profit is already profit realised in a capitalist fashion from the surplus labour of the 'free' workers; in the second case profit is still largely what Marx called 'profit upon alienation', which was typical of commercial capital in feudal society and was made up of the difference, in particular market conditions, between buying and selling price. Thus in the first case the capitalist has every interest in dismantling the various barriers and guild privileges in feudal society and in extending and broadening the market, while in the second case the commercial capitalist on the contrary has every interest in maintaining the *status quo* of the society on which his profit upon alienation rests.

This is the historical interpretation that Dobb gave the passage we quoted from *Capital*. According to his *Studies*, examples of Way No. 1 are the textile manufactories of John Winchomb at Newbury, and of Thomas Blanke at Bristol. Enterprises of this kind were more numerous in mining and production of salt. Finally he includes so-called 'domestic industry' in Way No. 1.[21] Examples of Way No. 2, if we may cite a more familiar example outside England, are the *manufactures royales* of Colbert's epoch in France. This example was advanced in support of Dobb's thesis, which he argued nearly exclusively from English material, by Takahashi, who cited works by Lefebvre, Labrousse, and Tarlé. It was these studies which first made it evident that the form of industrial organisation with the greatest future was not that exemplified by the privileged manufactures of Colbert, but was that of the smaller enterprises with a more clearly capitalist character – not the 'industrie des villes' but the 'petits producteurs de campagne'.

Sweezy, however, advances another interpretation of the passage quoted from *Capital*. In his opinion, 'What Marx was contrasting was the launching of full-fledged capitalist enterprises with the slow de-

[21] Dobb, *Studies*, pp. 138 et seq.

velopment of the putting-out system'.[22] In other words Way No. 2 is equivalent to the putting-out system (*Verlagssystem* in German) in which the merchant-entrepreneur commissions the various phases of the product's manufacture from independent artisans. Way No. 1, which is faster and, for that reason, more revolutionary, by-passes this intermediate phase and establishes directly a more rational system of production, of the type that was emerging – Takahashi argues – in Colbert's *manufactures réunies*. Sweezy does not seem to believe that different social strata (producers on the one hand and merchants on the other) necessarily corresponded to these two different ways, though he admits that this interpretation is possible. On the contrary, he appears to maintain that the same people and the same strata were equally present in the two ways. In other words, while for Dobb the difference between Way No. 1 and Way No. 2 consists essentially in the fact that they were promoted by social forces with distinct interests and distinct policies, for Sweezy the difference consists in distinct types of productive process (putting-out vs combined manufacture). Sweezy's assessment of the role of small enterprises – the 'small men', the 'petits productures de campagne' – in the origins of capitalist industry, is thus the opposite of Dobb's. In his view, the direct precedent of the capitalist factory proper should be sought not so much in the concerns of these small producer-capitalists as in those of the more substantial industrial enterprises on the model of Colbert's manufactories.

A notable contribution to the clarification of this complex question was made by Takahashi. Intervening in the debate between Dobb and Sweezy, he paid especial attention to the problem of the 'two ways'. In particular, he argued that the passage from the third volume of *Capital*, taken in context, does not confine itself to indicating the existence of the two ways, but asserts an opposition between them. Thus Way No. 1 is characterised by the subordination of commercial capital to industrial capital, of the market to production; conversely, Way No. 2 is characterised by the persistent dependence of production on the market, of industry on commercial gain. Way No. 1 necessarily leads to a definitive rupture with feudal relations of production, Way No. 2 to an accommodation with these relations, in so far as – to use Marx's phrase – 'it cannot by itself contribute to the overthrow of the old mode of production, but tends rather to preserve and retain it as its precondition'. The Japanese historian makes the timely observation that we have

[22] 'A Critique', p. 54.

here a *historical* characterisation of two distinct phases in the origins of capitalism. It is precisely in so far as they are distinct and opposite historical phases, that the two ways are not (as Sweezy seems to think) two separate solutions to a single problem; they do not answer to the same interests, but correspond to different problems, different interests, and different social strata. The *manufactures réunies* were created by the *haute bourgeoisie* that was tied to and integrated within the feudal order; as such they disappeared with the end of this order, in the French Revolution. In the same way, the 'charactered manufacturers' of the Stuart period were opposed to the Puritan rebellion, which was supported instead by small capitalist producers in town and countryside.

From this point of view, the opposition between the two ways and the two opposed modes of production with which they are linked is reflected in political struggle and in parties: independents vs royalists in the English Revolution, Jacobins vs Girondins in the French Revolution. Thus Takahashi, with a broad historical perspective, interprets predominance of either of the two ways in a particular country as one of the characteristics of the social structure of that country in the capitalist era. He comments that the predominance of Way No. 1 in France and England goes a long way towards explaining many of the differences in social structure between these countries and those in which Way No. 2 prevailed, such as Germany and Japan. For that matter, on the level of specific historical analysis, Takahashi's essay is a notable contribution, even when compared with Dobb's *Studies*. In particular he criticises as erroneous Dobb's ascription of the putting-out system to Way No. 1 rather than to Way No. 2. This system was in fact for the most part the work of merchants who, inasmuch as they furnished the material to individual producers first and then assured the sale of the final product, '"controlled" production only from the outside, and in order to continue this domination, as merchant capitalists, maintained the traditional conditions of production unchanged'.[23] The case of the putting-out system was thus not to be confused with that of domestic industry composed of 'independent small and medium enterprises', as Dobb had done.

It is interesting to note that the debate between Dobb and Sweezy on the origins of manufactures also had its counterpart in the Soviet Union. From 1948 to 1950, the journal *Voprosy Istorii* published numerous articles on the nature of Russian manufactures in the epoch of

[23] 'A Contribution to the Discussion', p. 92.

Peter the Great. The most recent of these articles, written by Borisov,[24] developed themes and arguments similar to those of Takahashi. Polemicising against preceding articles and monographs, Borisov rejects the notion that Russian manufactures at the time of Peter the Great were capitalist in character. They contained capitalist 'germs', but were not themselves a capitalist 'form' (*kapitalisticheskii uklad*, according to the term employed by Lenin in his *The Development of Capitalism in Russia*). Borisov distinguishes 'commercial' (*kaufmannisch*) manufacture from 'capitalist' manufacture. Like the Japanese historian, he attaches much importance to the relation between commercial and industrial capital, and between production and the market, for a historical account of manufactures.

We thus conclude our survey of the principal texts and themes of the debate on the transition from feudalism to capitalism. The reader will have seen that this debate was a complex of extremely varied discussions and themes. Within the context of the general problem, numerous particular questions were discussed: the question of the role of commerce in the development and supersession of the feudal mode of production; the question of the character of the English Revolution; the question of the 'two ways' and of the origins of capitalist manufacture.

In this sense the debate provides a summary of current historical approaches to the problem. Of course, its interest as well as its limitation is due to the fact that it is not a mere empirical registration, but an attempt to provide a reconstruction in the light of a new historical outlook. The debate was never, as has been noted, exempt from heterogeneity: the relationship between source and interpretation, material and exposition, remained necessarily external. All the participants in the discussion were aware of this fact, which was specially emphasized by Hilton. In this respect, the discussion is not merely a summary of existing knowledge. It represents a set of orientations for historical research into the solution of particular problems. These orientations are already beginning to bear fruit, particularly in England. Let us hope that knowledge and study of these problems may prove equally fertile for historical research in our own country.

Of course, the problems of the history of Italy are quite different from those of the history of England or even of France. It is evident, however,

[24] Compare the essay by Borisov, 'Uber die Entstehung der Formen der Kapitalistischen Ordnung in der Industrie', in the volume *Zur Periodisierung*, which surveys Soviet work on the subject.

that many of the elements that have emerged in the course of the discussion on the transition from feudalism to capitalism can be used to cultivate certain areas of research and to pose and answer certain problems in our own history. It is obvious, for example, that the role of commercial capital in the development and decay of Italian medieval society is a theme of particularly great historical interest to us. The same can be said of the problem of the origins of industry and manufacture, and of the character of domestic industry. Those who are familiar with Gramsci's *Prison Notebooks* will know that these contain many reflections on the themes of the debate with which we have been concerned. Every reader will recall Gramsci's comments on the economico-corporative character of the Communes, and the historical evolution of the relationship between town and country.

Further Materials

Capitalism—What's in a Name?

Rodney Hilton

The history of capitalism was once studied by its supporters and its critics on the basis of reasonably common agreement as to what both meant by the term.

'The subject of capitalism', wrote Professor M. M. Postan;[1] 'owes its present place in political and scientific discussion to the work of Marx and the Marxians'. Many historians substantially follow him. Mr. E. Lipson in his *Economic History of England*[2] on the whole adopts Marx's definition of Capitalism. He agrees that its essential feature is the division of classes between propertyless wage-earners and entrepreneurs who own capital, in contrast to the characteristic medieval organisation of industry and agriculture on the basis of the small producer who owned his own means of production.

Definitions, both implicit and explicit, which are much less precise have become fashionable in recent years. A characteristic definition is given by Professor Pirenne describing 'the tendency to the steady accumulation of wealth which we call capitalism'.[3] Two leading French historians refer to capitalists and capitalism when writing of large scale landed property in the Carolingian era.[4] And it is surely a looser definition than that of Marx which leads Professor Armando Sapori, the historian of Italian industry and commerce in the middle ages, to write of a 'capitalist revolution' in the time of Thomas Aquinas.[5]

Pirenne's definition referred to the activities of European merchants in the 12th and 13th centuries. Such definitions face the history teacher

[1] *Economic History Review*, 4. A thorough discussion of the uses of the term will be found in M. H. Dobb, *Studies of the Development of Capitalism*, Chapter I.

[2] *Economic History of England*, passim, but cf. e.g. p. 468.

[3] *Belgian Democracy*, p. 30.

[4] L. Halphen, *Etudes critiques sur l'histoire de Charlemagne*, p. 265. J. Calmette, *Le Moyen Age*, p. 135.

[5] 'Il guisto prezzo nella dottrina di San Tomasso', in *Studi di Storia Economica Medioevale*, 1946, p. 191.

and student with the puzzling phenomenon of 'the rise of the middle classes' (associated of course with the growth of trade), which seems to start so early, to go on for so long, and to be the explanation of so many different historical movements and events. For although the urban middle class of medieval Europe is said to have begun its notorious career as early as the 10th century,[6] the teacher is faced with the problem of explaining why it was not until the 17th and 18th centuries that this class became the dominant force in society. Why did it take more than 700 years to reach this position if during the whole period it was 'rising'?

Not all historians equate the expansion of a class based on trade in a predominantly agricultural society with the expansion of capitalism. Nevertheless the assumption that the two movements were identical is generally made. It is made with care and reservations by the specialists, but usually more unreservedly by those who feel it necessary to simplify for general teaching purposes. The latter do in fact get plenty of justification from some of the eminent specialists writing on medieval trade. For example, Professor de Roover, an outstanding contributor to our knowledge of medieval banking, speaks of the 'commercial revolution at the end of the 13th century' which paved the way for 'mercantile capitalism, which in most European countries was not replaced by industrial capitalism before the middle of the 19th century'.[7] And most of the contemporary contributions by historians of medieval industry and commerce rest on the (usually implicit) assumption that what is being discussed is 'capitalism'.

Recent researches have shown that an older generation of economic historians who regarded the middle ages as a period of 'natural economy' were mistaken. These historians minimised the extent to which commodities were produced for the market. They also under-estimated the volume of international trade and the repercussions which it had on economic activity. Pirenne, both in his studies of the growth of medieval towns and in his more general works[8] has had a considerable influence on the teaching and study of medieval economic history. He emphasised that the growth of international trade played a key role in the transformation of feudal society. Many current assumptions about medieval capitalism are derived from his work, and his conclusions have been supported

[6] See 'The Tenth Century' by the Abbé Lestocquoy, *Economic History Review*, XVII, 1.

[7] *Money, Banking and Credit in Medieval Bruges*, p. 11.

[8] *Medieval Cities; Histoire de Belgique; Social and Economic History of Medieval Europe; Mahomet and Charlemagne.*

by a number of subsequent studies. Only a few need be mentioned here. The most important have been those which have explored the development of trade and industry in the most advanced economic regions of medieval Europe – Flanders and Italy. The researches of Espinas have shown how great was the industrial activity of the Flemish cloth manufacturing centres, adding detailed material to illustrate the more general remarks of Pirenne. Doren, Davidsohn, Sapori and others have shown how the industrial and commercial activity of the Tuscan towns was even further advanced than that of Flanders.[9] These centres were producing cloth for an international market. They bought their raw material far from the place of manufacture. Wool was imported from England, Spain and elsewhere. Dyestuffs were brought from as far afield as the Black Sea. Naturally this shipment of raw materials and the export of finished goods brought into being an elaborate trading mechanism. Up to the end of the 13th century, the great fairs of Champagne formed the greatest among a number of international emporia where buyers from the south met sellers from the north. In the 14th century merchant importers (Italians especially) established permanent agencies in the manufacturing and trading centres. To avoid the transport of bullion and to overcome the difficulties of currency exchange in coin, letters of exchange were elaborated. This permitted the development of credit not to speak of facilitating large and small scale usury and international public finance.[10]

Investigations which revealed the importance of international trade have been accompanied by studies of agrarian life which again have corrected the older impression of a world composed of closed 'natural' economies. The disintegration, from the 11th century onwards of the big estates of the Carolingian era, the sub-division of manorial demesnes, the reduction in the numbers of completely servile peasants and the growth of rent paid in money, rather than in labour or in kind, have been described in works written half a century and more ago.[11] Since then economic historians have tended to link up these features more definitely with the contemporary commercial expansion. Yet less detailed

[9] G. Espinas, *La Vie Urbaine de Douai au Moyen-Age; Sire Jehan Boinebroke* (Les Origines du Capitalisme); *Histoire de la Draperie de la Flandre Francaise*. A. Doren, *Florentiner Wollentuchindustrie*. R. Davidsohn, *Geschichte von Florenz* IV. A. Sapori, *op. cit.*

[10] Besides the works of Sapori and de Roover already quoted, see R. Doehaerd, *Les Relations Commerciales entre Gênes et l'Outremont*, I. and Y. Renouard, *Les Hommes d'Affaires Italiens*; also their *Relations des Papes d'Avignon et des Compagnes Commerciales et Bancaires*.

[11] e.g. L. Delisle, *Etudes sur la Condition de la Classe Agricole en Normandie au Moyen-age*; H. Sée, *Les Classes Rurales et le Regime Seigneurial en France au Moyen-Age*.

study has been made of the market aspects of agriculture than of industry or trade. One reason for this is that evidence for production for the market in agriculture is comparatively scanty, except for England. The break-up of the big landlord estates was delayed longer in England than France and Western Germany; and so they were the main participants in market production when the demand came, above all in the 13th century. Consequently records of this production for the market have survived in England, as they have not on the continent. Annual manorial and central estate accounts dating from about the middle of the 13th century exist in abundance. But although many valuable monographs concerning individual estates have been written, comparatively little systematic investigation of the exact scope of production for the market has been undertaken.[12] Even so, one modern historian at least has concluded that the 13th century English estates were examples of agricultural capitalism.[13]

There is clearly no little confusion in the study of early forms of capitalism. It is therefore well to look back to what Marx understood by the word. He used it to denote what he described as a 'mode of production' of the material wealth of society. He believed that social and political institutions, the ideas and achievements of any society ultimately derive from its 'mode of production'. He therefore saw the heart of the change from feudal to capitalist society in the change from a primarily agrarian society of petty producers, whose most important social classes were the landlords and their unfree tenants, to a society producing commodities for exchange on the market, whose principal classes were capital-owning entrepreneurs and propertyless wage-earners.

Marx' general views are well enough known and his chapters on the 'primitive accumulation of capital' in Vol. I of 'Capital' (Part VIII) are familiar to most economic historians. But of more special interest to the medievalist are three chapters of Vol. III,[14] which summarise his less well-known views on the genesis of capitalism.

His main argument is that commerce, in money or goods, however widespread, and however productive of accumulations of money capital, does not *by itself* transform feudal society. The speed and forms of

[12] The pioneer book of N. S. B. Gras, *The Evolution of the English Corn Market* requires special mention, though it does no more than break the ground.

[13] R. R. Betts, 'La Société dans l'Europe centrale et dans l'Europe orientale, *Révue d'Histoire Comparée*, 1948.

[14] XX, Historical Data concerning Merchant's capital; XXXVI, Interest in the Middle Ages; XLVII, The Genesis of Capitalist Ground Rent. The whole volume was compiled from Marx' notes after his death by F. Engels.

the disintegration of feudal society, on the contrary, 'depend(ed) on its solidity and internal articulation' as a 'mode of production'. It was rather the inherent contradictions within the society than the impact upon it (as from without) of commerce which were the prime causes of its downfall.

In his view, the only form of capital in the ancient and medieval world was the money capital accumulated by merchants and usurers. The typical medieval capitalist was the merchant who drew his profit from the monopoly of the carrying trade between economically backward and geographically remote areas. This profit might be derived from the import of articles of small bulk and high prices (such as spices) from the east; or from the exploitation of the different prices of commodities of everyday consumption as between one local market area and another. The usurer's profit also depended on the backward, rather than on the advanced features of the economy. It was drawn from the extravagance of the landowning classes, and from the perpetual bankruptcy of the peasant and the small artisan. It is only when capital 'takes hold of production' that merchant's and usurer's capital becomes subordinate to industrial capital, and only then that it becomes possible to speak of a capitalist 'mode of production'.

This attitude to medieval money capital led Marx to view with scepticism the claim that the growth of money rent in itself had any direct connection with the decay of feudal relationships. He distinguished 'feudal rent' from capitalist ground rent with the same care that he distinguished merchant from industrial capital. The 'feudal rent', paid by the peasant to the landowner, whether in labour, kind or money, is analogous to the 'surplus-value' which the capitalist derives from the wage earner. Ground rent under capitalism is not the main source of the income of the ruling class. It is merely a 'super-profit', derived by the landlord from the capitalist farmer by virtue of his monopoly of a force of nature, the land.

Marx emphasised the corrosive effect of money on the economy of feudal society, whilst he also pointed to some of the retrograde effects of the action of merchants' and usurers' capital. In the cloth industry, the domination of merchants' capital simply deteriorated the conditions of the artisans, so that in some respects they were worse off than the wage earners. Usury, especially in the countryside, caused a depression without altering the character of existing society. 'The indebted feudal lord becomes even more oppressive, because he is himself more oppressed'. But Marx regarded the growth of merchants' capital as one of the preconditions of the capitalist mode of production.

The most important of these pre-conditions, especially for the development of capitalist industry, was the concentration of moneyed wealth. In agriculture, the development of money rent assisted the stratification of the rural population, and the growth of capitalist farming. When money rent replaced labour rent, the peasants were able to devote all their time to their own holdings, and the richer among them were able to accumulate surpluses. The poorer peasants, on the other hand, were ruined by the effect of continuous demand for money rent, and by usury. When the rent from land was expressed in money, it became possible to put a money price to the land. This promoted the buying and selling of land; and, as more land came on to the market, the resulting disintegration of traditional holdings further assisted the social differentiation of the peasantry.

The test of any such analysis is not whether or no it sounds convincing, but whether it helps to interpret the facts and solve some of the problens which confront the historian of the middle ages. One of the foremost among such problems is how far older forms of economic structure and social organisation persisted, and how far they remained dominant.

The main new developments in the agrarian life of the later middle ages in Western Europe are well enough known. The legal claims of the lords over the persons of their tenants were reduced; a majority of tenants were freed from the obligation to labour on their lord's demesne; money rent predominated; and the total amount of rent paid over to the landlords decreased. In short, the landlords' control over their peasantry was weakened. Ignoring for the moment the exact relationship between these new developments and increased market production, let us briefly consider how far they involved a fundamental change in the character of society. The big demesnes tended to disappear or to shrink, but they had never constituted more than a fraction of the land under cultivation nor did the techniques used on them differ significantly from those which the peasant used on their own plots. Small scale peasant production continued as before. It is true that, from the 14th century onward, a number of richer peasants, and, a little higher in the social hierarchy, many of the lesser nobility, were beginning to farm on a larger scale. Both needed a certain amount of wage labour. But the amount was not yet enough to change the old system. Furthermore, although a landlord-tenant relationship based on the payment of money rent can be seen in the light of later events to have been an important transitional stage in the decline of medieval agriculture, the main features of feudalism persisted. The landlords continued to take rent from peasants by non-economic compulsion.[15] The peasants handed over to their lords a portion of their surplus under the same sort of legal and military sanctions as before (though the growth of the state machine made them much more efficient). The fact that the surplus had to be converted by the peasant into money instead of being rendered directly in labour or in kind did not *yet* alter the class relations.

Small scale production operated also in industry. It was a great change when to the activities of the scattered artisans in the villages was added the productive effort of large numbers or workshops concentrated in towns and organised in gilds. This was part of the general economic expansion of the 12th and 13th centuries. In certain centres producing for export, primarily cloth, groups of wealthy merchants seized hold of both ends of the process of production, the provision of raw material and the marketing of the finished product. In so doing they destroyed the independence of the artisan. But the big merchants of Douai, Ghent or Florence did not revolutionise production. Although some centralisation of the preparation and finishing processes was achieved, the greater part of the work of manufacture was done in the family workshops of the master craftsmen. Furthermore although a proletarian labour force of some dimensions existed in both the Flemish and Italian cloth centres, they were normally concentrated in groups of no more than four or five apiece in the central warehouses of the merchants. For the most part they were employed in the artisan workshops by the master craftsmen, by whose side they worked.[16]

In some respects the big merchants actually retarded the development of production. They were afraid of production for the market by the artisans themselves. Consequently they forbade any collusion between artisans at different stages of the production process. If weavers passed their product straight on to the fullers and dyers, there was risk to the merchant that an element among the craftsmen might control the process

[15] The wage-earner, in order to live, is compelled to work for the capitalist; the compulsion on him is economic. The feudal peasant, having his own means of production, has to be compelled by the immediate or ultimate threat of force to hand over his rent to the landlord. This is the reason for the medieval peasant's lack of personal freedom.

[16] The nearest approach to an organised proletariat was the Florentine Ciompi. Their weakness was revealed in the revolt of 1378 when their short-lived achievement of political power collapsed as soon as they were cut off from their allies among the artisans and petty tradesmen. Additionally it was a measure of their immaturity that the big bourgeoisie could so easily isolate them.

of production from within. This almost happened in Flanders in the 14th century. When the political power of the old merchant-draper patrician caste was broken, the weavers of towns such as Ghent threw up an entrepreneur element which would have taken over the organisation of the industry, had not political factors, the rise of the country industry and the decay of the Flemish cloth industry prevented them.[17] It was to avoid this that in Northern Europe and in Italy, the merchants supplying the raw materials insisted that after the completion of each stage of the production process, the product should be brought back to the central warehouse for re-issue to the next craftsman in the chain. Whilst the artisan remained subordinated to the merchant in this fashion, no change in the traditional small scale methods of production was possible.

As in agriculture, so in industry and finance, there was conservatism as well as change. Great concentrations of merchant capital and elaborate credit and exchange mechanisms were a new feature of the 13th and 14th centuries. They arose when European industrial exports restored the balance of trade between Western Europe and the East.[18] The human agents of this development were those great merchants of whom the Italian bankers were the finest flower. Yet, in spite of their seeming power as international financiers, they adapted themselves like their ancestors of the 11th and 12th centuries to the existing social structure. The very diversity of their interests as bankers, money lenders, and traders, in any and every commodity, made them the more adaptable, both politically and socially, to the feudal ruling circles. For these rulers were their principal market for their luxury commodities, the recipients of private and government loans.

Old methods and old relations of production must be emphasised. But there were none the less very great changes within medieval Europe between the 11th and 15th centuries. Without these changes, subsequent development would have been impossible. The point is that *in spite of* the expansion of production, of population and of trade in the 13th and early 14th centuries, the main features of the old social and political framework remained, not to disappear until the 17th and 18th centuries. Of course, forms of government and social relations

[17] See H. Van Werweke, 'Currency Manipulations in the Middle Ages' in *Transactions of the Royal Historical Society, 4th Series, XXXI.*

[18] See Marc Bloch, 'Le probleme de l'or au Moyen-Age' – *Annales d'Histoire Economique et Sociale*, 1933; 'L'or musulman du VIIe au XIe siècle', *Annales*, 1947, No. 2 by M. Lombard; and 'Monnaies et civilisations', *ibid.*, 1946, No. 1 by F. Braudel.

did change greatly during the middle ages. But the states of Europe continued to be ruled by and for territorial aristocracies represented by feudal monarchies. They were not ruled by or for merchants or industrialists. That is why there had to be bourgeois revolutions before the full expansion of capitalism was possible. Our insistence on the persistence of the old structure in industry and agriculture has been to show the economic basis for the continued dominance of the old classes. This is one reason why an uncritical acceptance of the view that capitalism gradually expanded from the 13th century onwards may lead to a falsification of the real history of capitalism as well as of the preceding epoch.

It follows from the line of criticism outlined above that a changed direction of research into capitalist origins is needed. This does not minimise the great value of work done by the various specialists in the history of commerce, banking and industry. The point is that a number of questions with which the contemporary historians have not dealt remain to be answered.[19]

In order to promote the solution of the problems both of the chronology of capitalism and of its earliest characteristics, an approach might be made under two main heads. First a chronology of the *predominating* methods and relations of production should be established, and co-ordinated with the much better known chronology of the growth of commerce. Secondly, the inter-relationships of the economic, social and political aspects of society should be studied. In particular, the significance and consequences of the unevennesses in the development of these varied sides of human life require investigation.

We are likely to obtain the truest insight into the end of feudal and the beginning of capitalist society if we pay attention first to the techniques and relations of production. Naturally the commercial expansion of the Middle Ages must be examined in the closest association with the investigation of changes in the mode of production. But the history of trade alone will not tell us how and when the characteristic relations of feudalism gave place to those of capitalism, how peasant agriculture and artisan industry gave place to large concentrations of capital and of wage

[19] It is interesting to note what Mme. Doehaerd, in the admirable work mentioned above, considers to be the phenomena 'qui constituent l'ossature de la vie economique internationale et locale de tous le temps'. They are: 'la question des produits qui font l'objet du commerce . . . celle de leurs centres de provenance ou de production, des places ou ils sont échangés, des centres d'exportation et d'importation, des voies et moyens de transport, des agents d'échange, des methodes d'échange, des moyens monetaires et du credit.' p. 142. It is remarkable that questions of production do not come into the problems of economic life.

labourers, profit by rent to profit drawn from the value given to the finished product by the worker.

Political conditions need closer attention. The political structure and political movements ultimately arise out of the social relations based on production, but economic and political changes do not develop hand in hand. Though they develop unevenly, they are integrally connected. It is not possible to talk of a capitalist *society* when political power is still in the hands of a feudal aristocracy. It is unwise to speak of a capitalist system when the political and legal superstructure of society is still one shaped by pre-capitalist economic conditions. Political power, even in the hands of a ruling class whose economic basis is decaying can still retard the development of new economic and social forms. The history of England under the Tudors and Stuarts and of central and eastern Europe in the 19th century illustrates this point.

What kind of problems demand the attention of the research historian? The growth of capitalist production cannot be measured simply by estimating the level of commodity production. Developments in technique, the growth of the volume of total production, and the manner of application of labour to production also require study. These problems are common to both agriculture and industry; indeed it must not be imagined that in studying capitalist origins, attention should primarily be concentrated on industry. The history of England up to the revolution of 1640 would be but half told if it ignored the growth of capitalism in agriculture.

Questions of technique ought not to be considered simply as problems of technological evolution. What matters is their economic and social effects. One of the main obstacles to the accumulation and investment of capital was the small-scale of the units of production in agriculture and industry. Therefore one of the central problems for the student of capitalist origins is to find out about the number, size and methods of operation of the larger farms held in the late 14th and 15th centuries by the thriving elements in the countryside – the big peasants and the smaller gentry. All that we yet know about such farming units is that they were considerably larger than the traditional average peasant holding of the 13th century, being often more than 100 acres in arable area; that they were heterogeneous in composition, including the farmer's ancestral holding, fragments of other peasants' lapsed holdings, and leased-out demesne; and that they must have required hired labour for working them. We also need to know more about the chronology and scope of the turn-over to sheep farming for wool production. It is probable that in the middle of the 15th century England was producing less wool than at the beginning of the 14th century.[20] Yet there has been much loose writing about England being 'covered . . . with sheep farms in place of corn fields.[21]

Problems of size of farms and type of farming immediately raise the question of the agrarian labour force of the later middle ages. Was there a proportionate decline or increase in the number of wage labourers in the countryside after the middle of the 14th century? In a recent article[22] Professor Postan has challenged the usual view that wage labour increased in importance during the period. From figures of rising real wages, he deduces a decline in the numbers of wage earners compared with other sections of the population. Landless labourers and small-holders were able, he believes, to move after the Black Death into the vacated holdings of victims of the plague. But who provided the labour on the enlarged holdings of the top stratum of the villeins, the yeomen and the lesser gentry? Whilst 14th and 15th century rentals and surveys confirm that the small-holding class had diminished relatively to other peasant groups, this type of evidence is naturally useless for estimating the number of totally landless. The best English evidence bearing on the subject is not entirely reliable. This is the Poll Tax return of 1381. Unlike earlier returns it gives the occupations of practically all of the taxed personnel. The lists are very incomplete, for there was a mass evasion of the assessors.[23]

But those who hid and were not counted were more likely to be the landless than those whose houses and holdings could not be concealed. The returns are therefore likely to minimise rather than to exaggerate the proportion of wage workers. Such returns as have been examined show a surprisingly high proportion of wage workers, but much further investigation of the returns needs to be done before any firm conclusions can be reached.[24]

[20] Estimate of 15th century wool production in E. Power, *Medieval English Wool Trade*, p. 37.

[21] E. Lipson, *History of the English Woollen and Worsted Industries*, 1921, p. 16.

[22] 'Some Economic Evidence of Declining Population in the Later Middle Ages' – *Economic History Review*, 2nd series, II, 3

[23] See C. Oman, *The Great Revolt of 1381*.

[24] e.g. in two Leicestershire hundreds, 28% of the taxed population were wage workers, excluding market towns and artisans in the villages. A comparison with 19th century Russia is here useful. The rise in wages was due not only to the shortage of labour but to the increase in pure wage-labour as compared with the incidental wage labout of small-holders; since part of their wages consisted of their small-holding, money remuneration could therefore be kept down, while the pure wage labourers' could not.

An estimate of the amount of wage labour in the late middle ages gives more than an indication of the growth of capitalist social relations. It is in addition indirect evidence for production for the market. As the peasants became landless, they not only became labourers. They became consumers with an income entirely in the form of wages (not all, but mostly money) who needed to buy in the market the goods which previously had not gone through the market.[25] The quantitative significance of the home market in early times is so difficult to measure that international trade (for which there is much better evidence in the form of customs and toll figures) tends to dominate our ideas about production for the market to the exclusion of a sufficient consideration of internal demand.[26] Furthermore, in order to estimate the significance of the production of commodities for the home market in its relation to the productive system as a whole, it is advisable to attempt an estimate of the relative quantities of goods produced for direct use and for the market. A useful addition to what we already know about regional variations in English history would be a survey of how much of the total peasant product in different districts was consumed by the producer, how much went on to the market, and how much was left to spend when the rent was paid.

Some of these considerations apply also to industry. Here too the size and nature of the productive unit is of great importance. The continuing organisation of production on the basis of the artisan family unit prevented the development of capitalist relations of production. But simply to estimate the distance travelled on the road to capitalism from this factor alone would be insufficient. One of the most fruitful ways of tackling the problems of the earliest stages of capitalism in industry would be to compare the history of the cloth manufactures in medieval Flanders and Central Italy with those of England in the 16th and 17th centuries.[27] The concentration of capital and labour, the organisation of the supply of raw material, and of the sale of the finished product by capitalists in the Flemish and Italian towns at the end of the 13th and beginning of the 14th centuries, was such that one could almost say that here were societies trembling on the brink of the capitalist mode of production. Yet modern capitalism derived its initial impetus from the English textile industry and does not descend directly from the

[25] See Marx, *Capital*, I, XXIV, 5; Lenin, *Selected Works*, 1, 223–5.

[26] Compare the remarks on 15th century Poland by M. Malowist, *IXe Congrès des Sciences Historiques, Rapports*, p. 314.

[27] For both of which there are many good secondary works.

principal medieval centres. Its foundations were laid in the rural domestic industry which had fled from the traditional urban centres. We know of course that gild restrictionism was one reason for the shift in the centre of gravity from town to country. But this is only one of many aspects of the problem.

One of the principal attractions in studying the failure of medieval Flanders or Italy to develop the capitalist mode of production is that it not only permits, but demands, the widest treatment. The problem is insoluble on the basis of a narrow concentration on technical and economic factors, for social and political developments were all important. How different were the Boinebrokes of Douai and the Bardi and the Acciaiuoli of Florence from the English entrepreneurs of the 17th century! These earlier capitalists had unspecialised commercial interests; they had close financial associations with the leading feudalists; they were so enmeshed in the political and social relationships of European feudalism that no breakthrough to a new form of society was to be expected under their leadership. In Flanders at the beginning of the 14th century they lined up with the king of France and the feudal nobility against the urban craftsmen and the peasants. In 14th century Florence, the classic pattern of the bourgeois revolution in its least heroic aspects is anticipated like the spectre of the future – the bourgeoisie allying itself to its defeated feudal enemies out of fear of the workers and artisans, and in so doing destroying its own future as a class.[28]

To use Marx' phrase, the 'solidity and internal articulation' of feudal society was still sufficient, even during this period of economic and political crisis, to prevent the new mode of production from establishing itself. But exactly how and why is a matter for further investigation.

It is not enough to study capital, wage labour, and units of production in their economic aspects. Since men make their own history, the historian must know what part the political and social consciousness of the various classes played in advancing or retarding the tempo of capitalist development. Since that consciousness is by no means a direct reflection of the economic activity of these classes, the historian cannot but concern himself with law, politics, art and religion. Neither feudalism nor capitalism are understandable simple as phases in economic history. Society and its movement must be examined in their totality, for otherwise the significance of uneven developments, and of contradictions, between the economic foundation of society, and its ideas and

[28] See the first two chapters of F. Antal's *Florentine Painting and Its Social Background* and N. Rodolico's *I Ciompi*.

institutions, cannot be appreciated. A failure to appreciate their significance is fatal not only to the understanding of the growth and final victory of the capitalist mode of production, but to an insight into the principle motive force of all human development.

From Feudalism to Capitalism

Eric Hobsbawn

Of the various stages of historical development listed by Marx in the Preface to *The Critique of Political Economy* – the 'Asiatic, ancient, the feudal and the modern bourgeois' modes of production, the feudal and the capitalist have been accepted without serious question, while the existence, or the universality of the other two has been queried or denied.

On the other hand the problem of the transition from feudalism to capitalism has probably given rise to more Marxist discussion than any other connected with the periodisation of world history. Thus in the 1950's there took place the well-known international discussion on this point by Paul Sweezy, Maurice Dobb, H. K. Takahashi, Christopher Hill and Rodney Hilton (supplemented by interventions from the late Georges Lefebvre, A. Soboul and Giuliano Procacci).[1] In the same decade there occurred a lively, but inconclusive, discussion on the 'fundamental law of feudalism' in the USSR, i.e., on the mechanism which *necessarily* leads feudalism to be replaced by capitalism, as the historic tendency of capital accumulation, in Marx's analysis, leads capitalism to its doom.[2] There are no doubt other such discussions, particularly in Asian countries, of which I am unfortunately ignorant.

The object of this note is not to provide yet another answer to the questions raised by the transition from feudalism to capitalism, but to fit it into the more general discussion of the stages of social development, which *Marxism Today* has re-opened. This can perhaps best be done by putting forward a few propositions for discussion.

(1) The first concerns the universality of feudalism. As Joan Simon stated in *Marxism Today*, June 1962, summarising the recent one-day debate on the subject organised by the journal and the History Group of the Communist Party, the general drift of Marxist discussion in recent

[1] See above.

[2] So far as I know this discussion has not been made available in English, and it appears not to be reflected in the recent *Fundamentals of Marxism-Leninism*, edited by O. Kuusinen.

decades has tended to widen the scope of 'feudalism' at the expense of social forms previously classified as primitive-communal, Asiatic, etc.

'In practice this means that "feudalism", having become a sort of residuary legatee, now stretches over a vast expanse – from primitive societies up to the triumph of capitalism, which in some countries is in this century, and from China to West Africa, perhaps even to Mexico'. (*Marxism Today*, 1962, p. 184).

Without necessarily agreeing that the present wide scope of 'feudalism' is entirely justified, it is clear that it is an extremely widespread social formation. It is true that the precise form of feudalism varies considerably. The closest parallel to the fully developed European version is no doubt that found in Japan – the similarities are very striking – whereas in other areas the parallelism is rather less close, and in yet others feudal elements are merely part of a rather differently constituted society.

(2) Now it seems clear that under these circumstances it is very doubtful whether we can speak of a *universal* tendency of feudalism to develop into capitalism. In fact, of course, it did so only in one region of the world, namely western Europe and part of the Mediterranean area. There is room for argument about whether in certain other areas (e.g., Japan and parts of India) such an evolution would eventually have been completed, by purely internal forces, had not their historic development been interrupted by the intrusion of western capitalism and imperialist powers. We may also debate how far the tendencies towards capitalism had gone in such areas. (In the case of Japan it may be that the answer to the first question is 'yes' and the answer to the second 'very far', but this is a subject on which the non-expert must hesitate to express an opinion). It may also be argued that the tendencies towards such development were present everywhere, though its pace was sometimes so slow as to be negligible. Certainly no Marxist will deny that the forces which made for economic development in Europe operated everywhere, though not necessarily with the same results in different social and historical circumstances. But there is no getting round the fact that the transition from feudalism is, on a world scale, a case of highly uneven development. The triumph of capitalism occurred fully in one and only one part of the world, and this region in turn transformed the rest. Consequently we have to explain primarily the special reasons which caused this to happen in the Medterranean-European region and not elsewhere.

(3) This does not mean that the problem is to be solved in purely

European terms. On the contrary, it is evident that at various crucial stages the relations between Europe and the rest of the world were decisive. Broadly speaking, Europe was for most of its history a region of barbarism on the extreme western margin of the zone of civilisation, which extended from China in the East through southern Asia to the Near and Middle East. (Japan occupies a similar marginal position at the east of this area, though much closer to the centres of civilisation). At the very outset of European history (as Gordon Childe showed) the economic interrelations with the Near East were important. This is also true at the outset of European feudal history, when the new barbarian (though potentially much more progressive) economy established itself on the ruins of the ancient Greco-Roman empires, and its most advanced centres lay along the final stages of the pipe-line of East-West trade through the Mediterranean (Italy, the Rhine valley). It is even more obvious at the outset of European capitalism, when the conquest or colonial exploitation of America, Asia, Africa – and parts of Eastern Europe – made possible the primary accumulation of capital in the area in which it finally broke through to victory.

(4) This area comprises parts (but not by any means all) of mediterranean, central and western Europe. Thanks to archaeological and historical work, mainly since 1939, we are now in a position to establish the main stages of its economic development. They are:

(A) a period of relapse, following the break-up of the west-Roman empire followed by the gradual evolution of a feudal economy and perhaps a recession in the 10th century A.D. ('The dark ages').

(B) A period of extremely widespread and rapid economic development from about 1000 A.D. to the early 14th century (the 'high middle ages') which form the peak of feudalism. This period saw a marked growth of population, agricultural and manufacturing production and trade, the virtual revival of cities, a great outburst of culture, and a striking expansion of the western feudal economy in the form of 'crusades' against the Moslems, emigration, colonisation and the setting up of trading-posts abroad.

(C) A major 'feudal crisis' in the 14th and 15th centuries, marked by a collapse of large-scale feudal agriculture, of manufactures and international trade, by population decline, attempted social revolution and ideological crisis.

(D) A renewal period of expansion from the mid-15th to the mid-17th century marked for the first time by signs of a major break in the basis and superstructure of feudal society (the Reformation, the elements of bourgeois revolution in the Netherlands) and the first clear break-out of the European traders and conquerors into America and the Indian Ocean. This is the period which Marx regarded as marking the beginning of the capitalist era (*Capital*, I, Dona Torr edn., p. 739).

(E) Another period of crisis, adjustment or set-back, the 'seventeenth century crisis' coincides with the first clear breakthrough of bourgeois society, the English Revolution. It is followed by a renewed and increasingly general period of economic expansion which culminates in –

(F) The definite triumph of capitalist society in the virtually simultaneous Industrial Revolution in Britain, the American Revolution and the French Revolution, all occurring in the last quarter of the 18th century.

The economic development of eastern Europe is somewhat different. Perhaps roughly comparable in periods (A) and (B), a break occurs with the conquest of large areas by Asian peoples (Mongols, Turks), and during period (D) and (E) parts of it are subordinated as semi-colonies to the developing western capitalist area, and undergo a process of re-feudalisation.

(5) The transition from feudalism to capitalism is therefore a long and by no means uniform process. It covers at least five of our six phases. The discussion of this transition has turned largely on the character of the centuries between the first clear signs of breakdown of feudalism (period (C), the 'feudal crisis'[3] in the 14th century) and the definitive triumph of capitalism at the end of the 18th century. Each of these phases contains strong elements of capitalist development – e.g., in period (B) the striking rise of the Italian and Flemish textile manufactures, which collapsed during the feudal crisis. On the other hand nobody has seriously maintained that capitalism prevailed before the 16th century or that feudalism prevailed after the late 18th. However, nobody can doubt that for all or most of the last 1000 years before 1800 economic evolution consistently took place in the same direction. Not everywhere, and not at the same time. There were areas which relapsed, after leading the field (eg., in Italy). There were areas which altered the direction of their evolution for a time. Again, not uniformly. Each major crisis saw formerly 'leading' countries drop back, overtaken by formerly backward but potenti-

[3] This crisis first attracted serious attention in the 1930's. Marxist discussions of it occur in M. Dobb, *Studies in the Development of Capitalism*, 1946, R. H. Hilton in *Annales E.S.C.* 1951, 23–50 (in French), F. Graus, *The first crisis of feudalism* (in German and Czech), 1953, 1955, M. Malowist (in Polish), 1953, 1954 and E. A. Kosminsky, 'Feudal rent in England' *(Past and Present*, 7, 1955).

ally more progressive ones, like England. But there can be no serious doubt that each phase in its way *advanced* the victory of capitalism, even those which superficially appear as periods of economic recession.

(6) If this is so, it is certainly probable that there exists a fundamental contradiction in this particular form of feudal society which drives it ever forward towards the victory of capitalism. The nature of this contradiction has not yet been satisfactorily clarified. On the other hand it is also clear that the forces which resist such a development, though weaker, are far from negligible. For the transition from feudalism to capitalism is not a simple process by which the capitalist elements within feudalism are strengthened until they are strong enough to burst out of the feudal shell. What we see time and again (as in the 14th and probably the 17th centuries) is that a crisis of feudalism *also* involves the most advanced sections of bourgeois development within it, and therefore produces an apparent setback. Progress no doubt goes on or resumes elsewhere, in hitherto more backward areas, such as England. But the interesting thing about the 14th century crisis (for instance) is not only the collapse of large-scale feudal demesne agriculture, but also that of the Italian and Flemish textile industries, with their capitalist employers and proletarian wage-workers and an organisation which has almost got to the verge of industrialisation. England advances; but the much greater Italy and Flanders never recover and temporarily total industrial production therefore diminishes. Naturally such a long period in which the forces of capitalism are rising, but time and again fail to burst out of the feudal integument, or are even involved in the feudal crisis, is difficult to describe in static terms. Much of the unsatisfactory nature of Marxist discussion about the period between the first general crisis of feudalism and the much later unquestioned victory of capitalism, reflects this difficulty.

(7) How far does this picture of a progressive replacement of feudalism by capitalism apply to regions outside the 'heartland' of capitalist development? Only to a very small extent. There are admittedly certain signs of comparable development under the impetus of the development of the world market after the 16th century, perhaps in the encouragement of textile manufactures in India. But these are more than offset by the *opposite* tendency, namely that which turned the other areas that came into contact with and under the influence of the European powers into dependent economies and colonies of the west. In fact, large parts of the Americas were turned into slave economies to serve the needs of European capitalism, and large parts of Africa were pushed back

economically through the slave-trade; large areas of eastern Europe were turned into neo-feudal economies for similar reasons. And even the temporary and slight stimulus to the development of commercial farming and manufactures which the rise of European capitalism may have provided here and there, was stopped short by the deliberate de-industrialisation of the colonies and semi-colonies as soon as they looked like competing with home production or even (as in India) attempted to supply their own market instead of relying on imports from Britain. The net effect of the rise of European capitalism was therefore to intensify uneven development, and to divide the world ever more sharply into two sectors; the 'developed' and the 'under-developed' countries, in other words the exploiting and the exploited. The triumph of capitalism at the end of the 18th century put the seal on this development. Capitalism, while no doubt providing the historic conditions for economic transformation everywhere, in fact made it more difficult than before for the countries which did not belong to the original nucleus of capitalist development or its immediate neighbours. The Soviet Revolution of 1917 alone provided the means and the model for genuine world-wide economic growth and balanced development of all peoples.

From Feudalism to Capitalism

Maurice Dobb

With Eric Hobsbawm's interesting treatment of the considerable variety of forms of feudalism, and with his conclusion that 'transition from feudalism to capitalism is a long and by no means uniform process', I think I am in almost complete agreement. He is certainly right, I think, to raise sharply the question 'whether we can speak of a *universal* tendency of feudalism to develop into capitalism', whatever the correct answer may eventually turn out to be; as he is also to stress the important consideration that the development of capitalism in the most advanced countries, such as Britain, served to retard development in other parts of the world, and this not *only* in the epoch of imperialism.

The only point on which I should like to comment is one which he touches upon but does not develop; namely the nature of the essential contradiction of feudal society and the part this played in generating bourgeois relations of production. The point is a quite simple one, and will be familiar enough to anyone who followed the *Science and Society* discussion of the early 'fifties to which he refers. But I believe it is crucial; and therefore I will make no apology for raising it again. If we don't start from it, I believe that we shall fail to think clearly about the important questions which his contribution raises.

The Essential Conflict

If we ask ourselves what was the essential conflict generated by a feudal mode of production, it seems to me that there can be only one answer. Basically the mode of production under feudalism was the petty mode of production – production by small producers attached to the land and to their instruments of production. The basic social relation rested on the extraction of the surplus product of this petty mode of production by the feudal ruling class – an exploitation-relationship that was buttressed by various methods of 'extra-economic compulsion'. The precise form in which the surplus product was extracted could vary, according to those different kinds of feudal rent distinguished by Marx in Volume III of *Capital* (labour rent, produce rent or rent in kind, money rent, which can still be feudal rent even if 'a dissolving form' of it): 'this is a lack of freedom', Marx wrote, 'which may be modified from serfdom with forced labour to the point of a mere tributary relation.' I have very little knowledge of the differing forms of feudalism in different parts of the world; but I believe I should be right in saying that these differences about which Eric Hobsbawm speaks with encyclopaedic knowledge largely turn on differences in the *form of extraction* of surplus product. Thus in Western Europe labour rent, in the shape of direct labour services on a lord's estate, predominated, in certain centuries at least[1] (also in Eastern Europe after 'the second serfdom'); but further east, in Asia, it seems to have been the tribute-form of exaction which predominated. 'The specific economic form in which unpaid surplus labour is pumped out of the direct producers determines the relation of rulers and ruled'.

It follows immediately from this that the basic conflict must have been between the direct producers and their feudal overlords who made exactions of their surplus labour-time or surplus product by dint of feudal right and feudal power. This conflict when it broke into open antagonism expressed itself in peasant revolt (individual or collective, e.g. in flight from the land or organised illegal action and force), which Rodney Hilton has shown to have been endemic in England in the 13th and 14th centuries.[2] This was the crucial class struggle under feudalism, and *not* any direct clash of urban bourgeois elements (traders) with feudal lords. The latter did, of course, occur (as witness the struggle of urban communities for political autonomy and control of local markets). But bourgeois traders, so long as they were purely traders and intermediaries, were generally parasitic on feudalism and tended to compromise with it; in many cases they were actual allies of the feudal aristocracy. At any rate their struggle, I believe, remained *secondary*, at least until a much later stage.

If I am right in what has just been said, then it is upon this *revolt among the petty producers* that we must fix our attention in seeking to explain the dissolution and decline of feudal exploitation. This rather than

[1] It has been a common mistake in the interpretation and dating of feudalism to identify the decline of labour rent (by commutation to a money rent) with the decline of feudalism itself.

[2] 'Peasant movements in England before 1381', *Economic History Review*, 1949, Second Series, Vol. II, No. 2.

vague concepts like 'the widening of the market' or 'rise of money economy'; moreover this and not the direct challenge of large capitalist manufactories which the Kuusinen volume emphasises (in Chapter , pp. 161–2).

Genesis of Capitalism

But what connection is there between the revolt of petty producers and the genesis of capitalism? Peasant revolt against feudalism, even if it is successful, does not mean the simultaneous appearance of bourgeois relations of production. In other words, the link between them is not a direct one, but *indirect*; and it is this, I believe, which explains why the dissolution of feudalism and the transition are apt to be long drawn-out in time and why sometimes the process is arrested (as in the case of Italy, mentioned by Eric Hobsbawm, and also the Netherlands, with its first flowering of bourgeois relations of production as early as the 13th and 14th century, if still in a very elementary form). It is true, and worthy of emphasis, that 'the transition from feudalism to capitalism is not a simple process by which the capitalist elements within feudalism are strengthened until they are strong enough to burst out of the feudal shell'. (E.H.)

The connection, as I see it, is this. To the extent that the petty producers were successful in securing partial emancipation from feudal exploitation – perhaps at first merely an alleviation of it (e.g. a transition from labour rent to money rent) – they were able to retain some element of the surplus product for themselves. This provided both the means and the motive for improving cultivation and extending it to new lands, which incidentally served to sharpen antagonism against feudal restrictions still further. It also laid the basis for some *accumulation of capital within the petty mode of production itself*, and hence for the start of a process of *class differentiation within that economy of small producers* – the familiar process, seen at various dates and in widely scattered parts of the world, towards the formation on the one hand of an upper layer of relatively well-to-do improving farmers (the *kulaks* of the Russian tradition) and on the other hand of a depressed layer of impoverished peasants. This social polarisation in the village (and similarly in the urban handicrafts) prepared the way for production by wage-labour and hence for bourgeois relations of production.

It was in *this* way that the embryo of bourgeois productive relations arose within the old society. But the process did not mature immediately. It took time: in England it took some centuries. In this connection it will be remembered that, in speaking of the transition to capitalism, and the role of merchant capital, Marx spoke of the rise of capitalists from the ranks of the producers as 'the really revolutionary way' of transition. When the shift to bourgeois methods of production is initiated 'from above' then the process of transition is apt to stop half-way, and the old mode of production is preserved rather than supplanted.[3]

Uneven Development

When expressed in summary fashion as I have expressed it, this may sound abstract and schematic – at best oversimplified. But it does serve, I suggest, to direct attention towards certain factors when looking for an explanation of that uneven development and of differences in the time-scale of the process which Eric Hobsbawm stresses. In the first place, as the strength of peasant discontent may be affected by the *form* which feudal exaction takes, so the success of peasant revolt may be influenced by the availability of new land and the presence of towns to act as magnets and refuges for peasants from the countryside, thereby creating labour scarcity on the feudal estates (and labour scarcity certainly underlay the feudal crisis of the 14th and 15th centuries). More obviously the military and political strength of feudal lords will determine their ability to repress revolt and to replenish labour reserves, if need be, by fresh exactions and the enserfment of peasants previously free (as in the reaction in eastern Europe). The frequency of feudal wars, again, may be a factor in heightening conflict and revolt by necessitating a larger feudal revenue and hence increased exactions on the producers.

When we come to the burgeoning of bourgeois relations within the petty mode of production, it is obvious that opportunities for this will be affected by the presence of markets, as represented by towns or interregional trade-routes. Here quite properly the market-factor, and such considerations as Pirenne's Mediterranean trade, come in – but they come in quite concretely and specifically as encouraging commodity-production (i.e. production for the market) *within the petty mode*, and hence stimulating the process of social differentiation within it. It seems to me also possible that the availability of land, while at an earlier stage it may facilitate revolt of the producers, may at a later stage serve to inhibit the growth of bourgeois relations by giving more chance to impoverished and/or dispossessed peasants of emigrating elsewhere (did not the migrants and 'beggars' of 16th century England often end

[3] *Capital*, Vol. III, Chapter XX, especially pp. 393–5, Kerr ed., Chicago.

up as 'squatters' in some other part of the country where parcels of land were more readily available?)

By contrast, a high ratio of population to land would tend to heighten the pressure upon the impoverished and dispossessed to find wage-employment, and hence make wage-labour more plentiful (and cheaper) for the *parvenu* capitalist-employer.

I am not suggesting that this is anything like an exhaustive list of the explanations we should look for in finding answers to our problems. They are mentioned merely as indicative of the *kind* of explanation to which the type of approach I have outlined seems to point. But unless we hold some clear picture of *how* we think the process of feudal dissolution and transition worked (even if this picture be modified or clarified as we absorb and discover more facts) I don't think we shall get far in finding clear and satisfactory answers to the sort of question Eric Hobsbawm's contribution raises.

Town and Country in the Transition to Capitalism

John Merrington

The centrality of the town-country relation in the transition to capitalism in the West and more basically the equation of urbanism with capitalism and progress were already explicitly formulated in the earliest theories of the origins of capitalism – those of 18th-century political economy. For the proponents of the new and revolutionary 'conjectural' history of 'civil society' – Smith, Steuart, Ferguson, Millar – the origins of division of labour and the market in the 'commercial stage' of civilisation were to be sought in the separation of town and country. (The highland-lowland division in Scotland provided first-hand evidence.) The separation of production and consumption brought about by rural-urban exchange was the cause of that 'revolution' whereby the self-sufficiency of the rural economy is undermined by urban consumption patterns, destroying the static order of patriarchal authority based on landownership in which 'consumption is not a reward but a price of subordination'.[1] This revolution was brought about entirely without foresight or intention, merely by the interaction of self-interests – gratification of 'childish vanity' on the part of the rural nobility, pursuit of gain by urban merchants – in other words by the free action of the exchange principle (man's 'natural propensity to barter and exchange'), realising a *higher unity* out of the clash of separate interests in the market place. The progressive role of the market is thus realised: it destroys coercive bonds in the country, creates independence for rural commodity producers and establishes 'regular government' in place of internecine territorial feuds. The same principle of division of labour between specialised producers for the market simultaneously increases productivity in its application to manufacture. Moreover, in contrast to the physiocrats in France, for whom rent was the sole form of surplus value, the progress of

[1] Smith, *Wealth of Nations*, Book III, ch. 3–4; Steuart, *An Inquiry into the Principles of Political Economy*, 1754, vol. I, ch. 20.

agricultural productivity is a victory for urban capital over rural backwardness: 'Cities, instead of being the effect, have been the cause and occasion of the improvement and cultivation of the country'.[2]

The city is the dynamic principle of progress, the country inert and passive, requiring an external stimulus, the 'market pull' exerted by towns as concentrated nuclei of exchange transactions and capital wealth. This in turn provided a powerful underpinning for the ideology of the ascendant bourgeoisie: the victory of capitalism as the victory of urban civilisation and the principles of market freedom.[3]

But it is also evident that the subordination of the country to the capitalist 'market' has already in this case reached an advanced stage: Smith's reference to the nobility dismissing their retinues as 'unnecessary mouths', when placed alongside the clearances in the Highlands, makes this clear. This example of total destruction of a rural economy and demographic recomposition already indicates the extremely one-sided nature of capitalist urban progress. This problem can be initially posed if we start from Roupnel's reminder that 'Western civilisation is strictly speaking *rural*: towns only represent a later phenomenon, their form and material physiognomy conserving their rustic origins'.[4]

If we bear in mind these rural origins it is clear that capitalist industrialism has involved not only a massive shift of human and material resources in favour of urban concentrations, but also a *conquest* over the countryside, which becomes 'ruralised', since it by no means represented in the past an exclusively agricultural milieu. From being a centre of all kinds of production, an autonomous primary sector that incorporates the whole of social production, the country becomes 'agriculture', i.e. a separate industry for food and raw materials, separated in turn into various specialised types of farming, districts, etc. All towns imply, of course, some kind of town-country differentiation: the extraction of food and manpower from the country is implied in the very definition of a town. But in every previous case the agrarian economy established the historical limits of town development until capitalist urbanisation broke this Malthusian dependence. 'The town only exists . . . in relation to a form of life subordinate to its own . . . It has to dominate an empire, however small, in order to exist'.[5]

[2] Smith, I, p. 392.

[3] E. Chill ed., *Power Property and History*, Intro: 'Barnave as a Philosophical Historian', p. 1–74: D. Forbes, 'Scientific Whiggism: Adam Smith and John Millar', *Cambridge Journal*, Vol. 7, 1953–4, pp. 643–70.

[4] G. Roupnel, *Histoire de la Campagne Francaise*, Paris, 1932, cited in G. Friedmann, ed. *Villes et Campagnes*, Paris, 1954, p. 3.

In precapitalist formations the victory of towns was always precarious, easily reversed; the growth of the cities was arrested, or wiped out altogether, according to their political domination of the country and the capacity to extract the agricultural surplus and fresh manpower which was their life blood. Under what conditions does urban growth acquire social forces and a momentum of its own that can break this dependence on the country for good? And where/when do we situate this 'urban revolution' as a key aspect of the transition to capitalism?

One answer is given by modern urbanisation theory. But the typology of 'generative' and 'parasitic' cities as functional or non-functional to 'growth' (Hoselitz) assumes development as the paradigm against which we 'measure' the numerous urban failures to meet value criteria derived from industrial capitalism. It cannot *explain* these disparities as an intelligible diversified unit which can provide a basis for global comparison: instead it offers a proliferation of descriptive models, classifications of sub-species and multiplication of factors *ad infinitum*. The category 'pre-industrial', to which feudal towns are assimilated by Sjoberg, is similarly too inclusive: it cannot grasp the specific form of town-country opposition that led to capitalism in the West. Nor can quantitative and ecological classification (size and distribution of urban networks, applied by J. C. Russell to the European Middle Ages) provide any more than *indices* of urbanisation, which cannot *explain* the countless cases of involution, regression and qualitative alteration in the hierarchy of size ratios in which urban history is so rich.[6]

The most powerful strand of explanation goes back to Weber and Pirenne, arguing the peculiarly 'generative' character of the medieval European town based on its corporate, communal organisation as a capitalist nucleus with the capacity to act as the solvent of feudal social relations. Thus 'capitalism and towns were basically the same thing in the West' (Braudel); the European towns' corporate autonomy and the relative openness of their communal structure allowed them to 'develop as autonomous worlds according to their own propensities' (Weber). According to Pirenne's enormously influential studies of medieval towns and commerce, the closing of the Mediterranean trade routes was the key to the substitution of an agrarian economy in the 7th–9th centuries: 'For an economy of exchange was substituted an economy of consumption. Each demesne . . . constituted from this

[5] F. Braudel, *Capitalism and Material Life 1400–1800*, London, 1973, p. 374.

[6] G. Sjoberg, *The Pre-Industrial City*, Glencoe, Ill., 1960; J. C. Russell, *Medieval Regions and their Cities*, Newton Abbott, 1972.

time on a little world of its own . . . a closed domestic economy . . . of no markets. They did not sell because they could not sell, because markets were wanting'. Conversely, the reopening of long-distance trade from the 11th century – the counter-attack of Christianity against Islam – revived towns and markets (Italy, Flanders) and broke down the 'rigid confines' of the demesnial system. 'As in antiquity the country oriented itself afresh on the city'. But in this case the division of labour between town and country transformed the countryside: by 'arousing his desires' the city multiplied the peasant's needs, raised his standard of living and so caused the end of serfdom, which 'coincided with the increasing importance of liquid capital'. Urban trade drew agricultural production towards the town, 'modernised it and set it free'. While the burghers' own conception of freedom was still that of a privileged order, a corporate monopoly, 'nonetheless to that middle class was reserved the mission of spreading the idea of liberty far and wide and of becoming, *without having consciously desired to be*, the means of the gradual enfranchisement of the rural classes . . . It had not the power to arrest an evolution of which it was the cause and which it could not suppress save by itself vanishing'.[7] Smith might have had doubts about the timing but he would certainly have fully concurred with the substance.

This immediately poses, like all evolutionary theories of the 'rise of capitalism', the problem of the long period of capitalist gestation in the towns and the multi-secular rise of the 'middle class' – an evolution interrupted by spectacular false starts, reverses, backslidings and betrayals to the old order before this class became the dominant force in society.[8] For Pirenne this untidy breach of continuity was solved by the constant need to replenish or releaven the capitalist 'stock' in order to maintain its adaptive, aggressive spirit of risk and innovation.[9]

But there is also a more general objection: to read the progressive role of the urban bourgeoisie backwards into history is to pose the market as the *only* dynamic force, the principle behind all movement, all change. Capitalism (and its urban nucleus) is the only formation with a capacity for development, identified with historicity itself. Hence the need to discover an external, contingent source or 'prime mover' that

[7] H. Pirenne, *Medieval Cities*, New York, 1956 (first edition 1925), pp. 31, 72, 153–8. My italics. Max Weber, *The City*, New York, 1958, ch. 2, 'The Occidental City'.

[8] R. H. Hilton, 'Capitalism – What's in a Name?'. See above, p. 146.

[9] H. Pirenne, *American Historical Review*, vol. XIX, no. 3, April, 1914, 494–5.

can account for its genesis: the opening of trade routes, first in the Mediterranean, then in the Atlantic, a development contingent and external vis-à-vis feudal relations in the country, which intrinsically have no capacity for ulterior development. The capitalist world market is not only the teleological outcome of history: it is also its starting point. The market and exchange principle are the self-generating 'motor' behind *all* development whether ancient, feudal or capitalist: their absence denotes stasis. Karl Polanyi long ago pointed out the fallacy of orthodox economic history according to which the market is the end of *all* economic activity and the world market is a 'natural result of the spreading of markets'.[10]

More recently this became the central issue in the debate within Marxist historiography on the transition from feudalism to capitalism, occasioned by Sweezy's criticisms of Dobb's *Studies in the Development of Capitalism*, published in *Science and Society* in 1950–53.[11] Sweezy reiterated the classic thesis of Pirenne: the external pull of urban markets based on long-distance trade as the motor and dissolvent of the feudal mode. Dobb had already criticised the disjunction that this presupposed between 'natural' and 'exchange' economies as 'two economic orders that cannot mix' in his *Studies*. He rejected this dualistic model as an ahistorical abstraction of the market, divorced from the conditions of its realisation: in other words as an extension into history of the fundamental assumption underlying neoclassical economics.[12] At the same time he did not deny the role of towns and trade in the decline of feudalism as against 'internal' contradictions: the role of commodity circulation in extending rural specialised production for the market and accelerating socio-economic differentiation within the peasantry and within/against the urban guilds was reintegrated by Dobb as a 'subordinate coefficient' in the crisis and decline of the seignorial economy. Nor did he fully deny the capitalist nature of towns in the feudal mode.[13] The tendency of historical enquiry since

[10] K. Polanyi, *The Great Transformation*, Boston, 1968 (first edition, 1944), chs. 4–5.

[11] See above. Further relevant discussion is to be found in the colloquy organised by the *Centre d'Etudes et de Recherches Marxistes* in 1968 with preparatory material by C. Parain and P. Vilar: *Sur le Féodalisme*, Paris, 1971; E. J. Hobsbawm, Intro. to Marx, *Precapitalist Economic Formations*, London, 1964; and the recent original synthesis by Perry Anderson on divergences in the formation of the absolutist state: *Lineages of the Absolutist State*, NLB, 1974.

[12] Dobb, *Studies in the Development of Capitalism*, London, 1946, pp. 27–8, 34, 38–9.

[13] Dobb, 'A Reply', above, pp. 60–61; see also Procacci's excellent survey of the debate, above.

has been to situate towns within the feudal mode, arguing the compatibility of towns with feudalism in Europe, the feudal origin of towns and indeed the integral role of merchant capital within the feudal mode.[14]

This is in line with a tendency to reject the dualistic model of the transition to capitalism – capitalist urban markets against the static feudal 'economy of subsistence' in the countryside – and the attempt to discover specific dynamic 'laws' governing the development and crisis of the feudal mode, analogous to those inherent in capitalist accumulation.

This, however, raises a problem. Given the specificity of the medieval town and merchant capital *within* the feudal mode, what are the determinants of the 'urban revolution' in Western Europe which allowed the dissolution of this mode to lead to the ulterior conquest of the countryside by the city? How can the towns be 'internal' and 'external' at the same time? What is the specific form of town – country opposition *both within and against* feudalism in the West? The radical discontinuity that is implied if we reject – as we should – the dualistic hypothesis, both in terms of the history of the market and of capitalism and towns, was already theoretically established by Marx. In his first outline of the history of civil society in *German Ideology*, the division of labour between town and country, between capital and landed property, is the central motor in the autonomous, materialist development of contradictions in civil society towards a class-divided market. This is in contrast to Hegel, for whom the polarisation of towns (the sphere of corporate, finite organisation) and the countryside (the 'seat of ethical life resting on nature and the family') is only a moment – the 'phase of division' – in the higher realisation of universality in the state.[15]

In a passage in *Capital* (Vol. I, Ch. 14) Marx refers back to this earlier outline, defining the separation of town and country as 'the foundation of every division of labour that is well developed and brought about by the exchange of commodities'. However, he goes on to show that

[14] F. Polyansky in *Vosprosy Istorii*, 1953, no. 1; A. B. Hibbert, 'The Origins of the Medieval Town Patriciate', *Past and Present*, February 1963; C. Cahen, 'A Propos de la discussion sur le feodalité', *La Pensée*, no. 68, July–August, 1956; G. Duby, *Guerriers et Paysans*, reviewed by Rodney Hilton in NLR 83, January–February, 1974. On the other hand, for a restatement of the Pirenne position see H. van Werwecke, 'The Rise of the Towns' in the *Cambridge Economic History of Europe*, vol. III, ch. 1, in which the towns of North-West Europe 'where the purely economic factor was most fully operative' are given an almost exclusive prominence.

[15] Marx and Engels, *German Ideology*, London, 1965, pp. 64–77; Hegel, *Philosophy of Right*, ed. T. Knox, Oxford, 1952, pp. 152–5.

this separation, as a foundation of *every* social division of labour, is common to the most diverse formations – for example, in the Indian communities where it acts with the 'irresistible authority of a force of nature'. This social division merely establishes the existence of towns as such. It follows that it cannot be confused (as in Smith) with the capitalist *market* division of labour and hence the *capitalist* city, which implies the breaking up of all established specialisations based on reciprocal dependence, crystallised by tradition, and their reallocation by the indirect medium of market price movements. Nor can it be equated with the technical organisation of detail operations in manufacture, since in this case 'only the combined product is a commodity', implying 'the direct authority of the capitalist over men who are but parts of a mechanism that belongs to him'. Hence there can be no linear evolution of the 'market' from the social division of labour. There is no evolution of the capitalist city – and the town-country opposition/subordination corresponding to it – from ancient or feudal to capitalist. The dominance of the capitalist city, like that of the factory based on wage labour as its *raison d'être*, is the product of an historical rupture – the 'original sin' of capital, its 'original accumulation'. Nor can the factory be evolved from society.

What then are the discontinuities or 'stages' in this transition? Marx defined the specificity of the feudal town in the West as follows: 'The history of classical antiquity is the history of cities, but of cities founded on landed property and agriculture: Asiatic history is a kind of undifferentiated unity of town and countryside (the largest cities must be regarded here as royal camps, as works of artifice created above the economic construction proper); the Middle Ages (Germanic period) begins with the land as the seat of history, whose further development then moves forward in the opposition between town and countryside; the modern age is the urbanisation of the country, not ruralisation of the city as in antiquity'.[16]

This sybilline indication (it is no more) of the dynamic character of the opposition of town and country specific to the feudal mode should be supplemented with Marx's analysis of merchant capital in Volume III of *Capital*. Marx rejects the evolutionary history of capital based on the categories of bourgeois exchange (the sphere of the 'free trader vulgaris') since those categories – the freedom and equality of the market place – are merely the phenomenal form of social relations of produc-

[16] Marx, *Grundrisse*, Penguin/NLR, 1973, p. 479.

tion, expressed through the distorting lens of relations between products of labour. The sphere of circulation, on which merchant capital – the 'first free form of capital' – arises and which is the basis of the urban accumulation of the middle ages, is transferred by bourgeois political economy 'from its prehistory into the present', thereby establishing 'the eternal right of capital to the fruits of alien labour . . . from the simple and "just" laws of equivalent exchange'.[17] The procedure should be 'quite the reverse'.[18]

While merchant capital in the feudal mode certainly has a dissolvent effect, it is 'incapable by itself of promoting or explaining the transition from one mode of production to another'. The mere existence of commodity production and capital based on circulation is not sufficient for the process of dissolution to result in capitalist production. 'Or else ancient Rome, Byzantium etc., would have ended thieir history with free labour and capital', whereas 'this dissolution led in fact to the supremacy of the countryside over the city'. Where the corrosive action of merchant capital will lead, in other words, 'what new mode of production will replace the old, does not depend on commerce, but on the character of the old mode of production'.[19]

Indeed the autonomous development of commercial capital, which is based on price differentials between *separated* markets and spheres of production (buying cheap and selling dear) is 'inversely proportional to the non-subjection of production to capital'. Its *externality*, vis-à-vis production, is the very condition of its existence, since it interposes itself as 'middleman' 'between extremes which it does not control and between premises which it does not create'. Merchant capital can only redistribute surplus value by windfall profits: hence its key role in the original accumulation of capital. But it cannot be a source of a permanent, self-reproducing accumulation. While it has a key *preparatory* role, together with its 'domestic' forms of usury, speculation on scarcity, etc., it cannot play a determinant, endogenous role in the transition.

These considerations enable us to define more precisely the unity/opposition of towns and urban 'capitalism' in the feudal mode. The 'capital' and 'markets' on which feudal urban growth was based were in no sense the linear ancestors of the capitalist world market. It is wrong to interpret the 'freedom' of the medieval towns in a one-sided, unilateral sense outside the feudal context which both determined the

[17] *Ibid.*, pp. 247–8, 504.
[18] Marx, *Contribution to the Critique of Political Economy*, London, 1971, pp. 213–14.
[19] Marx, *Capital*, Moscow, 1962, vol. III, op. 321–2, 326; *Grundrisse*, p. 506.

'externality' of this freedom of merchant capital and defined its limits. The town's autonomy was not that of a 'non-feudal island' (Postan); its freedom and development as a corporate enclave was not 'according to its *own* propensities' as in Weber's historicist formulation. It was grounded on and limited by the overall parcellisation of sovereignty, based on *the coincidence of political and economic relations of subordination/appropriation* which defined the feudal mode. It was the existence of this corporate urban autonomy as a 'collective seigneur' within a cellular structure based on sovereignty 'in several degrees' that precisely encouraged the fullest development of merchant capital in the medieval town. Hence urban 'capitalism' was both internal and external to the feudal mode – or, more precisely, the former was the *condition* for the latter. The 'internal' versus 'external' terminology of the Dobb-Sweezy debate should be reinterpreted in this light. The 'opposition' of these towns was an opposition of economic-corporative spheres of sovereignty: this must be seen as an element as internal to feudalism as the rise and decline of the seignorial economy – indeed as defined by this coexistence. Far from being immobile, let alone exclusively 'rural', feudalism was the first mode of production in history to allow, by its very absence of sovereignty, an autonomous structural place to urban production and merchant capital.

This 'internal externality' that allowed the independent growth of urban capital, the conquest of trade routes, etc., in Europe is in marked contrast to the 'Eastern city', fixed in a continuity of relationship with the fortunes of imperial power and where political fragmentation was absent except in periods of internal anarchy. In China 'city air' made nobody free: the walls of the town did not represent the ramparts of its juridical autonomy vis-à-vis the countryside as in Europe, but the outward military-administrative defence of a higher tribute-collecting authority, represented in the morphology of the city by the separate, fortified 'inner city' reserved for officialdom. The town had no social autonomy: its social structure, based on clans, lineages, religious sects, was an extension of that of the countryside.[20] It is illuminating to compare this with the growth of independent trading communities in Japan alongside the castle-towns of the nobility during the decentralised Ashikaga period (1339–1573), with the spectacular growth of the commercial free port of Sakai to over 50,000 inhabitants – the 'Venice

[20] E. Balazs, *Chinese Civilization and Bureaucracy*, New Haven, 1964, ch. 6; M. Cartier, 'Une tradition urbaine: les villes dans la Chine antique et médiévale', *Annales*, July–August, 1970, 'Histoire et Urbanisation', pp. 835–7, 841; Weber, op. cit.; Braudel, op. cit., ch. 8.

of Japan' to the Jesuit missionaries.[21]

Feudal town growth was in the closest correlation with the development of the seignorial economy. Far from being a static system of 'production for use', the latter, based on the direct appropriation of surplus labour and rent from the peasant cultivators, in conditions where the means of production were in the hands of the direct producers and the 'political relation of master and dependant is (therefore) an essential part of the economic relation of appropriation',[22] was the real, underlying motor of the feudal mode and its crisis from the 14th century. The resistance of the peasants to surplus labour on the demesne, the struggle to devote labour to the family holding and to keep as much as possible of the product of that labour, the constant expansion of allodial property and the struggle for rural enfranchisement (the rural communes of Italy and France) were scarcely 'secondary' struggles, movements of 'protest' without incidence on social relations, let alone imitative of urban initiatives. The transformations of feudal rent which they engendered – from labour rent to rent in kind or to money rent – while these did not in themselves alter the basic nature of feudal rent as direct appropriation of unpaid surplus labour by the landlord, nonetheless, by fixing this surplus labour to a constant magnitude, stimulated the growth of independent commodity production and differentiation within the peasantry itself. Marx himself noted the dynamic possibilities inherent in the feudal mode, not only in an extensive-territorial sense, but in terms of this struggle for the share-out of the surplus product. It was this that determined the limits of the seignorial demesne economy and hence the alternative outcome of the 14th-century crisis (victory of landlord appropriation of forced labour in the 'second serfdom' in Eastern Europe; victory of peasant commodity production with the emergence of a class of peasant farmers – yeomen or *laboureurs* – in the West).[23] The peasant uprisings, which reached a crescendo with the intensification of labour services in the context of labour shortage in the 14th century, were 'as inseparable from the seignorial régime as strikes are to large-scale capitalism' (Bloch). The enduring historical myth of the passive peasantry (despite the obvious contemporary evidence to the contrary) must be

[21] J. W. Hall, 'The Castle Town and Japan's Modern Urbanization' in ed. Hall and Jansen, *Studies in the Institutional History of Early Modern Japan*, Princeton, NJ, 1968, ch. 10, pp. 171–9.

[22] Marx, *Capital*, III, ch. 47, p. 771; Lenin, *Development of Capitalism in Russia*, Moscow, 1956, pp. 190–2.

[23] Marx, *Capital*, III, ch. 47, pp. 772–7.

set against this key role in bringing about the crisis of the demesne economy, the survival of the peasantry in most of Europe and – above all – its victory in France in 1789.[24]

This myth is matched by the myth of the revolutionary urban bourgeoisie. Yet, as Hilton has pointed out, compared to this fundamental rural struggle over the generation of the surplus product, that of the urban communes merely concerned the 'share-out of the surplus once it had been taken from the basic producers'.[25] Similarly, Porchnev's pioneering work on French peasant uprisings in the context of the 17th-century crisis, which ranged the urban bourgeoisie alongside the nobility in defence of the social order based on the extraction of rent, showed that these uprisings were the 'motor' behind the refeudalisation of the bourgeoisie in the context of the new 'state feudalism' of absolutism.[26]

This absence of revolutionary vocation on the part of the towns, the constant 'betrayals' of the bourgeoisie to the old order (as the *creditor* of the old order), in which Engels saw an analogous process in Germany in 1525 as in 1848, must be seen in terms of their objectively *convergent* interests vis-à-vis the exploitation of the countryside so long as rent remained, in its various forms, the principal mode of appropriation of the surplus and capital remained external to the productive process.

In this context, the position of the town as a 'collective seigneur' was – and remained when backed by the absolutist state – that of a corporate monopoly. 'Towns became distinctive economic and social units just when and because certain places were set apart and defended by laws and privileges making them market or production centres and denying some or all such rights to the countryside around'. Trade was 'strictly reserved to those who had joined the trading community of (a given) town'.[27] Pirenne's free trade liberal bias inclined him to see this restrictive monopoly character of the medieval towns as an obstacle to free circulation represented by the 'dynamic' element of long-distance trace. On the contrary, the exclusivism of towns must be seen as precisely the *precondition* for the development of merchant capital at this stage. We must not lose sight of this feudal character of early 'capitalism'; circulation based on the free exchange of equivalents belongs to the

[24] For most of the above points, see Rodney Hilton's decisively important work, *Bond Men Made Free*, London, 1973.

[25] Hilton, 'Warriors and Peasants', NLR 83, p. 81–2.

[26] B. Porchnev, *Les Soulevements Populaires en France de 1625 à 1648*, Paris, 1963.

[27] See the excellent general account by A. B. Hibbert, 'The Economic Policies of Towns', ch. 4 of the *Cambridge Economic History of Europe*, vol. III, cited, pp. 197–8.

full development of the capitalist market. Even as late as the 18th century, the market remained limited in most of Europe to a given range of commodities, wages were frequently paid in kind and the commercialisation of the agricultural product was still only partial. Autoconsumption, sales by barter and payments in kind commonly reduced the range of monetary transactions and hence the dominance of the market. In 1751 Galiani estimated that in Naples 50% of transactions took place outside the market: 'the peasants who form three quarters of our people do not settle a tenth of their consumption in hard cash'.[28]

The market was a restricted prize and the 'capture' of it entailed the *enforcement* of a productive and trading monopoly against the countryside and against the encroachments of rival towns. So long as the market depended on price disparities between separate spheres of production in which the producers were not separated from the means of production and subsistence, trade existed only in the interstices of the system, monopolising supply of a limited range of goods, and was dependent on political indulgence: it was 'more of a tribute structure than a trade structure'.[29]

Trade by no means escaped this monopolistic framework: it depended on the town's success in securing a favoured position as middleman by means of staple policies, concentrating and diverting exchange transactions to its market, enforcing sale and excluding foreigners from direct access by means of 'hosting laws', etc. In the Mediterranean, the urban economy was based on monopoly of supply of key commodities, defended by embargoes, alliances, war and piracy against rival towns: war, diplomacy and trade were synonymous. (The fate of Pisa, which first lost to Genoa – in 1284 the latter built a mole across the mouth of the Arno and choked the port with silt – then later to Florence, is eloquent.) This also meant exclusion of the countryside from the town's monopoly of exchange and from the guild monopoly of craft production: prevention of low quality production outside the town's *ban* was especially marked in the Flemish textile centres from the 13th century with punitive expeditions to destroy looms and fulling vats in neighbouring villages, an attempt to create an industrial vacuum and private hinterland for raw materials and sale of urban goods.

[28] F. Braudel, op. cit., p. 355.

[29] Hibbert, op. cit.; O. Lattimore, 'The Frontier in History', *Relazioni del X Congresso di Scienze Storiche*, Florence, 1955, pp. 124–5; I. Wallerstein, *The Modern World System*, New York, 1974, pp. 20–1.

In Scotland the royal burghs were surrounded by their liberties, within which 'only burgesses could carry on any kind of retail trade even in native commodities', a monopoly only broken, and then partially, in the late 17th century. In the case of Flanders the failure of the textile cities to develop a 'city-state' form has been attributed to 'the exclusive preoccupation of the bourgeois with the town and their urban interests', their 'tendency to seal themselves off from the country', failing to establish a viable economic unity of town and country.[30] As Polanyi put it, the town both 'enveloped the market and prevented its further expansion'. The growth of the town depended on its *ban*, the safeguarding of its monopoly against the country, which allowed it 'to exploit the country economically by its monopoly prices, system of taxation, guild organisation, direct commercial fraudulence and usury'.[31] The growth of underprivileged suburbs (*ban-lieu*) was to house those poorer labourers and artisans outside the walls and hence often outside the privileges of the town.

While this monopoly and the juridical conditions allowing it made the town as a collective, corporate body an anomaly vis-à-vis the vertical articulation of feudal power in the countryside, the town nonetheless depended on this 'feudal setting' for the defence of its privileges. In England, where these monopolies were in any case limited, the setting for town growth was 'a society dominated by lay and ecclesiastical lords, who took a share of the profits and gave their own stamp to many of the towns, before loosening their grip – if they ever did'. Even so, self-government and economic privileges were the key to growth, as witnessed by the fate of towns which failed to gain key rights, for example to their own corn or fulling mills – Warwick, St. Albans, Wells, Bury St. Edmunds, etc. – the growth of which was arrested.[32]

In Italy, where the city-state made the town a full seigneur, the map remained one of 'wide feudal lordships, in the interstices of which the communes struggled to maintain a fugitive independence'. Vassalage continued in most of rural Italy and the towns depended – both militarily and for supply – on key local feudatories. Hence the rise of *condottieri* dynasties over the city itself: the lordships of the Romagna, the Estensi over Ferrara, the Visconti over Milan, etc., which were the

[30] Hibbert, op. cit.; T. C. Smout, *A History of the Scottish People*, London, 1972, p. 147; D. M. Nicholas, 'Town and Countryside: Social and Economic Tensions in 14th century Flanders', *Comparative Studies in Society and History*, vol. X, 4 July, 1968, pp. 458–85.

[31] Marx, *Capital*, III, p. 781.

[32] R. H. Hilton, *A Medieval Society*, London, 1966, p. 177.

norm rather than the exception.[33] Similarly the trading privileges of the Hanseatic towns at the height of their power was dependent on the feudal protection of the Order of Teutonic Knights.[34]

Nothing reveals better the limits of this municipal economy than its decline and involution in the context of the growing world market and the establishment of territorial state sovereignty from the 16th century. This coincided with a speculative boom of merchant capital based on colonial trade and fiscal credit: the decline of the Mediterranean corporate cities, which followed their subjugation by the new monarchies (defeat of the *communeros*, capture of Florence, Hapsburg domination of Italy) was not a contingent event (due to 'Atlantic discoveries', in which Italian capital in any case fully participated; the Atlantic, as Braudel showed, was initially a commercial extension of the Mediterranean.) Rather it was due to the objective limitations of merchant capital itself and hence its failure to develop an adequate expanded productive basis for capital accumulation. This failure, except in North-West Europe, to move *beyond* guild and municipal exclusivism and hence production of high quality goods for an increasingly narrow market, was singled out by Cipolla as the main factor in the decline of the Italian urban economy. The same 'limits' that allowed the fullest autonomy of merchant capital in the feudal mode now became fetters on the subsequent development of capitalism: 'the situation reversed itself . . . The cities which had formerly fought for the establishment of a new, progressive economic system now became a nucleus of interests fighting against the new type of development'.[35]

This was accompanied by an internal involution towards *rentier* forms of wealth, the flight of urban capital into land, state bonds and tax-farming (*Casa di San Giorgio* in Genoa, the *monti* in Florence) which transformed the urban élite into a landed or rentier aristocracy, merged in turn with the absentee nobility itself. This 'refeudalisation' of the town by the transformation of merchant capital into rent should not be seen as a 'defection' or 'betrayal' on the part of the bourgeoisie as a result of hunger for social status (which implies an opposition of class interests which can be 'betrayed'); let alone, as in Peter Burke's recent

[33] D. Waley, *The Italian City Republics*, London, 1969, pp. 110–23; 221–30.

[34] M. Malowist, 'The Problem of the Inequality of Economic Development in Europe in the later Middle Ages', *Economic History Review*, 2nd series, vol. 19, 1966, pp. 25–6.

[35] C. Cipolla, 'The Economic Decline of Italy', *Econ. Hist. Review*, 2nd series, vol. V, 1952; A. Pizzorno, 'Three Types of Urban Social Structure and the Development of Industrial Society' in G. Germani ed., *Modernization, Urbanization and the Urban Crisis*, Boston, 1973, p. 125.

study of élites in Venice and Amsterdam, in terms of 'shifts in life style' from an entrepreneurial to rentier outlook geared to conspicuous consumption. This merely accepts the contemporary verdict of moral decline, a subjectivist and élitist abandonment of historical explanation[36]

Rather it should be seen – as with the decline of Spain – as a product of the precarious, speculative nature of this boom of merchant capital, witnessed by its reversal in the 17th-century crisis, which favoured the influx of urban wealth into usurious forms of rent and tax-farming: the outcome of this 'rentier feudalism' – the fusion of merchant capital and landed property – was the fiscalisation of rent on a national basis (Porchnev) in the absolutist state, which accentuated the gap between town and country based on an absentee credit-debt nexus. Just as the transition to money rent is only a change in the *form* of rent – *other things being equal* – so the influx of urban capital into land and purchase of titles, farming of seignorial revenues, etc., need in no sense lead to capitalist tenant farming – the English 'direct path' to capitalist agriculture in Marx. Urban commercialisation of agriculture can equally lead to a reinforcement of an external rentier relation of urban dominance, merely crystallising feudal obligations, seignorial revenues and ecclesiastical tithes on a commercial basis, which the receivers of this revenue had no interest in destroying. Indeed the commercialisation of agriculture was generally accompanied by seignorial reaction. Exactions grew heavier, resulting in the wave of peasant uprisings against fiscal and absentee-landlord exploitation which reached its climax in the mid-17th century. The absolutist state was first and foremost a machine for the extraction of rent, in which the towns had as much interest as the nobility.[37]

The action of urban capital on rural society was principally by way of usury capital, exploiting shortage of credit in the country (intensified by the transition to money rents and the demands of fiscality), speculating on harvest prices and on scarcity, mortgaging feudal dues and services. Usury 'feeds off' the old mode without altering it. It depends, like merchant capital, on a precapitalist market and petty commodity production, aggravated by fiscal appropriation. The tax farmer and usurer characteristically go hand in hand (Duby). The dominance of

[36] F. Braudel, *The Mediterranean in the Age of Philip II*, London, 1973, vol. II, pp. 728–33; P. Burke, *Venice and Amsterdam*, London, 1974, which is based on the explicitly anti-Marxist model of circulation of élites borrowed from Pareto.

[37] R. Villari, *La rivolta antispagnola a Napoli: Le Origine 1585–1647*, Bari, 1967, pp. 228 ff. See also Porchnev and Anderson, op. cit., P. Goubert, *The Ancien Régime*, London, 1973, ch. 6.

rentier capital (based on both proprietary and 'constituted' rent, i.e. *usurious* forms of rent) is well illustrated by that 'intermediate' type of lease – *mezzadria* or sharecropping – widespread in Italy and southern France: here urban capital shares the product with the peasant cultivator as a return on their respective outlay of investment. This 'transitional' form, associating merchant capital and peasant agriculture (Marx, *Capital* III, Ch. 47) was clearly not 'transitional' in an historically dynamic sense: the development of this usurious rent took place within, rather than against, the feudal structure of rural society. In spite of a precocious development of capitalist farming in the irrigated Po basin, urban capital investment in Italian agriculture tended towards a re-feudalisation of agrarian relations.[38] This urban transition to rentier wealth was scarcely due to a decline of 'entrepreneurial outlook': in the given conjuncture, investment in seignorial titles and revenues gave more secure returns. Genoese investment in southern Italian wheat, oil, silk and other commercial crops enjoyed returns of over 30%. The migration of the Venetian aristocracy to the *terra firma* was not merely due to a delight in Palladian architecture, but was accompanied by a more intense seignorial farming system based on commercial cultivation of maize and canapa and the rearing of livestock.[39] The paradox of this 'capitalist' or more precisely 'rentier' feudalism is due to the fact that in most of Europe the commercialisation of agriculture fortified rather than weakened feudal burdens on the peasantry.

In Eastern Europe there was an analogous decline of the privileged 'free' cities based on guild production: here, where the autonomy of towns was closely hemmed in by the seignorial economy, and weakened by their role as intermediaries in the transit of goods with the West, the growth of the world market led to the subordination of the urban bourgeoisie within a seignorial export economy based on *corvée* labour. The presumed antithesis of feudalism and trade, deriving from the dualistic model of town and country as separate modes of production and the ecological-spatial correlation of towns and feudal 'decline' that this implies (Sweezy: 'Near the centres of trade the effect on feudal economy is strongly disintegrating; further away the effect tends to be just the opposite'), cannot account for the varied forms of this feudalism of commercial agriculture – and not only in the East – from the middle ages onwards. In Central Europe (Bohemia, Saxony, Austria) where the

[38] R. Zangheri and E. Sereni in *Agricoltura e sviluppo del capitalismo*: Istituto Gramsci, Rome, 1970, pp. 682–703. Marx, *Capital*, III, ch. 36.

[39] P. Villani, *Feodalità, riforme e capitalismo agrario*, Bari, 1968, pp. 116–25.

internal market developed advantageously up to the Thirty Years War, a 'half-way' position emerged; the response to labour shortage on seignorial estates took either the form of high wages or intensification of *robot* services, while the free towns were undercut by cheaper production in the 'domain townships' which grew up on feudal estates unencumbered by guild regulations. The free towns, with their own extensive estates, tended to 'follow the same . . . economic policy as the aristocratic magnates'.[40]

In France, where the dominance of rentier urban wealth was reinforced by the confirmation of the town's privileged status in the *ancien régime*, the 'external' relation of the town to the country was widened: the rentier became 'more and more removed from the source of his income . . . more and more a stranger to the fields, those 'deserts' despised ever since the age of Molière: he belongs to the town, even the capital, whether provincial, national or royal . . . The interests and residence of rentier and rent-payer put them all too clearly on opposite sides.'[41] This explains the limited and episodic resistance of the towns to royal centralisation – urban participation in the *Ligue* or the *Frondes* – and the fact that urban concentration of landed wealth was enormously accentuated by royal absolutism. Arthur Young's astonishment at the contrast between the Breton countryside and the opulence of the port of Nantes – 'no gentle transition from ease to comfort . . . from beggary to profusion in one step' – testified to a fundamental weakness in the conditions governing original accumulation in France.

The crisis of the 17th century, first delineated in Hobsbawm's article of 1954, was revelatory of the weaknesses of this world market based on speculative merchant capital and feudal productive relations in town *and* country. 'Economic booms multiply activities: crises select them' (Vilar). The reversal of the boom dragged down the feudal and mercantile town economies that had promoted it, to a secondary, subordinate role (Spain, Italy, later the Netherlands) owing to their weak productive home base. Only in Britain was this speculation based on colonial trade able to provide the launching-pad for a fully autonomous productive accumulation and growth of the home market. Otherwise the dominance of merchant capital – whether in trade or production – remained a redistributive mediation between producer

[40] J. V. Polisensky, *The Thirty Years War*, London, 1971, pp. 38, 40, 44–9; A. Klima, J. Macurek, 'La Question de la Transition du Féodalisme au Capitalisme en Europe Centrale', *XI International Congress of Historical Sciences*, *Rapports*, vol. 4, pp. 99–102.

[41] P. Goubert, op. cit., pp. 136–7.

and consumer, dependent on disparities between cost price and sale price, as long as production itself was organised externally to capital and the integrated world market (and its average or long-term prices) was non-existent: in conditions where the world economy was (to quote Braudel) 'vast but weak'.[42]

Conversely, the 'original accumulation of capital engenders its own destruction' (Vilar). The advent of a world market by the evening out of cost-price differentials – the establishment of world prices – coincided with cotton and increased exploitation in the home economy. This 18th century *productive* response to inflationary pressure (that of capitalist factory production) revolutionised the existing division of labour and the existing hierarchy of towns, subordinating commercial windfall profits to market price discipline and reducing them to the mere income of the distribution sector.[43]

The demographic imbalance owing to this weak productive base and the instability this engendered was compensated by the growth of large capital cities: the earlier hypertrophy of Naples or Constantinople became in the 17th century the European norm. This disproportionate growth of the metropolis was fed by the proletarianisation and surplus population of the country, the lure of wages in all seasons and the concentration in the capital of rentier and government revenue with attendant multiplication of services. The high proportion in this growth of fringe occupations, servants, unmarried or widowed women, prostitutes, uprooted indigents and abandoned children, tells its own story. Contemporary moralists inveighed against this eminently non-productive concentration of revenue with its accompaniment – the swollen proletarian underworld of 'non-work'. Defoe, the Fieldings and Cobbett denounced London's ostentatious squandering of wealth, its 'idleness', 'profligacy' and corruption of the national character. Mercier feared the *canaille sans nom* to whom he attributed the evils

[42] F. Braudel, *Chapters in Western Civilization*, NY, 1961, vol. 1, p. 260. Immanuel Wallerstein, though correctly indicating the interdependence of neo-feudal cash-cropping régimes and the process of proletarianization/expropriation in the 'core' countries in the phase of original accumulation, seems obliged by his reliance on the static core-periphery model of A. G. Frank to argue the *continuity* of a fully fledged capitalist world 'market system' from the 16th century. He also rejects the key Marxist distinction between *merchant* and *industrial* capital (which precisely allows a grasp of periodization, structural contradictions and crisis in the progress of original accumulation): he regards this distinction as 'unfortunate terminology'. See *The Modern World System*, ch. 2 and 'The Rise and Decline of the Capitalist World System', *Comparative Studies in Society and History*, vol. 16, 1974, pp. 387–415.

[43] P. Vilar, *La Catalogne dans l'Espagne Moderne*, Paris, 1962, vol. III, esp. pp. 9–12, 562–5; and *Sur le Féodalisme*, cit., pp. 42–3; Marx, *Capital*, I, ch. 15.

of the revolution in Paris, convinced that only the unhealthiest elements of the rural population came to the capital. To Rousseau it was inconceivable that 'there has been no one able to see that France would be much more powerful if Paris were annihilated'. Governments legislated in vain to confine the poor, to prevent mobility and curb this growth, seen as a danger to social order. But, as Braudel puts it: 'Was it after all wise to suppress the safety valve indispensable to the simmering of the great kingdom?'[44]

According to Sombart this concentration of consumer wealth, the common ability of these capitals to live above their means, accelerated the growth of capitalism. Wrigley has argued that in the case of London, the 'great wen' (with 11% of the national population by 1750 against 2½% for Paris), the consumption of the capital exerted a healthy, generative influence on the formation of the national market. But it would be rash to apply this to all cases: the difference between London, as the capital of a highly developed agrarian capitalism and entrepôt of world trade, and, say, Naples or St. Petersburg was vast. London's supply hinterland was as assured as the world market it dominated: consumer unrest was not centred on bread prices (as in Paris) but on a more varied consumption pattern and on wages. Whereas in Naples, where fear of the mob made the authorities 'not only liberal but prodigal', supplies were subsidised by royal monopoly at a loss. The relation between cheap grain and oil and the popularity of the Bourbon *re lazzaroni* was a political index of this precarious problem of supply, which drained resources from a vast area. The demographic instability of these cities, maintained by a permanent stream of rural immigrants to compensate for higher mortality and 'crowd epidemics', was a witness to this basic disequilibrium.

The formation of the home market centred on the metropolis is well attested by Steuart: 'Every superfluity becomes money . . . without one supernumerary or useless mouth', whereas far from the city 'there is an abundance of things superfluous which cannot be turned into money'. He adds: 'It is good to have an estate far off when you wish to live upon it; it is better to have one near the great town when you do not'. (*Inquiry*, Vol. I, 55.) But this 'generative' capitalist pull of the urban market is dependent on a further circumstance which Steuart calls' the

[44] See Braudel's excellent survey of this metropolitan growth in *Capitalism and Material Life*, ch. 8; *The Mediterranean*, vol. I, pp. 344–52; Raymond Williams, *The Country and the City*, London, 1975, ch. 14; Richard Cobb, *The Police and the People*, Oxford, 1970, pp. 266–7.

separation between the parent earth and her laborious children', which must 'naturally' take place in proportion to the development of industry and commerce (Ch. 10). The full development of a capitalist market requires, as Dobb rightly insisted, the expropriation of the immediate producers from the means of production and subsistence, i.e. the land, itself 'freed' by the separation of agriculture as an enterprise from the ties of landownership. The organisation of agriculture as an industry producing exchange-values is part and parcel of the same division of labour that produces the factory based on free wage labour. This *creation* of the conditions of an agrarian-industrial market based on exchange of equivalents shows 'what an extremely different development of the division of labour and productive relations is required so that corn can be produced as an exchange-value pure and simple, entering entirely into circulation; what particular economic processes are required to produce instead of a French peasant an English tenant-farmer'.[45]

Nothing illustrates better the limitations of the concept of 'urban economy' (Karl Bücher) and the economic dualism of town and country which it pre-supposes, than the fact that capital first seizes control of the productive process *outside* the town: 'in the countryside, in villages lacking guilds' (Marx). This is true not only of factory-based industry, which gave rise to an entirely new urban hierarchy *outside* the limits of municipal control of the established corporate towns (as in the case of Manchester or Birmingham, which were under manorial jurisdiction and offered no hindrance to freedom to exploit the labour market). It is also true of rural domestic industries or 'putting' out systems from the Middle Ages on, which escaped guild control and undercut urban monopolies. As Clark and Slack put it: 'The disincentive (for industry) of existing urban controls was a more important factor than the positive incentives of the rural economy . . . growth seems to have been encouraged by the absence of stringent community controls'.[46]

This rural migration of industry corresponds to the first historical form of capitalist control of production, that of *manufacture*. Manufacture enormously expands the social productivity of labour by the multiplication of detailed functions, subordinating whole areas of the country and branches of production to the urban capitalist. The subsumption

[45] Marx, *Grundrisse*, German ed., p. 906, quoted by R. Rosdolsky, *Genesi e Struttura del 'Capitale' di Marx*, Bari, 1971, p. 221.

[46] P. Clark and P. Slack, ed., *Crisis and Order in English Towns 1500–1700*, London, 1972, Intro: pp. 11, 33–4; M. J. Daunton, 'Towns and Economic Growth in 18th century England', paper presented to the *Past and Present* Conference on 'Towns and Economic Growth', July, 1975.

of labour to capital, however, remains external and formal. Production is only modified by subdivision of tasks; the labour process itself is merely taken over from preceding modes of production. With the advent of machine production this framework is qualitatively altered; capital seizes hold of the real substance of the labour process, dynamically reshaping and diversifying all branches of production by the technical-organisational transformation of the productive process. The removal of all fetters on the mobility of labour and the separation of one secondary process after another from agriculture (given the corresponding revolutions in transport) opens the way to an accelerated, permanent urbanisation based on the 'concentration of the motive power of society in big cities' (Marx) and the subordination of agriculture as merely one branch of industry. The dominance of the town is no longer externally imposed: it is now reproduced as part of the accumulation process, transforming and spatially reallocating rural production 'from within'. The territorial division of labour is redefined, enormously accentuating regional inequalities: far from overcoming rural backwardness (seen as a legacy of the past, as in Smith), capitalist urbanisation merely reproduces it, subordinating the country on a more intensive basis. The creation of the 'reserve army' of cheap labour and the rural exodus could scarcely be seen as 'progress' from the rural standpoint.

The tendency of capitalist enlarged reproduction is to revolutionise all fixed divisions of labour (in contrast to *manufacture*); it recomposes the labour force by constant 'variation of labour, fluidity of function and universal mobility', undermining the existing relation between the worker and his job – the use-value of his work, tending towards the subordination of universal undifferentiated labour at the service of accumulated dead labour (constant capital), bringing the countryside into the factory and the factory to the countryside in its restless search for fresh manpower. In this levelling and mobility of the labour market, the 'factory city' already prefigures the sprawling conurbation, the 'megalopolis' of the 20th century, the absolute *negation* of the 'city' to humanist critics and planners. The capacity of fully socialised capital to appropriate earlier utopias based on the ideal of a balanced environment, to transform them into a 'technical matter at the service of neo-conservative established powers', is demonstrated by the 'garden city' ideal (derided by the Fabians as a pipe-dream in 1898) and its reality in the *planned deurbanisation of the metropolis*, dissolving the city into the 'urban region' in the town and country planning of the 20th century.

('Town and country', wrote Howard, 'must be married and out of this union will spring a new life, a new hope, a new civilisation'.) The mobility of mature social capital presupposes this capacity to reconstitute the town-country division on an ever-renewed basis: while the town-country opposition becomes that of *agricultural versus industrial prices* – an increasingly political, rather than market-price determination (subsidies, quotas, price-fixing) since the need to control the cost of reproducing labour power – the price of reformism in our own day – clashes with the interest of agricultural producers.[47]

We can, then, discern the two major breaks or discontinuities in this history, which cannot be accounted for by a unilinear conception of 'urbanisation' as a process correlated with economic growth, nor by the autonomous action of an 'urban economy' acting externally upon the country. The first coincides with the extension of the market in the territorial state, which reduced the urban merchant economies of the feudal mode to a shrinking sphere of operations, undermining guild production by the growth of manufactures and rural industries. Original accumulation largely takes the form of a capitalisation of feudal relations, mercantile activity remains external to production and national accumulation is seen in 'zero-sum' terms as an aggregate of revenue-producing capacity for fiscal-military purposes (as in the calculations of Petty, King and Vauban). The growth of capital cities and towns generally remains an unstable one in the absence of capitalist agriculture: the town's dominance is that of a rentier, dependent on external political and military conditions. Its dependence on a fragile supply system and on rural immigration, even to maintain its population at a constant level, makes this clear. The second break, which occurs with factory cities, expanded reproduction of the proletariat and capitalist agriculture, marks the take-off into an *autonomous* urban growth: it overcomes the corporative limits to urban development by seizing the entire productive process and subordinating it to the dictates of the law of value. This in turn reduces the earlier corporates cities of mercantile and guild activity to secondary distributive centres and resorts for the gentry. It is evident that these qualitative re-definitions were not the result of 'towns' as protagonists of history: it was the dominant mode of production that determined the global conditions within which given towns prospered or not. Towns, in spite of their role as *cultural* pace-

[47] M. Bookchin, *The Limits of the City*, New York, 1974, ch. 4; Marx, *Capital*, I, ch. 15. Cf. the wave of farmers' protest throughout Europe in 1974.

makers, reflected the conditions of rural accumulation as much as contributed to it. Similarly, the despotism of the modern metropolitan agglomerations based on wage-labour 'will be abolished only by the abolition of the capitalist mode of production itself' (Engels).

It must also be made clear that the transition to a capitalist urban-based market did not come about without crisis and mass resistance. The extension of this market was marked by a 'type of crisis' (first analysed by Labrousse) engendered by failure in the subsistence sector – a crisis which provoked the most violent polarisations of town and country in modern history. In England, the local response to the advancing intrusion of the metropolitan and export market characteristically took the form of the food riot, a popular pricing movement in defence of local regulated markets backed by the moral conception of a 'just' economy of provision. The medieval defence of the urban consumer interest – supported by laws to fix prices, ensure open sale on the market place and eliminate middle-men, forestalling and engrossing – was revived in the 17th–18th centuries as a movement of resistance against the corn-factors who served the London market.[48]

In France, with its delicate patchwork of local controlled markets served by poor communications and aggravated by fiscal barriers ('exports went with the river current; imports had to be pulled against it' [Cobb]), the resistance to free trade and struggle for a controlled economy of provision went much further. The precarious nature of local supply areas and dependence on a single subsistence crop which underlay the tottering economy of the *ancien régime* was peculiarly prone to breakdown in case of dearth, and totally thrown out of gear by free trade grain policies – as Turgot found to his cost in 1775. The revolutionary 'crisis of subsistence', combined with the dismantling of all these economic controls as relics of the old order, rapidly led – in the context of inflation and war – to what Cobb has described as a subsistence war between town and country. The alliance of peasants and bourgeoisie against the common enemy of 1789 – the seignorial régime – gave way to the urban economic terrorism of Year II – price controls, requisitioning and the collective brigandage of the Revolutionary Army, combined with the urban assault of dechristianisation and military recruitment. This crisis, in which each local provisioning area fought against the next, towns against country, towns against

[48] See E. P. Thompson's vivid and perceptive reconstruction of these movements, 'The Moral Economy of the English Crowd in the 18th century', *Past and Present*, 50, February, 1971, pp. 76–136.

towns, and all towns against the economic imperialism of Paris, revealed the extent of dependence of the consumer in *both* town and country. The dominance of the towns was starkly reflected by the uprooting of masses of rural consumers, who migrated to the towns in search of provisions. With the dismantling of price controls after the defeat of the popular movement in Year III, the rural producer took his revenge. If the country, according to the *sans-culotte* creed, should be 'made to feel the full weight of a town-made Terror directed by townsmen', the country resisted by production strikes and the counter-revolutionary and federalist rebellions in West and South. As in Russia after 1917 (war communism), this breakdown and the hatred and polarisation it engendered lasted in popular memory long after; it conditioned the anti-republicanism of the French peasantry up to the Third Republic.[49]

The abolition of the antithesis between town and country is a classic objective of revolutionary socialism from the *Communist Manifesto* onwards. Faced with the backwardness of rural social relations and institutions in much of Europe and the persistent political weight of the 'landed interest' as the armature of the state, the problem of class alliance, of 'carrying the class war into the countryside' (Lenin) gave this goal an immediate, pressing relevance. Against the populist and romantic belief in the separation of the rural social world from industrialism, the social democracts exalted the capitalist development of the countryside and elimination of small property, seen as the premise for the conjunction of rural and urban class forces under the leadership of the urban proletariat. In other words, the *immediate* perspective was one of furthering capitalist development to overcome the disjunction of a backward rural structure. With what concrete slogans could social democracy lead the 'rural revolution' against the rival claims of peasant organisations? The bias against land parcellisation and the tactical uncertainties to which this gave rise are well illustrated by the waverings of German social democracy on the land question, faced with the fully integrated capitalism of the Junker estates. Moreover, the tendency to see in rural backwardness an obsolete precapitalist survival, external and inimical to capitalist development, overlooked the numerous cases where this backwardness was quite functional to the overall process of accumulation.

The existence of a separate 'agrarian problem' was seen as the legacy of

[49] Richard Cobb, *Les Armées Revolutionnaires*; and *The Police and the People*, Oxford, 1970, part 3, which contains a brilliant analysis of the town–country antagonism and politics of dearth in the French revolution.

the historical failure of the bourgeoisie to carry through its democratic-revolutionary vocation in the countryside, a task which now fell to the proletariat as the spearhead of urban progress. Beyond all tactical differences and oscillations, the underlying basis of many Communist 'bids for power' from the 30's onwards lay in this belief that the working class had both the task and the capacity to resolve or 'make good' the *limits and insufficiencies* of capitalist development. Fascist régimes were proof of the historical bankruptcy of the bourgeoisie, compromised through the alliance of monopoly and financial interests with the 'agrarian-bureaucratic caste' and hence unable to ensure any ulterior development or progress.

The conception of Fascism as an alliance of finance capital with the most backward rentier elements in society (Dimitrov) allowed the corresponding openings (Frontism, the New Democracies) to alliance with progressive capitalism; just as a similar dualism transferred to the Third World countries found the 'national' bourgeoisies ready to take the progressive role against feudal rural residues. Sweezy's hypostasis of the dynamic of capitalist development corresponds to an evolutionist projection within Marxism of the need for unilateral completion of the capitalist 'stage', requiring the infinite extension of capitalism as the vehicle of progress against all precapitalist obstacles, with, ultimately, the 'rational' completion of this evolution entrusted to socialism.

In reality, the gap between productive industrial capital and the rentier-based 'finance aristocracy' was already closed by Marx – and by the real historical movement of capital – by 1857. The discovery by Marx of the mechanism of mature capitalist crisis as a product of the contradiction between money as a commodity and money as capital, coincided with the world crisis of 1857. This crisis was provoked not by any failure in the subsistence sector but by the contradiction between 'bank and factory', between money and capital as a contradictory unity on an international scale. In France the St. Simonian 'utopian' solution to the disjunction of capital and landed property, which envisaged the victory of the *industriel* over the *rentier*, had to await the breakdown and working-class threat of 1848, which united land and capital in the 'party of order'. It took 'Bonapartist socialism' (Marx), the 'government of liquidity, of monetary Proudhonism and the *Credit Mobilier*', to recompose landed rentier income and savings within industrial development, just as Lasalle's 'state credit' had to await Bismarck. Marx was accordingly obliged to rework his earlier critique of utopian credit schemes in the *Grundrisse*; he abandoned his earlier Manchesterian model of the 'parasitism' of finance capital for an analysis of money and credit as an *immanent* articulation of the socialisation of capital and the motor of its crises.[50]

To conclude: the dualistic tendency to separate urban progress and rural backwardness, seen as a relic of the past, must be set against the fact that 'urbanisation' and 'ruralisation' are opposite sides of the same process of the capitalist division of labour. But, of course, the conception of towns as the historical agency behind all change has deep and enduring cultural roots. These have been traced by Raymond Williams in his survey of the town-country contrast in English literature, with its ambiguous shifting between idealisation of rural innocence, the lost Arcadia, and urban disdain for 'rural idiocy'.[52] Williams has some powerful words to say about 'metropolitan socialists' who have swallowed the myth of rural passivity and the urban bias of capitalist progressivism. This salutary reminder of the evolutionist inroads made by urban ideology into socialist thought suggests the need for a critical return to Marx.

50 See Sergio Bologna's penetrating analysis of this transition to a fully socialised capital in Marx's writings of the 1850s: 'Moneta e Crisi; Marx corrispendente della "New York Daily Tribune"', *Primo Maggio*, no. 1, 1973, shortly to appear in translation. An extended version of this essay is included in S. Bologna, P. Carpignano and A. Negri, *Crisi e organizzazione operaia*, Milan, 1974.

51 Raymond Williams, *The Country and the City*, pp. 50–1.

NECESSARY READING

THE BRENNER DEBATE
Agrarian Class Structure and Economic Development in Pre-Industrial Europe

Edited by **T.H. Aston**
C.H.E. Philpin

Few historical issues have occasioned such discussion since at least the time of Marx as the transition from feudalism to capitalism in western Europe. *The Brenner Debate,* which reprints from *Past and Present* various articles stemming from Professor Brenner's original, bold and wide-ranging article in 1976, is a scholarly presentation of a variety of points of view, covering a wide range in time, place and type of approach. Weighty theoretical responses to Brenner's first formulation followed from the late Sir Michael Postan, John Hatcher, Emmanuel Le Roy Ladurie and Guy Bois; more particular contributions came from Patricia Croot, David Parker, Arnost Klima and Heide Wunder on England, France, Bohemia and Germany; reflective pieces from R.H. Hilton and the late J.P. Cooper. The debate has already aroused widespread interest among historians and scholars in allied fields as well as among ordinary readers, and may reasonably be regarded as one of the most important historical debates of recent years.

NECESSARY READING

STUDIES IN THE DEVELOPMENT OF CAPITALISM

Maurice Dobb

Maurice Dobb, who died in 1976, was a Fellow of Trinity College, Cambridge, and Reader Emeritus in Economics in the University of Cambridge. He was also a Fellow of the British Academy. In these studies, he examines what have been the leading factors in ecomomic development in the epoch of modern capitalism.

'Individually and taken together Mr. Dobb's studies are a most valuable contribution to economic literature, and to the understanding of the problems of our time.'—*New Stateman*